IN PRAISE OF MICHAEL LUCKMAN

Michael Luckman is one of those rare individuals who radiate confidence with an iron clad positive outlook on life.
– Larry Allen, President Allen Portrait Arts

Michaels helped me realize that my fears from childhood are still holding me back in adulthood, and it's time to not only become aware of them, but set SMART goals to remove them from my life.
– Josephine Hanan, Career Transition Specialist

Michael touches on the fears in the deeper recesses of the mind that when addressed and overpowered can make a positive difference in your life.
– Bill Leonard, CEO Ignite Marketing

Michael is an excellent communicator. He takes his subject, simplifies it, and then creates wonderful stories to help the listener learn to face and overpower their fears.
– Steve Peck, President, SJP Commercial Real Estate Services

The exercises that Michael created helped me to better understand my fears and address their long lasting effects. Great stuff!
- Jeff Nott, Action Coach

Since enrolling in your training program our business is running a four-fold increase over what we did previously – and still continues to grow as we put more and more of what we learned into action. Thank you.
- Ed Correia, President Sagacent Technologies

The best part of my training is that my trainer is Michael Luckman. He's both my coach and my mentor, dedicated to my success.
-Carole Rose, Master NLP Practitioner

Michael's topic of Overpowering Fear is one which all people, not just salespeople, should address throughout their professional career.
– Erin Benford, Benford & Benford Real Estate

i

DEDICATION

To my beautiful daughters Melissa and Jennifer. When you were growing up I wasn't always there for you. And nothing I could say or do can change that. But today I stand in awe of the incredible wives, mothers and good citizens you have become. And what I want you to know is that I am so very proud to be your Dad. To both of you I dedicate this book.

ACKNOWLEDGEMENTS

Many years ago, when I was going through a very difficult time in my life, I met a gentleman who gave me an incredible book that has literally changed my life. On the first blank page he had written this quote by Charlie Jones, "You will be the same person in five years except for the people you meet and the books you read." He went on to say, "My life has been enriched by meeting you." The book was *The Greatest Miracle in the World* by Og Mandino. Through multiple moves I have lost the book, but I am forever grateful to this man.

This was my introduction to Og Mandino whose writings had a tremendous impact on me. *The Greatest Miracle in the World*, especially the chapter entitled *The God Memorandum*, moved me to tears because it brought me such great comfort. Another Mandino book, *The Greatest Salesman in the World*, among the world's greatest sales books, is a must read for anyone who sells for a living.

Another author whose writings introduced me to the vast power of the universe is U.S. Andersen, a former Stanford University football player and World War II Naval officer whose 1954 book is *Three Magic Words*. The secret of those three magic words? You are God.

My greatest regret in life was that I never had a mentor. Someone who would have taken an interest in me, given me honest feedback and guided me along life's path of challenges and triumphs. On the other hand, I was very fortunate to work for some very demanding bosses. At the time I reported to each of them, I did not always see the deeper, life changing lessons that were there for me to learn. However, I did learn the value of a job well done, a solid work ethic, and the joy that comes from providing the customer with not only a top quality product, but outstanding customer service. Those high standards shaped my life and will stay with me forever. Gentlemen, thank you for those lessons.

I want to thank my incredible editor and publisher Nance Rosen and her wonderful staff. As a new author, I appreciate how Nance made what could have been a very difficult process into a true labor of love.

I also want to thank all the great people at Sandler® Training, both in the home office and in the network, for the past 10 years as a Sandler trainer. David Sandler was a genius in understanding salespeople and for putting together what I know to be the best sales training program mankind has ever developed. My one regret is that I was not introduced to this unique sales methodology many, many years ago; when with sweaty hands I picked up a telephone and made my first cold call.

And finally, I want to thank my wife Arleen. We met while I was going through my darkest hours. She has always been there for me, supported me, and believed in me. Without her love this book would probably never have been written. I love you.

TABLE OF CONTENTS

> *Courage is resistance to fear, mastery of fear -*
> *not absence of fear.*
>
> — Mark Twain

INTRODUCTION

I have been thinking about writing this book for at least the past ten years. From the onset, it was going to be a guide for salespeople about the one subject that no sales training course, no college course and no life course that I've taken or ever heard of has ever been taught: how to face and overpower our fears. We all feel our fears. We all fight them. And we all succumb to them. But why did I start out writing this book just for salespeople? The answer is quite simple. I'm a salesman. I've sold all my life. Even as a small boy you could find me selling stuff to my neighbors. In fact this year marks half a century of selling, if you include my jobs in high school and college.

For the past ten years my labor of love has been to train salespeople how to get in front of more qualified prospects on a consistent basis, how to qualify or disqualify an opportunity early in the sales process, and how to easily close the prospect once you determined 1) a reason to do business, 2) their budget, and 3) how they make a decision. I was a Sandler® Training franchisee in Silicon Valley, California. I trained people on a methodology that I wish I had been introduced to at the start of my career. If I had, my life would certainly have been different, more productive and richer than it was.

So why write about fear when I am an expert in selling skills?

Over my career I've hired, trained and managed thousands of sales-people. But I was often baffled. Why did some people whom I thought would land in the top 10% of producers fail to achieve the results I expected of them, while others whom I thought of as less talented, rose up to be my best people? Why did some of my students who learned the Sandler® methodology, and could have taught the course for me, fail to use it in the real world? In debating this with friends and colleagues I came to the conclusion that the top producers in any company were those individuals who are able to face their fears and do what is necessary to achieve their goals. These are the men and women who instead of calling at the buyer or user level within a pro-spective company, would make their initial contact with the CEO, president or owner - even though they may have been frightened or intimidated by talking to the person at the top. These are the people who overpower their fears and outsell their colleagues by huge mar-gins, often selling a broader selection of their companies' products and services. These are the salespeople who stand-up, face their fears, and do whatever is necessary to get the business.

Working with my amazing editor, publisher and friend, Nance Rosen, this book started to take shape. As Nance and I discussed what I'd written each week, we came to the realization that this book is not just for salespeople (although salespeople face more fears in a month than most people do in a year), but a book for everyone. We're all human beings and human beings all have these primordial fear sensors built in to protect us from danger. And that's great, should we ever run into a raging wild beast that would like to make us his dinner. That's when the fight or flight responses should kick in, for good reason – we need to run away! But most fears we experience on a daily basis have nothing to do with survival and a lot to do with our own egos. We don't worry about being eaten alive, but we do fear having someone hang-up the phone on us or rejecting our invitation to dinner!

Few of us began our day fearing we would be killed in battle, but you may have awakened with the fear of getting up in front of a group of people and making a speech. If statistics are correct, you don't fear death as much as walking up to a complete stranger and introducing yourself. Our fears for the most part are totally irrational. Products of our own delusional thoughts. And the real shame of all this is that the vast majority of what we fear never happens. **IT NEVER HAPPENS.** But even knowing that, we still feel fear.

At this point you might be saying, "So what? I feel fear. We all feel fear. What's the big deal?" The big deal is that fear prevents you from having, being and doing the things that will bring joy, happiness, love and prosperity into your life. When fear prevents you from making a sales call on a CEO, your competitor's salesperson may have the nerve to dial that top dog and win the business while you and your company have lost income now and in the future. If you're single and out to meet someone new at a dance, and you see the perfect person across the room, but fear freezes you in place: you never get to meet that person and the two of you may have lost your happily ever after. If a perfect job opens up at your workplace but you're afraid to ask the hiring manager to consider you, you've lost not only the job, but also the prestige and income that position would have provided you. It is in these everyday occurrences that you win or lose, and the choice is always yours. It just may not have seemed like you had a choice to overpower your fears, until now.

Consider how the losses mount up and what that means to the quality of your life, if you can't overpower your fears.

The majority of books written about fear are authored by psychiatrists and psychologists. I am neither. I'm just a fear-based person, born into a fear-based family. Fear has been my constant companion for the majority of my life. From my earliest memories, I was always afraid of new situations. My family, teachers, and friends never provided the support or insight I needed to release myself from those fears. In fact, they validated a lot of them. I was afraid I wasn't smart enough. Afraid to fail. Afraid of being found out that I really wasn't that good at what I did. Afraid of the shame and embarrassment that might come my way if I tried and failed. Afraid that others would believe I didn't know what I was doing. Afraid of not knowing what to say. Afraid of flubbing my words. If there was a fear out there, I had it!

While many of my friends, classmates and colleagues believed that bad things would never happen to them, I was certain if something awful could happen to anyone, it would happen to me. I saw nothing about myself that made me feel special, brilliant, ambitious, courageous, and untouchable or above the fray. I never thought I had any unique talents. I was everyman, maybe less. I never saw myself as a man with a great mind. In fact, when I was acknowledged for an award, it threw me into a panic.

When I began almost every new job, I did respect and nurture my own ideas by doing rigorous research and creating solid plans. Unfortunately, I did not treasure and nurture relationships with people who needed to approve my ideas or collaborate with me on my plans. My fear of authority built a chip on my shoulder, and turned me into a serially argumentative and often unpleasant person.

Years later, I watched my ideas turn into products that became huge successes, but not at the companies where I worked nor in a company I owned. I was afraid to go out on my own, take the risk, and succeed on my own merit. I never was at the helm – in fact, I was not even involved – in those highly visible successes.

In the past, I let my fears run most of my relationships and ruin some of them. Because I was so afraid of being counted out, I was consumed with proving myself and often steamrolled over the concerns of others. Oftentimes, I didn't take time to develop trust or rapport, because I thought it was only my plans and products that people would buy and not me as a valuable member of the team. This became a self-fulfilling prophecy. I did not always have empathy – because I had never seen empathy. Instead, I almost always focused on taking a project straight from point A to point B. Then, when I needed help, the people I turned to weren't in my corner.

So now, you're probably wondering how did I ever succeed in business with all these fears and their fallout? And succeed I did, when I did not let fear stop me. Obviously, I'm not saying that I faced every fear and won – especially at the moments when winning would have been sweetest. There were plenty of times I allowed fear to win. And when fear won, I lost. And those times were way too many to even count. I've been very successful in my life --- but certainly, not as successful as I could have been, should have been, or deserved to be.

As I mentioned, I have been thinking about writing this book for many years, but until I had overpowered my own fears it would have been disingenuous of me to write a book about helping others to overcome theirs.

Here's how I knew I was ready to write. In the spring of 2010 I lost an account. The company's monthly payments to me were sizable. Why I lost this account doesn't much matter. What matters is the fact that in my final meeting with the CEO, as he was telling me why he was canceling our contract, I felt no fear. In my lifetime I have been fired from several jobs and in my ten years as a Sandler® trainer I have lost a few accounts. Typically, in the process of being fired I would be overcome by fear. My heart rate would increase as the fight or flight hormones surged through my body, and my mind would focus on catastrophe. What was I going to do now? How was I going to replace the income?

But this time was different, I felt that a door had opened. I finally understood what was standing in my way – and it wasn't this CEO not approving of my plan or even of me. In the past, I would have gotten argumentative. I could have "enlightened" him about his shortcomings, including how his management style or lack of leadership would cost the company. Of course, he would have gotten angry and defensive. I've seen this lose-lose approach play out many times before.

However, this time with a clear head, I was thinking logically and not reeling with fear. I realized the CEO wasn't attacking me or my plan. He was reacting to his own fear, facing a fractious board of directors. That fear was impeding his ability to think clearly. It was then I realized I would start writing this book, because I finally understood the magnitude of fear that was running and ruining so many people's lives, while I had learned to overpower my own.

As I began writing the stories of my life, focusing on when I was challenged by fear, sometimes winning – sometimes losing, I became more convinced than ever that this book is not just for salespeople, but also for everyone. From teenagers facing high school bullies to seniors facing inevitable life changes, and everyone in between. Could others benefit from what I've learned over a lifetime? From what I lived through? I believe so. You see we are all not so different. The homes we grew up in, although a little dysfunctional, were for the most part filled with good intentions and love. And yet, when most of us are faced with challenges, the first emotion that wells up is fear. This may be your reaction. You feel self-doubt. You believe you are alone, that nobody feels what you feel. Because you don't see how to get past your fears, you enter into a negative spiral. You give up on your dreams and the happiness you deserve.

HOW THIS BOOK IS ORGANIZED

In the first section of this book, I am going to share some life lessons and show you some choices you may not realize you are making. As my friend, my student, and my colleague, you deserve to know what I know as soon as possible. Therefore, in the first section of the book, I'm going to let you in on all the big and little secrets I know, about how to create a life full of what you want and not full of fear.

In the second section of this book, I invite you to come on the journey of my life. I have laid it out bare so you would be able to see the mistakes I made. It is my fervent hope you realize you are not alone when you make mistakes. Instead, I want you to see yourself as perfectly human, as I am, as we all are. We are no different than anyone else who lives with fear and allows it to narrow our options.

In the third and final section of this book, I'll turn the focus back to you. You'll find ten exercises that will transform the thoughts and feelings you have been harboring. You will see how you can create a positive and powerful reality. You will be able to put away your fear, overpower it when it rears its head, and get to the most magnificent time of your life: the now you intentionally create.

Some of the exercises may make you feel uncomfortable. That's good. It means you are bumping up against your comfort zones. The only way to grow is to expand those comfort zones. But if you can't do an exercise now, that's okay too. Take from this book what feels right for you at this point in your life. Sometime down the road you may return to it and find the exercises that were too uncomfortable at first, now bring you comfort.

Eventually, you'll see how it serves you to do all the exercises. It is harder to begin a journey when you lack a clear idea of where you are starting from. You'll learn about your own personal starting point from completing the exercises. When I ask you to write down your fears make sure not to pre-judge them. Don't say to yourself, "This fear is not too bad so I won't write it down." Or, "I only feel this fear when faced with a particular situation, and since I don't experience that situation too often I won't put it down." The purpose of this book is to help you overcome ALL your fears. Not just some.

Now on to your fearless future! A future of joy, happiness, abundance and unlimited opportunities.

– Michael Luckman

LIFE'S A JOURNEY...SO SIT BACK AND ENJOY THE RIDE!

Why do so many of us fail to grab the brass ring? Is it because to grab the brass ring you have to grab a lot of iron rings first, and sooner or later you just give up, believing that you'll never reach that coveted ring? Or, do you believe that you don't deserve to have the brass ring, because someone, at some time, convinced you that people like you never get the brass ring, so they tell you to settle for what you do have? Iron rings. Or, do you not even try, because your fear of falling off the wooden horse is greater than your desire for the brass ring?

Life is the carousel and the brass ring represents your full enjoyment of that life. But yet, how many of us live our lives to the fullest, by enjoying every single minute of it? For some people, life is always in the past. They're either reliving their glory days, or recounting their past mistakes and the guilt that always accompanies them. Others believe the future is the time when everything will be exactly as they want it. You know them well because they punctuate their conversations with the word "someday." Someday I'm going to do this and someday I'm going to have that. Often forgetting that yesterday's someday, is today.

The past is gone. You've lived it and you cannot change it. If it's your past mistakes that haunt you, then you must understand that all of us are human. But, you must do what is divine: forgive yourself. Mistakes are for learning and not meant to condemn you to a lifetime of guilt and regrets. You've lived the past and now it's time to let it go.

The future isn't here yet. When it comes it will certainly take care of itself. And yet, so many of us fear tomorrow. We live in hope that tomorrow will be better than today, but secretly we fear that it won't be.

The tree outside your window does not fear the fall when it is going to lose its leaves and face a barren winter. Instead it transitions to the future in a burst of glory. I'm sure the squirrel living within that tree doesn't look to its future with dread. Instead the squirrel lives each day, doing the things it loves to do, without a mere thought to its future. Only man squanders his "now" either reliving yesterday or worrying about tomorrow and things that may never come to pass.

Life is not lived in the past and it's not lived in the future. It is always lived in the moment. Only this moment is important. Only this moment counts. Only in this moment can you create the future that you want and deserve. This moment is called the present. And that is exactly what it is; it is a present from God, Jesus, Infinite Spirit, Universe, Universal Subconscious Mind, or from whichever higher power you believe in. In this book I will use all of the above at various times. To me they are just different names to describe God. The present is given to you with absolutely no strings attached. What you do with it is simply up to you. You can use it to dwell upon what happened in the past or what could have been. Or, you can use it to worry about what may happen in the future. Or you can use it as the magnificent gift that it is, to create the most perfect life for yourself, where everything comes your way and where everything goes your way.

Most religions tell us God created us in his image and then blessed us with his gift of free choice. But what exactly is free choice? If you believe in a chaotic universe where random things just seem to happen, where does free choice come in? It doesn't seem like you have a choice because if you did, bad things wouldn't happen. But they do. If you believe in an orderly universe where you can create exactly what you want in your life, then free choice has a far greater meaning than good or bad. Every day you make thousands of choices, most of them are decisions. From the very mundane, "What should I have for lunch today?" to some of the most important decisions of your life, "Is this the person I want to spend the rest of my life with?"

Each decision you make in a day typically begins with multiple choices. You get to choose the option you believe is the most suitable one. But yet, you don't always make the most appropriate choice. In fact, in many, many instances, you choose the exact opposite of what you really want. You do this by making choices based upon what's the most expeditious. What's the easiest? Or, what's the least you can do and get by? For example, you might be an individual who is chronically late for work. When your morning alarm goes off you're faced with two choices, 1) get out of bed or, 2) press the snooze alarm for 10 more minutes. You rationalize in your mind that you were up late last night so you deserve a few more minutes of sleep. And so, you choose to press the snooze alarm. Then 10 minutes later you press it again, until finally you do get out of bed and then rush to get to work, only to walk in late. When your boss finally has had enough of your tardiness you get fired. Now who do you blame? Certainly not yourself. You might choose to believe that you live in a chaotic world, what with traffic and accidents or mishaps creating delays that chronically impact you.

Take a look around you. Are you living the life you dreamed about as a child? Is your life easy or is every day a difficult battle? Does money flow effortlessly to you or is it a struggle just to make ends meet? Are your days filled with love and contentment or anger and strife? Is your outlook one of unlimited opportunities or one of lack and limitations? If your life is not what you want, then change it! You may not believe what I'm going to tell you next, but it is the truth. You have, and always have had, the ability to create the life you want. A life that is filled with all the joy, all the happiness, all the good health and all the abundance you could possibly want. The sad part is that no one has ever told you or me this truth. No one ever showed us how to create this life. And so we live the lives that we do, always hoping, always wishing, always dreaming.

I want you to make note of the date and time that you are reading these words. For this is the day and time of your rebirth. At this exact moment in time you are nothing more nor less than the choices you made in the past. Every choice you have ever made brought you to this point. But here is the good news. And good news it is. If you don't like the life you are currently living, you can change it, and create the life that you really, really want. You and I can always create the life of our dreams. Everyone can. And it doesn't matter if you are male or female, rich or poor, young or old, black, white or brown, you can have, be and do whatever you desire. And you do it simply by changing the things you think about. Change your thoughts and you change your life.

Instead of thinking thousands of random thoughts every day, most of which are negative, you can learn to choose which thoughts you desire to allow into your mind to take root, and which thoughts you choose to discard. It's as easy and as hard as that! But please don't worry. I promise to show you how to do it.

One thing you must do is to live your life now, in the present. Do I always live my life in the present? I'd like to believe that I do, now. But it wasn't always that way for me. In fact the things I am going to teach you I didn't begin learning until I was into my forties. But it doesn't matter at what age you start. Because the life you have been seeking has always been seeking you in return. It's out there, with your name on it, just waiting for the two of you to meet up.

But before I begin to tell you my story let me first tell you of the amazing things that happened to me when I started to live and create my life in the present. Life becomes easier. Why? Because I no longer rail against life. Instead of forcefully swimming upstream, I now find myself going with the flow instead of against it. For so many years, instead of turning my life over to God, I believed that I knew best what God's plan was for me. So when my life was not going the way

I wanted it, I became angry. The angrier I got the harder it was for me to create the life that I really wanted.

What I want you to do now and always, is: ask your higher power to always place you in the right place at the right time, saying and doing the right thing at the right time. And then know that wherever you are, whatever you are doing, this is where God wants you to be. Then accept it. Life is like a river. It often takes the path of least resistance. When you're standing on the river's edge the river looks like it is straight as an arrow. But look at it from the air and you'll see that it meanders left, then right, and at times it even reverses itself. When these reversals happen they are often just detours along the path. Accept them as exactly that, detours. The Universe knows where you're going and will always provide you the perfect path for getting there.

Since life is always in the moment, why would you not want to use this moment to create what you want to come into your life in the next moment and the moment after that? I call this the Luckmans's Law of Deliberate Manifestation. Jesus knew how to do this. He could turn water into wine, feed the multitudes with only several loaves of bread and take a sick and dying person and restore them to perfect wellness, and do it all in an instant. We all have the power to evoke miracles, just not always on demand.

So how do you manifest the things you want in your life? First you need to know what you want. Often we are so caught up in the moment we forget to define exactly what we want that moment to be like. In *A Course in Miracles* it is said that God wants his children to have everything, and that it is not that we ask God for too much, but that we ask him for too little. So know exactly what you want God to bring you and then ask him for it. I ask God for the big things, but I also ask him to guide me in all my daily activities. It is here that you are reminded that God is the Universe, is Infinite Spirit, and that God is all around you.

- When I get up in the morning I ask Infinite Spirit for a perfect day. A day where everything comes my way and a day where everything goes my way. I definitely have many more good days than bad days.

- When I sit down at my computer I ask God to guide me in all my work and that whatever my output, it be perfect. When I sit down to write I ask of God, that the words I write be his, written through me. I know when the words are coming from God and not me. Writing is a whole lot easier.

- Before I step into a meeting I ask Infinite Spirit for the exact meeting I would like to have. Then I just relax and let the meeting take place. And it typically happens exactly as I envision it. With the outcome I had asked for.

- When I am training I begin by asking God to help me achieve a perfect workshop, where I have imparted real knowledge to all my students. I'll often ask that in that training the words that I speak be God's words spoken through my lips.

- When I make a phone call I ask God for a perfect conversation. If the call is going to be more important than a simple conversation I discuss it with God and let him run the call.

- Whenever I buckle myself in, and before I put my car in drive, I always ask Infinite Spirit for a safe and enjoyable drive to wherever I am going. Often I'll look at my clock to see how much time I've given myself to get to my destination, and if I didn't allow myself enough time I'll ask Spirit to get me to my destination at a certain time. Nine times out of ten I'll look again at the clock upon my arrival and see that Infinite Spirit brought me safely to my destination exactly to the minute I asked to arrive. I call this bending time – and believe me it works. In fact, let me tell you a story.

This took place in 1992 shortly after I had separated from my second wife Susan and I was still living in our home in Danville, California, about 40 miles east of San Francisco. I was invited to a singles dinner in San Francisco on a Friday night that was called for 6:30 PM. Depending upon the time of day it could take anywhere from 45 minutes to 90 minutes to get into the city. I wanted to leave home at 5:00 PM, just to give myself enough time because Friday night traffic could be horrendous. Unfortunately, I couldn't get out of the house until 5:30. Once in my car I asked Infinite Spirit to provide me with a safe and enjoyable drive into San Francisco and I asked that I get to my destination no later than 6:30 PM. Traffic was a breeze. An obstacle like going through the Caldecott Tunnel when only one bore was available in my direction was a snap. Traffic on the Bay Bridge reminded me of Sunday morning. Everything flowed exactly the way I wanted it to. I arrived at the restaurant at 6:20. 50 minutes door-to-door. An hour later a friend of mine arrived. Carol lived about a half mile from me, and if I had known she was coming, I would have invited her to ride with me. She arrived frazzled. Complaining bitterly how bad traffic was. The tunnel took forever to get through and the Bay Bridge was packed. When I asked her when she left her house she responded, "5:30." Exactly when I left my house. Ask for what you want and it shall be given.

Going to the mall and finding a place to park can be pure hell. Wouldn't it be nice to find a spot within seconds after entering the lot? I usually do. In fact I have actually amazed friends when I've asked the Universe to provide me a parking space right away, and then almost miraculously, someone is backing out as I enter the lot. In fact I do more than just ask for a space, I ask for one close up so I don't have to do much walking.

When I go out to any social function I always ask Infinite Spirit for a perfect event. I ask that I have fun and that I meet really interesting people. And guess what, I typically have a great time and I do meet some wonderful people.

If you're traveling I'm the one you want to travel with. Before each leg of a trip I ask Infinite Spirit for exactly what I want. On the drive to the airport I ask Spirit for a safe drive and to get me to the long term parking lot at the time I choose. Before I arrive, I ask Spirit for a parking space right away, and for it to be near where the shuttle bus picks us up. Next it's asking for a safe ride to the terminal. Once inside I ask that the check-in line move quickly. Next I want to get through security without long lines and a lot of hassle, so I ask Spirit for a quick screening. Then it's off to the gate. Once our plane has pushed back from the gate I ask for a safe and uneventful flight. Before landing I ask for a safe and uneventful landing. Then to find my bag quickly.

Then a safe and quick ride to the car rental where I ask for a quick check-in and the perfect car. Finally, I ask Spirit for a safe drive to my destination. This is Luckman's Law of Deliberate Manifestation, and you can make the same powerful law for yourself.

I don't leave anything to chance when I travel. Is every trip I take perfect? Of course not. But most are relaxing and enjoyable. A far cry from what they used to be.

How would you like to live your life without fear, uncertainly and doubt? The dreaded threesome that I call the FUD Brothers. What would your life be like if you were totally fearless? Would you change jobs or career? Would you ask the person you've been admiring from afar out on a date? Would you stand up for what you believe in? Would you get up in front of a group of strangers and advocate for your position? Would you change the way you approach risks? Would you have the courage to say no to people? Would you do things to build your business like make 50+ cold calls a day? Would you invest your money differently?

If you would love to love your life, this book was written for you. It is a guide to living the life you have only dreamed of. It is also the story of my life, the challenges that I've faced and what I ultimately did to overpower my own fears, doubts and uncertainties. I'm sorry it took so long to get it into your hands, but I couldn't write it until I had actually lived it.

It is my fervent hope that what I've done to change my life will help you to change yours. After all, you and I aren't so different.

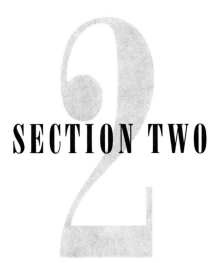

SECTION TWO

LUCKMAN'S LAWS

CHAPTER 1

- ✔ Don't be afraid to ask for whatever you want. You just might get it.
- ✔ You are rarer than rare. Of all the people who have ever lived on earth there has never been anyone like you.
- ✔ Learn to bond and build rapport with other people. This skill will change your life.

CHAPTER 2

- ✔ If a truck brought it a salesperson sold it. Selling is truly a noble profession.
- ✔ The streets of America are still paved with gold. Don't believe those who want to convince you our country's best days are behind us.
- ✔ So they rejected you. So what? Tomorrow they won't even remember it and neither should you.
- ✔ If you know how to sell you can always make a living. And if you're really good at it, you'll make more than just a living.

CHAPTER 3

- ✔ If you want to be happy for the rest of your life - move away from your immediate family. Even if it's just to the next town.
- ✔ Being perfect is not all it's cracked up to be.
- ✔ Given the choice I'll take physical abuse over emotional abuse. With physical abuse it only hurts for a little while.
- ✔ You might think it normal to lose your temper now and then and start yelling. But for those closest to you it scares the hell out of them.
- ✔ Children should never have to fear their parents.

CHAPTER 4

- ✔ Children can be especially cruel. The greatest gift you can teach them is tolerance.
- ✔ It is never your plan, but God's plan for you. Let go and let

God do his work.

- ✔ Hidden within every adversity is a nugget of opportunity. But unless you look for it you'll never find it.
- ✔ If you expect to make a mistake you will. If you expect to screw-up you will. If you expect to fail you will. The Universe gives you everything you ask for.

CHAPTER 5

- ✔ Never ever walk into someone's office without knowing at least a little bit of the history of the company.
- ✔ It is absolutely amazing how many people and companies make money for quite a while before their lack of knowledge catches up with them.
- ✔ Be friendly to everyone. The guy in the corner pushing the broom today could be your buyer tomorrow.
- ✔ Life would be perfect if we could be like little children who naturally accept others regardless of race, culture or religion.

CHAPTER 6

- ✔ When faced with the choice more people prefer death than public speaking. Luckily for them, they won't have to give the eulogy at their own funeral.
- ✔ When standing face-to-face with your greatest fear remember that the worst part is already over. It was the days and weeks of worry leading up to this moment that were excruciating. Now it's just a matter of doing it.
- ✔ Never be afraid to make mistakes. We're all human and that's how human beings learn.
- ✔ Fear is a lot like dark threatening rain clouds. From afar they look intimidating but up close they have the consistency of cotton candy.

CHAPTER 7

- ✔ Others may bully you and trash your ideas, but don't think you can out bully them.
- ✔ Examine your anger at others, especially when you feel like

name-calling. Ask yourself, what in my background is handicapping me – and how can I choose another way.

✔ Arrogance has its roots in believing your own press or the stories you make up about yourself in order to feel more important or better than other people. It is then that you become a legend in your own mind.

✔ It has been said that people rise to their own level of incompetence. Don't let your competence in one area be undermined by your fear of taking steps to change your attitude or behavior.

CHAPTER 8

✔ Life is so very fragile. One day you're king of the world. The next day you're following the elephants with a shovel in your hand.

✔ If you believe that things never happen to you, but only to people like "George," be careful and count your blessings. For someday you may wake up and be George.

✔ When we screw-up it's bad. When a doctor screws-up it can be catastrophic.

✔ You are never alone. Wherever you are God is right there with you.

✔ No matter how bad things may seem, there are good people out there ready and willing to help.

CHAPTER 9

✔ Parenthood should come with an instruction manual. Nobody ever showed me what a good dad was like.

✔ Anger, resentment and parenting don't mix.

✔ Children should be seen, listened to and loved unconditionally.

✔ We cannot always depend on someone to love us unconditionally. In its absence we need to accept ourselves and love ourselves unconditionally.

✔ Everyone should have friends they can confide in. If they did the world wouldn't be such a lonely place.

✔ Much of life is a balancing act. It works better when you have a trustworthy partner to help maintain your equilibrium.

✔ Life itself can be exhilarating when you learn how to truly live it.

CHAPTER 10

✔ God created us perfect, and then our egos get a hold of us.

✔ If you allow your roles in life to affect how you feel about yourself, then expect your life to be like a roller coaster. One minute up, the next minute down.

✔ Some people accidentally shoot themselves in the foot. And then there are those who take off their shoes and socks, put their feet up on the desk and proceed to shoot off their toes one-by-one.

✔ A company's salespeople should always be seated in the front seats on the bus. They, more than anyone, need to see what's coming down the road.

✔ Once, a very smart man told me, "If you want to get even with a prospect…let them buy from you!"

✔ Treat your boss like a prospect.

✔ The truly amazing thing is that we as humans are capable of doing and being so much more than we are. A whole world opens up when you release the brakes of fear, uncertainty and doubt.

✔ The success you never achieve is typically waiting in the moment after you accept the belief that you cannot go on anymore and quit.

CHAPTER 11

✔ When your gut is telling you one thing and your mind another, nine times out of ten your gut is right.

✔ When opportunity knocks it helps to open the door.

✔ Never own a company with three people on the board. One has only to sway one other person to shift the balance of power against you.

- ✔ When someone is with you and tells you things about another, who do you think they talk about when they are with that other person?
- ✔ Fear of missing out on something is the number one reason most people go against their gut instincts.
- ✔ Don't let anybody bully you, including your own ego.

CHAPTER 12

- ✔ By your very existence you DESERVE to have the BEST of EVERYTHING.
- ✔ You were created for Greatness and nothing less.
- ✔ God created an abundant Universe so that you His child would have everything.
- ✔ Do not ever feel guilty for asking for what you want. As a child of God you deserve to have, be and do everything you desire. Ask and have faith that your choices will be delivered to you.
- ✔ Life is not a zero sum game where if you win someone else must lose. The Universe sees that everyone is a winner.
- ✔ Nothing happens until you ask for what you want when you want it.

CHAPTER 13

- ✔ Everything you see around you started out as an idea in somebody's mind. The only difference between their idea and your idea is their belief that their idea would come true.
- ✔ You have been created by God to create. Don't disappoint Her.
- ✔ Well-meaning friends often have a hidden agenda when rationalizing to you why your idea won't work. They're afraid that if you do succeed you will choose not to be their friend anymore.
- ✔ One of the key reasons why successful people are successful is because they don't allow negative people into their lives.
- ✔ True friends build you up and encourage you to reach for the

stars. False friends tear you down by reminding you of all you're not good enough.

CHAPTER 14

✔ Life has a way of knocking us down. It happens to everyone. Failure is when we don't get back up.

✔ How can you know success if you've never known failure?

✔ If you're an entrepreneur in Silicon Valley and you have not failed at least once, venture capital people will look at you funny.

✔ A horse won't respect you if after it's thrown you, you fail to get back in the saddle.

✔ We are what we think, so choose your thoughts wisely.

CHAPTER 15

✔ A math problem for men: In the past week there were 3 Susie's you wanted to meet. You were afraid to go up and talk to any of them. How many Susie's will you be going out with this weekend?

✔ A math problem for women: There's a cute new guy at your office building you'd like to talk to but you're afraid you'll stumble over your words. Will you be giving yourself a manicure or a pedicure, or both, this coming Saturday night?

✔ Mom and Dad advised you never to talk to strangers. But that was when you were a little kid. Now that you're all grown-up it's okay to talk to strangers.

CHAPTER 16

✔ Fear and ego are a lousy combination. Fear tells you what you can't do. And then if you do it anyway and fail, your ego reminds you that YOU are a failure. When in fact it is what you did that failed. NOT YOU.

CHAPTER 1

"Men are born to succeed, not fail."
– Henry David Thoreau

A LITTLE ABOUT ME

My name is Michael Luckman and I'm proud to be a peddler. I even come from a long line of proud peddlers.

What is a peddler? The dictionary defines to peddle as a transitive verb meaning to sell goods, especially while traveling from place to place. And nowhere was it more prevalent than in the old West as pioneers crossed the Midwestern plains and the western mountains to settle the new territories. Often these farmers and ranchers settled in areas even before there was a town nearby. Without a retail store to provide these rugged pioneers with needed essentials, entrepreneurs would go

LUCKMAN'S LAWS
- Don't be afraid to ask for whatever you want. You just might get it.
- You are rarer than rare. Of all the people who have ever lived on earth there has never been anyone like you.
- Learn to bond and build rapport with other people. This skill will change your life.

from homestead to homestead, at first by walking, then with wagon-loads of products; selling pots and pans, tobacco, fabrics to make new clothes, and hundreds of other everyday products. Sort of like a mini Wal-Mart that came to you. These rugged entrepreneurs eventually settled down and opened what was referred to as dry goods stores. These mom and pop shops later became our department stores of today.

So I am a salesman, and very proud of it. I've sold all my life. As a kid I was a cub scout and then a boy scout and every scout had to have a subscription to Boy's Life magazine. On the back of every issue was an advertisement for a company that sold consum-able products, and its way of going to market was to hire boys 8 to 12 years old to sell for them. In **What was your first job?** the spring I sold flower and vegetable seed packets for my neighbors' gardens. In the fall it was boxed greeting cards for the holidays. I wasn't paid in cash, instead I earned points. You saved up your points and then turned them in for a bicycle, baseball glove, football, camping equipment or a myriad of other products every kid wanted. It was my first taste of entrepreneurship – and FEAR. I had to climb the steps of each of my neighbors' houses, and with a trembling hand ring the doorbell, while practicing in my mind what I was going to say, and pray I didn't stumble over my words. It was my first lesson in learning that selling and fear go hand in hand. But even though it was scary what propelled me to push myself through the fear was what I dreamed of at night, earning enough points for a bicycle. Not just any bike but a Schwinn. The Cadillac of bicycles.

I've got to be honest with you, I never earned that bicycle. And it wasn't until years later in a college marketing course that I learned why I never got the bike. It had nothing to do with working hard. I worked hard. I forced myself to ring those doorbells. No it had to do with something market- **Which is sweeter: instant or delayed gratification?** ers refer to as gratification, instant and delayed. At the end of each year, when looking at the total points I had earned, I was faced with this dilemma; should I save my points and bank them for some unknown time in the future when I would have enough points for the bike (delayed gratification), or should I use them to purchase something I wanted now like a football or a baseball glove (instant gratification)? Well, since I already told you I never got the bike, it's obvious that I succumbed to the intoxicating pull of instant gratification. I earned it. I want it. And, I want it now. Isn't that the American way?

When I was 15 years old I got a job at Mister Junior, a boy's clothing store on Chicago's north side near Devon and California streets. No more being paid with points. I was in the workforce. I was not only a full-fledged salesman, but I was being paid 75¢ an hour to do it. I not only loved what I was doing, but I was good at it. I was in high school and working two evenings a week (stores were only open Monday and Thursday nights then) and Saturday. Once I got over my fear of approaching customers I found that I had a genuine gift for sales, and I was having fun. I was a Mister Junior silver tongued devil and it wasn't long before I was their number one part-time salesperson.

But since this is a book on overpowering fear you probably want to know how this 15 year old kid learned to get past his fears. At that age you are somewhere between childhood and adulthood. Old enough to be working but still young enough where interactions with adults still scared me. Ringing my neighbors' doorbells and selling them seed packets was a piece of cake compared to walking up to a complete stranger and introducing myself, and then engaging them in conversation.

Working on the floor with 3 other salespeople we would rotate turns approaching potential customers as they walked through the door. Since this was a children's clothing store the majority of our walk-ins were parents accompanied by their children looking for new clothes.

What does fear feel like?

When it was my turn to walk up to a customer I could feel the fear begin to rise through my body. Starting in my lower gut and moving up through my chest until I could hear my rapidly beating heart thundering in my ears. It took everything I had to take my first faltering steps towards the new customer and keep my voice from cracking as I said hello and asked them if I could help. Since I was the new "kid" I was still learning the inventory and the different boy's sizes, not remembering what size I had worn at any age growing up.

Who was the first person you shared your fears with?

I found that once the conversation started the fear I was feeling would usually dissipate to a point where I began to feel more and more comfortable in the buyer-seller relationship. But, I think it was the assistant store manager, who seeing my discomfort, took me aside one Saturday morning and asked me how I was doing. I was more than a bit embarrassed when I told him that I was scared approaching customers. His response after a short laugh was to tell me that it was perfectly natural to feel some fear. That it was almost the same as an actor walking out on stage at the beginning of a play and the butterflies they experience. He then told me something that made perfect sense. He said these people are coming into our store because they want to buy new clothes for their child. They're here and looking for help. Your role as a salesperson is to find out why they came into our store and then provide them the help they need in picking out the right items in the right size. And he finished our little pep-talk with this touchstone; just before you approach a new customer say to yourself, "Show time!" Feel the butterflies and add, "It's OK to feel some fear, Michael. Just go ahead and do it."

He was right. The fear would last maybe a minute or two, and then it became fun. Yes, fun. I wouldn't want to go back to working retail now because the thought of standing on my feet for 8 hours would be pure hell. But I miss the opportunity to meet new people and see how fast I could develop some rapport with them, and then of course, how much I could sell them.

When did you ask for your first pay raise?

I worked there about six months when a new men's clothing store opened up not far from my house at the Howard and Western Shopping Center. It was a men's clothing store owned by an Austrian holocaust survivor by the name of Max Kassner. Max was a tough man to work for, but a very successful entrepreneur who had just opened his fifth Kassner's California Men's Shop. It was also my first introduction to marketing. You see nothing in the store was even remotely tied to California. But these were the days of the Beach Boys and the Mamas and the Poppas' California Dreaming, and everybody wanted to live in California. So having the word California in your store's name was pure marketing genius.

With six months sales experience under my belt I applied to Max for a job in his new store. When he asked what I was being paid I bumped up my hourly wage by a third and told him I was making $1.00 an hour (keep in mind prospects lie, salespeople embellish. I embellished my income). He agreed to give me a chance and offered me the job at $1.00 an hour. I was thrilled. Not only was the store within walking distance from home but it was a step up from what I was selling. It wasn't kids' clothes anymore. It was the big time. I was selling men's clothing to men and women who valued my services and liked the fact that I had a flare for putting together just the right look. And what I mean by that was I could sell the husband a suit, then take them over to the dress shirts and find just the right shirt to go with the suit, then the perfect tie and then a new pair of dress shoes. I suggested and they bought. I could up-sell and cross-sell, before I even knew what those phrases meant.

What is your God given talent?

It's funny; I don't know where this talent came from. The joke in our family, even to this day, was that as a family we were devoid of talent. Nobody could sing, nobody could dance, most of us when it came to art could only draw stick figures (certainly me), no one had a gift for writing and no one had any musical talent. So where did this talent for putting together outfits and matching and blending colors come from? Maybe it was in my blood since I come from a long line of merchants. And maybe it was just a God given talent, although I wouldn't know what it was called. Either way I loved what I was doing and it probably helped that I really liked people and truly enjoyed helping them.

My best sale came one Sunday the week following Father's Day. It just so happened that my Dad dropped in to visit me while I was working at Kassner's store in downtown Skokie, IL. A gentleman came in to return a sweater he had gotten as a gift. I returned the sweater for him and since we were hitting it off and I was beginning to understand his tastes, started showing him other items I thought he might like. When it was all said and done the total of his new purchases came to **When did you see pride in your parents's eyes?** just over one thousand dollars. Today $1,000 may buy you one suit, but in the early 1960s when a Petrocelli suit set you back $250 and a mohair cardigan sweater could be had for about $20 and an Enro white-on-white shirt was $12.99, you got a whole lot of clothes for $1,000. I'll never forget the pride I saw in my Dad's eyes as he watched me sell. Those moments stay with you forever.

I was asked afterward how this came about. How was I able to go from returning an item to making a $1,000 sale? I would typically reply, "I guess he just liked me." But looking back on it now there was definitely more to the story. Getting people to like you is not an easy task. One, you have to genuinely like people. I do. I love talking to people and finding out about them, their lives, their work, their dreams, etc. Two, you can't just ask them questions about themselves without opening up about yourself. The more things you share about yourself the **What was your first success? How did you do it?** more comfortable they'll feel about opening up to you. And, three, put a smile on your face and in your voice. Be friendly. Be approachable. Be the first to stick out your hand and say hello. I know it's scary sometimes. But if you want to get people to like you you are going to need to do these things. The more you do them the easier it gets.

In grade school I was not quite in the popular group. That group

13

was made up of the kids who were the best athletes, the jocks. Nor was I in the nerdy group. I fell somewhere in between. Starting high school is a fearful event for most of us and it certainly was for me. But within several months of acclimating myself to this new environment I discovered something about myself that I hadn't known before. I had this ability to make people laugh. I had what was referred to as a quick wit.

Quick witted is defined as: mentally alert and sharp; keen. What it really meant for me was that I could think on my feet. I could quickly

What were you like in High School?

come back with a retort when someone said something or asked me something, and this usually meant a smartass answer. Of course there is a time and a place for smartass answers, and school was not one of them. But being funny boosted my popularity. At Sullivan High School in Chicago there was a chair with my name on it, right outside Mr. Fenn's office, the Assistant Principal. He would see to it that I would only have a four day school week, because one day a week I was suspended.

I found while working at Kassner's that this ability can work in your favor when used to establish bonding and rapport with customers. I wish I could give you a short course in quick

How did your first job effect your long term career choice?

wittedness but I don't think it's something that can be taught. Although, you may have this innate ability already, but fear prevents you from using it. Fear that you'll embarrass yourself and perhaps say the wrong thing. And believe me that can happen. If you are quick witted around your family and friends but not prospects, then you need to get over your fear and let the real you come out. Prospect's will probably like that about you and that's how you create a bond, build rapport and close the sale.

I worked for Kassner's California Men's Shops part-time during the school year and full-time during summers, for the rest of high school and during most of college. I was a good employee who not only sold well, but at 16 years old was mature enough to take over management of the different stores while the managers went on their summer vacations. I loved selling. I loved the thrill of making the sale, but I also enjoyed the challenge of bonding and building rapport with the customer. After 43 years in sales, with the last ten training salespeople, I believe that building rapport and developing a bond with the prospect is the most important thing you can do in a sales call. Bonding and building rapport creates trust. All things being equal people want to do business with people they trust. The more trust the easier the sale.

Now you're probably asking, "Well that all sounds pretty good, but what does that have to do with fear? It doesn't sound like you experienced much fear working retail." First, let me state unequivocally, I am a fear based person. I was born into fear and it has been a constant companion throughout most of my life.

When I say I was born into fear let me describe to you my birth. I was the second child of Adeline and Melvin Luckman. My older sister Ramona was one month shy of her 4th birthday and the Japanese had just surrendered the week before ending World War II. Mom was 25 years old and the times were looking up. I've got the details of my birth down pretty good, and I'll tell you why. As every September 9th rolls around Mom in painstaking detail describes the saga of my birth to me.

What is your first memory of fear?

It was a stifling hot Sunday morning in early September when Mom's water broke. I want to say Dad whisked her away to the hospital in his car, but I don't think he owned a car at the time. I think he took my grandfather's car. Either way Dad took Mom to Illinois Masonic Hospital where, after admittance, she was placed on a gurney and wheeled in to the delivery room area. Now this was the beginning of the baby boom and delivery rooms were often crowded. Since Mom had not dilated all that much the nurses felt she could wait in the hallway while another new mom got the delivery room. As it was,

I decided not to wait. With no one around and Mom all alone on that gurney I came into this world at 7:30 AM Central Daylight Savings Time.

That all sounds pretty sterile and straightforward. But for a moment let's think of Mom. What was she feeling that early September morning? Mom was scared to death. Screaming and with no drugs to ease the pain. And, no one around to come to her aid. Mom was never like those Native American women who gave birth by just leaning up against a tree and dropping the little papoose onto the ground. Nor was she a Rosie the Riveter during the war. Mom was a housewife.

What was your birth expierence?

So, as you can imagine, the very first rush I ever felt was from mom's adrenaline coursing through my tiny little body. It was FEAR. Pure unadulterated FEAR. And, I felt it then and every day since.

So let's take a look at what I was afraid of. My earliest fear recollection was of being with my mom shopping on Lawrence Avenue. As with most preschoolers, I was much more interested in looking in the store windows and watching the people go by, then following my mother as she was walking away. It wasn't long before I realized that she wasn't there anymore, and fear and panic gripped my little body. I began crying and running down Lawrence Avenue calling for my mother, with the belief forming in my mind that I would never see her again. Of course, she wasn't too far away, and heard my screams and came to my aid. The stern lecture I got about paying attention was outweighed by my relief of being found. But, the fear of abandonment stayed with me. Every time my parents would leave the house after that and a babysitter would stay with my sister and me, I would fear that my parents would never come home.

How do you feel when your lost?

I know that most kids have some apprehension about their first day of school. The little 5 year old boy walking with his mom in front of my mom and me, on my first day of kindergarten, vomited on the steps of our new school. At least I kept my lunch down. Actually, kindergarten wasn't so scary. It was the first day of first grade that fear of school took hold. The teacher passed out a large sheet of construction paper and with a crayon we were asked to write our numbers from 1 to 100. As my classmates and I began our assignment fear gripped me and panic began to set in. I was OK from 1 to 10 but that was it. I was lost from that point on. No one had taught me how to count past 10. Wasn't that what school was for?

How was your first day of school?

Up until that point in my life I never gave intelligence a thought. In fact, I thought I was pretty smart. Isn't that what mommies and daddies tell us? But not anymore. My new belief, and one that would last most of my life, was that I wasn't very smart. My new belief was that others (just about everyone) were smarter than me. Others learned new things quickly. I, on the other hand, struggled. Now what happens to children who have this belief about themselves? It becomes a self-fulfilling prophesy. If you believe that you're not smart and that it's hard to learn new things, then learning new things becomes a struggle and school is not a pleasant experience.

I should probably share with you my parents' conversation with me after every parent teacher conference they ever attended. "Mike, Mrs. (every teacher) thinks that you are not working up to your potential. That you're capable of much better work." Well, you certainly could have fooled me. I thought I was working up to my potential. It was just that my potential was not quite as high as most of the other kids in my class. I didn't tell them that. That was my secret. But, I always ended these conversations with a promise that I would work harder. But how do you work harder at something that fear tells you, you can't do?

What did teachers say about your parents?

That's what fear does to us. It reminds us of our shortcomings. It tells us we're not good enough, not smart enough, not talented enough, not bright enough, not athletic enough, not creative enough, not handsome enough, not beautiful enough, not coordinated enough and certainly not deserving enough. We are just plain **NOT ENOUGH**! But, others, yes others, they are. They are everything we are not. We desire to be like them. They are the people who don't suffer like we do. By some magical gift of birth they've got it all together. They don't feel fear. They face every day's challenges head on, and succeed at everything that we fail at. They don't struggle, we do. They are everything we are not. They are what we want to be.

Who has told you, you are not enough?

So who are **THEY**? These mythical perfect people who live amongst us? Actually, **THEY** are us. You see, when we came into this world, we were each given a little gift. Now, I know, there are some of you who will argue that this gift came later, when we, as toddlers, separated ourselves from our primary caretakers. But I like to think it came with our name. Because our individual unique name defined us to the world. It was our "I." "I" am Michael Luckman. You are you. And along with our name came this protector of our "I" from other people's "I." We call this protector our ego.

Let's begin by understanding; your ego is **NOT** your friend. Friends say and do things that make us feel good about ourselves. Egos say and do things that make us feel bad, sometimes real bad.

Who does your ego compare you to?

Your ego is of the body. When you die your ego dies with you. It's not something you can bequeath to others, nor would others want it. They've got their own egos to deal with. Our egos are there to constantly compare us to others. They are the ones that remind us of all of our not enoughs. Now where does the ego get this garbage from? They get it from others. Others who have judged us, either rightly or wrongly. They are our parents, grandparents, siblings, friends, school mates, teammates, teachers, boyfriends, girlfriends, spouses, employers and the list goes on and on. Sometimes these things have been told us with love, "Don't worry about this honey; some kids are just better at math than others. You'll be good at something else." And sometimes, they have been told us with malice, "We don't want Luckman on our team. He couldn't catch the ball even if we put it in his hands." Either way, your ego remembers these things and in an instant will remind you of them, and to hell with how you feel.

How does your ego threaten you?

As I said, your ego is not your friend. When faced with new challenges the first thing our ego does is to whisper to us, "You can't do that. You're not (fill in the blank) enough. You'll be found out that you're not too (fill in the blank). Everyone will laugh at you. You won't be able to take the embarrassment and the humiliation. You'll lose your job. You'll lose your friends. Your life, as you know it, will be over." And with these words of "endearment" comes the fear. The fear that grips our hearts. The fear that becomes the knot in our bellies. The fear that sets our minds racing with one delusional thought after another. The fear that forces us to give up the things in our lives that we truly want and that we truly deserve. It is this fear that makes us compromise our dreams. The fear that makes us settle for less. This senseless irrational fear that keeps us plodding along the ground with

What have you settled for?

turkeys instead of soaring with eagles where we truly belong. We were each destined for greatness if only, if only, we could overpower our fears.

Later, in an exercise in Section 3, we'll talk about how to get rid of this unwanted and unneeded "friend," our ego.

CHAPTER 2

WHY I LOVE SALESPEOPLE!

You have got to admit, most people don't like to deal with salespeople. And some, just plain don't like salespeople. These people often fear us. What they fear is that we, the silver tongued devils that we are, are going to sell them something that they don't want, they don't need, and that they certainly cannot afford. They believe that at the bottom of the deepest ocean is fish and whale muck. And on top of that is either a salesperson or an attorney, depending upon the tides. In fact, I even sold for a company whose owners not only didn't like salespeople; they didn't even like their own salespeople. They thought of us lazy and in it only for the commission. Duh? In it for the commission, of course. Lazy, absolutely not. If they could find a way

LUCKMAN'S LAWS
- If a truck brought it a salesperson sold it. Selling is truly a noble profession.
- The streets of America are still paved with gold. Don't believe those who want to convince you our country's best days are behind us.
- So they rejected you. So what? Tomorrow they won't even remember it and neither should you.
- If you know how to sell you can always make a living. And if you're really good at it, you'll make more than just a living.

to get their products into the market without us, we would all have been gone in a heartbeat.

Now, I consider selling a noble profession. I am proud of what I do. Many years ago I was given a bumper sticker that I immediately affixed to one of my oversized rolling sample cases. In bold letters it proclaimed, *If a Truck Brought It a Salesperson Sold It.* Think about that. Could there be a more **Are you proud of what you do?** truthful statement? Look around you. Everything you see. The chair you are sitting on. The light that brightens your room. The paint on the walls. The table in front of you. All were sold by someone who believed in their product and convinced someone else to purchase it. What could be nobler?

Like most Americans, my ancestors came to this country looking for a better life. They had heard that in America the streets were paved with gold and if you worked hard you could have everything that you have ever dreamed of. In the early 1900s my mother's paternal grandmother, a widow from a small shtetl in Russia, left her children and journeyed to this new land seeking that better life. A cousin, already living in Chicago, brought my great grandmother to that bustling city. A city filled with opportunity. With what few dollars she had brought with her from the old country, she bought a horse and wagon and went into the used furniture business.

Through all kinds of weather, hot and muggy in the summer, freezing cold in the winter, this tough little lady drove her wagon through the cinder paved alleys of Chicago, and in her broken English, bought and sold used furniture. Within several years she had enough money saved to send for my grandfather, her eldest son, and brought him to America. As it was, it was just in time. For in those days the **How did your family support itself in the "old days?"** Czar filled the ranks of his army with poor Jewish boys from shtetls throughout Russia. And, if you were Jewish, the length of your enlistment was 30 years or death, whichever came first.

With my grandfather in the business they eventually earned enough money to rent a storefront with the space necessary to display their wares. At first the furniture was all used. But as time went on they added some new pieces to their mix and their business grew. With an ever increasing income they brought over the remaining children left behind in Russia. I am not going to bore you with the ups and downs of the furniture business, but I want to share this. From those humble beginnings my cousin now runs the largest furniture retailer in the Chicago land area; Harlem Furniture.

I'd like to add one more reason why I think sales is a noble profession. In the Great Depression that rocked our nation starting in 1929 and ending when we entered World War II, my grandfather lost his store. He not only lost his means for earning a living and providing for his wife and two small children, he also lost his apartment building where they lived, to foreclosure. My mother always recounts with sadness and shame the day the Sheriff's officers came and moved them out of their apartment with all their possessions, and put them out onto the street. Life changed dramatically for my mother, her dad and mom and little brother when they were forced to move in with relatives just to have a roof over their heads.

Has financial hard times effected your family?

The reason I bring this up, is not to dwell on what happened to my grandparents during this awful time, but how my grandfather fell back on his sales skills to feed his family. With what little money they had left my grandfather bought a horse and wagon and going up and down the alleyways of Chicago, began selling fruits and vegetables. My mother likes to tell about how difficult it was for my grandfather in his broken English to say banana, but yet he earned enough to survive the Depression. After the war the streets of America were once again paved with gold, and he opened up a new store and left a legacy that lives on today.

How has your family dealt with difficult times?

Before I move on I want you to stop and think about what it took for my grandfather to get up each morning and before dawn go down to the wholesale fruit market and buy his fruits and vegetables. Then go up and down the alleys in all types of weather to earn enough to keep his family from going hungry. Here was a man who epitomized the American Dream. An immigrant, who built a successful business and was well respected in his community and industry, relegated to selling produce from a horse drawn wagon. Obviously, my grandfather had to face some humungous fears. I'm sure he felt the fear immediately upon waking up and it probably stayed with him until he arrived home at night, weary and tired. And what about the embarrassment? Losing everything and seeing all your worldly possessions out on the street next to the gutter.

But my grandfather had tasted success. He knew that no matter how bleak things were at the time, better days were ahead. He believed in himself and he realized that he could not let fear stop him. I'm sure that if he were alive today and needed to grow his business he would be on the phone making cold calls. And, nobody, and I repeat nobody likes to make cold calls. In fact, most of us dread picking-up the phone and calling a complete stranger. Even our mommies and daddies warn us against talking to strangers.
Yet, how are we to grow our book of business?

The reason we don't like to make cold calls **Are you** is they engender fear in us. We fear interrupting **afraid to make** someone's day. That we're a pest as if Orkin has to **cold calls?** come out and spray to get rid of us. We fear stumbling over our words. We fear forgetting what we were going to say and then having those God awful pregnant pauses. And then believing that the person on the other end of the line is thinking that we are some sort of idiot. And the biggest fear of all; having somebody reject us.

Are they rejecting you? They don't even know you. No, they are rejecting only what you stand for, a salesperson wanting to sell them something. Yet, if you believe that what you are selling, product or service, will dramatically change their life – will in some small way (or big way even) make their life better, then you have every right to speak with them and to use those few moments to introduce them to your company and product line. When they hang up on you, when they tell you they're "not interested" even before you tell them who and what you represent, they are bruising your ego. And what did I tell you about your ego? Your ego is not your friend. Your ego will prevent you from living the life you want. All the joy. All the happiness. All the wealth and riches will go to someone else, because your ego got bruised. Think of it. Your competitors will be living the life that you want and that you deserve. Does this make any sense?

What is your ego "protecting" you from?

My grandfather, Sam Berman, lived with his fears for a decade until World War II pulled us out of the Great Depression. He did what he had to do. Or, as Susan Jeffers says in her wonderful book, *Feel the Fear and Do It Anyway!* Or, as Nike says, *Just Do It.*

Do you understand now why I believe that selling is such a noble occupation? My grandfather proved that if you could sell you could always make a living. Robert Kiyosaki, bestselling author of *Rich Dad, Poor Dad*, believes that everyone, not just salespeople, should learn how to sell. Selling skills can help when you have to persuade your boss or co-workers to buy-in to your way of thinking, or even in your closest relationships to sway a spouse or child to your ideas. Even if you hate salespeople and would never want to sell, these skills can and will improve your everyday life.

CHAPTER 3

MY GROWING UP YEARS

To understand my fears and where they came from you would have to know a little more about my childhood. I was the second child of Adeline and Melvin Luckman born on September 9, 1945. Mom was a housewife and Dad was a junkman, but we preferred to call him a scrap metal dealer. I have an older sister Ramona who is four years older than me and twin brothers, David and Richard, 7½ years younger. My sister, brothers and I were brought up in a nice middle-class neighborhood called West Rogers Park on the north side of Chicago. My parents bought their ranch style house in 1954. Up until that time we lived in an apartment. The last one on the third floor.

LUCKMAN'S LAWS
- If you want to be happy for the rest of your life - move away from your immediate family. Even if it's just to the next town.
- Being perfect is not all it's cracked up to be.
- Given the choice I'll take physical abuse over emotional abuse. With physical abuse it only hurts for a little while.
- You might think it normal to lose your temper now and then and start yelling. But for those closest to you it scares the hell out of them.
- Children should never have to fear their parents.

Mom and Dad married in 1940 much to the dismay of Mom's parents. They didn't much care for my father and cared even less for my dad's family. Mom's parents were wealthy, while Dad's parents barely made a living. But my folks were madly in love and nothing was going to stand in their way.

How do your grandparents feel about your parents' choices?

Neither Mom nor Dad graduated from college. Dad had a number of jobs after they were married and even tried working for his father-in-law in his furniture store, but that was a total disaster. Dad was the third generation in the scrap business (today we call it recycling). He loved that business and he flourished in it. To Mom's parents it was a dirty business, calling on factories buying their scrap and working on trucks. They had expected better from their daughter and they never let her forget it.

It was certainly far from idyllic on the other side. Dad's parents, especially his mother and his sister Rena, didn't like Mom. They knew that Mom's parents looked down on them and that they despised Dad. They blamed Mom for this. There was no winning for Mom or Dad. But here's the kicker; every weekend we spent one evening with one set of grandparents or the other. Some weekends were a double header; we saw one set of grandparents Friday night and the other set Sunday afternoon and evening.

Are there bad feelings, slights and insults among your family members?

For those of us who as adults moved away from our immediate families, we have it a whole lot better. We get to choose with whom we want to be with on the weekends. We can visit with friends or just go out as a family. We have choices. But for my mother and father they had none. I often imagined what it must have been like for them. If we went to my mother's parents Dad would have to put up with my grandfather who hardly acknowledged him. Mom would be in the kitchen helping Grandma and listening to her criticisms of Dad, sometimes to the point of bringing her to tears. And then there was my Uncle Leo and his wife Marilyn. Leo was a manic depressive. When he was manic he was the biggest son-of-a-bitch ever created. He was snide, arrogant, condescending and could cut you to pieces with his words. When he was in a depressive state he wouldn't come out of his bedroom. We liked him better that way. He, more than anyone, made my dad miserable.

Is there mental illness in your family that effects others?

His wife Marilyn went to "college" and came from a family where her mother was a "Yankee." Mom's parents admired that and kowtowed to Marilyn's parents. What's a "Yankee?" A "Yankee" is not a "Greenhorn." OK, I'll tell you what these terms mean. A "Greenhorn" is an immigrant, one who was born in the old country. A "Yankee" on the other hand was born in the United States. "Yankees" didn't speak English with a Yiddish accent. My grandparents, although very well off, looked up to "Yankees." My dad's dad was born in Worcester, Massachusetts, but that didn't count because he didn't make a success of himself like it was expected of "Yankees." My grandmother would frequently boast about Marilyn and her parents to Mom, often at the expense of Mom's feelings.

But Mom had a solution. If she couldn't get that unconditional love that she craved from her parents by just being their daughter, she would get it through her oldest son, me. It started when I was very young, maybe when I was a toddler. I was groomed to be this perfect little boy. My grandmother came from a large family and many of her brothers had no children of their own. On the Sundays we spent at their house we'd often have 3 to 4 couples of great aunts and uncles. Mom would have me kiss all my great-aunts and shake hands with all my

How were you treated as a child?

great-uncles. Mom relished Monday conversations with her mother. Grandma would relay to Mom all the compliments she got from her brothers and sister-in-laws about me. And of course Mom would then tell me what Grandma said. It became so that I learned at an early age, how to manipulate people to like me. I was so cute. This miniature little man. Kissing up and paying compliments to the adults. I really became quite good at it. But it had a huge downside.

The downside was I felt like I was put up on a pedestal, this perfect little boy. And as the years went by I grew afraid of falling off that pedestal. If I did, would I then be found out that I was a fake? Would people discover that I wasn't who I pretended to be? Being on that pedestal became my identity. And if I did fall off, who would be left? Would my mother still love me? Would people shun me? It was a scary thing to carry around, especially for a little boy. And the worst part, I couldn't tell anyone. It was not something you shared with people, and so I hid it from all others. My little secret.

Have you been afraid to let your family know how you feel?

My dad took after his mother or maybe it was his grandfather, certainly not his father. My dad was a rage-a-holic. You never knew what would set him off. And when he'd rage you'd better watch out. Funny, all three of his sons became rage-a-holics too. I wonder where that came from?

I have many wonderful memories of my dad, and a few very scary ones. When he'd rage the fear would course through my body in an instant. Sometimes he'd only scream and curse at me, other times he'd grab me by the left arm with his left hand, and use his right hand to give me a swat on the bottom. He never punched me or slapped me in the face, although one time he got so mad he picked me up and threw me. Fortunately, hitting the wall broke my fall and I landed on the bed.

Were you ever scared of your parents or caregivers?

I think Dad hated fixing things around the house. When his boys were old enough each of us became the family handyman. I remember one time in particular, I was about 9 or 10 and Dad was on his back under the kitchen sink cursing a screw that wouldn't budge. He asked me to hand him a screwdriver and I did, but it was the wrong one. His response just scared the crap out of me. "Not that one Goddamnit the Phillips one," he screamed. Whenever that happened my eyes would well up with tears and I'd feel so afraid.

Have you ever said to your children wait until your father gets home? Maybe in your household that meant your child was going to get a stern lecture. Or maybe, some sort of time-out. In my house it meant I was going to get a spanking when Dad got home. All day long I lived in fear of when my father would return from work. And when he did, my mother would greet him at the door and tell him what his first task of the evening would be. My bedroom was in the back of our house next to the kitchen. I'd hear him as he walked down the hallway. He'd already have his belt out of his pants and it would be folded over so he could make those snapping noises with it. It was like hearing the fall of the guillotine and knowing I was next.

Have you "walked on eggshells" to avoid setting off a parent's rage?

As an adult I was very fortunate to be part of a men's group. I was one of ten and we all were close in age. I remember talking about my father and his rage, but I didn't believe I came from an abusive home. My friends just laughed. Obviously, I didn't think walking on egg shells around my dad so as not to set him off, or being used by your mother to find love from her parents was abusive. I guess everything is in the eye of the beholder.

I mentioned that I was a rage-a-holic and looking back on my life I sure scared a lot of people. Especially my wives and children. I never hit my children but they definitely lived through moments when they thought I would. Even my employees would tiptoe around me at times. When Phyllis, my first wife, was pregnant with Melissa, our first child, we would lie in bed and talk about how having a child would change our lives. We talked about how we would raise our children and

What is your definition of a good parent?

I mentioned that I thought it was right that children grow up fearing their fathers. You would not believe the look Phyllis gave me. My belief is that everything we learn about other people and the world around us we learn over the kitchen table. All the good things and all the bad. My mother feared her father and my Dad his mother. It was natural that our children should fear us. Looking back I have to ask myself, what the hell was I thinking?

I mentioned that both my brothers were rage-a-holics too. I remember being in Chicago on business and having dinner at my brother David's house. When I arrived David had just left to pick-up dinner and I was in the kitchen talking to my sister-in-law, while their two boys were downstairs in the basement family room playing video games. This was during the NBA playoffs and David was an avid Bull's fan. Upon arriving back to the house he immediately went downstairs to see if his VCR was recording the game. When he discovered that his sons, when turning on their game system, had inadvertently shut off the VCR, he went into a rage. Upstairs I heard him. His voice, yelling and screaming, sounded just like my dad. In an instant I was transported back to my childhood and instantly felt the same sense of fear and dread I did as a boy. Both my brothers have two boys, now in their 20s. I hope they don't sit down with their pregnant wives someday and share with them their belief that children should fear their fathers.

What is or would be your parenting style?

From what you just read you probably think my parents were the most horrible people on earth, but they were not. They were both caring and loving and provided me with some wonderful childhood memories. My Dad passed away in 1994 and in his later years tried to apologize for the father he was. My mother is going strong at 91 and she often will apologize for the way things were for us children growing up. I would usually tell them both that I understood, for I was fortunate to know their parents. The apple doesn't fall far from the tree.

CHAPTER 4

AND LUCKMAN, YOU PLAY RIGHT FIELD

As a kid I don't remember a day that I did not feel some form of fear. I wasn't athletic and I didn't think of myself as very smart. I always believed everyone else was smarter than me. Consequently school was a fearful place. A place where I would be laughed at and ridiculed for a wrong answer, a slip of the tongue or a low grade on a paper. But inside the school building was a piece of cake compared to what transpired outside those brick walls.

Let me give you an example. Try to picture an early spring day in Chicago. The cold frozen winter ground has slowly warmed up from sun filled days and temperatures in the 50s and 60s. Almost every

LUCKMAN'S LAWS
- Children can be especially cruel. The greatest gift you can teach them is tolerance.
- It is never your plan, but God's plan for you. Let go and let God do his work.
- Hidden within every adversity is a nugget of opportunity. But unless you look for it you'll never find it.
- If you expect to make a mistake you will. If you expect to screw-up you will. If you expect to fail you will. The Universe gives you everything you ask for.

What subject or sport made you nervous - or got you left out?

child waking up to this beautiful morning would be looking forward to a fun filled day playing with their friends at recess or a gym class moved outdoors. But not me. No, I was thinking about the gym class, but not in the same way as the others. It was spring and that meant softball. Sixteen inch softball to be exact. No gloves and just your bare hands to catch that brand new hard as hell Clincher softball.

Now my childhood body was deceiving. I was of normal height and weight and I looked athletic. But I was anything but. When it came to sports, any sports, I had to work three times as hard as the other kids just to be mediocre. I wasn't fast. I wasn't agile. And, I wasn't particularly coordinated. So was I feeling the thrill of spending gym class outside playing baseball on that warm sunny spring day? Anything but. I felt nothing but fear. Fear of having to perform in front of my classmates. Fear of being judged. Fear of failing. Fear of letting my teammates down. Fear of humiliation. If you can think of any other fears, jot them down and send them to me for I'm sure I had them too.

First, came the picking of teams. Of course the gym teacher picked his favorites to be team captains. Those who were the best athletes.

If captains were picking teams when did your name get called?

How I hated them. In my world they were everything that I was not. Of course their first choices were always their friends. Usually other good athletes. Then they started choosing from the remaining pool of boys. Those who weren't great softball players, but weren't really that bad. I waited anxiously in this group hoping to hear my name called out. As each captain picked his team the pool of the unchosen got smaller and smaller until there was just me and the real nerdy kids left. Finally, my name was called. But certainly, not very enthusiastically. My team captain knew what he was getting when he chose Luckman. The humiliation and fear had just begun.

Next for the team captains came assigning the nine positions. It wasn't necessary for me to even listen; I knew where I was going. But finally here it came, "And Luckman, you play right field." Of course, where else would they put the kid who would probably drop every fly ball that came his way?

As we walked out onto the still moist field to our assigned places my mind would be racing with one horrifying scenario after another. A fly ball would be hit to me and my ears would be filled with the screams of eight 10 year olds (and probably the gym teacher too) all yelling, "Luckman don't drop it." And of course I would. Or, it would be a grounder, and as I picked up the ball to throw it to the infield I would hear the chorus yelling to me where I should throw it, but of course, I would throw it to the wrong person. Or, when it came time to bat (and you know I was the last to bat), I would strike out. It was at this tender young age that I learned the meaning of self-fulfilling prophesy. For sure enough, my scenarios became my reality. And with it every fear and humiliation a young boy could feel.

Were you afraid of being embrassed in front of your classmates?

WHAT I KNOW NOW THAT I WISH I KNEW THEN

When I was about 20 years old I was in an automobile accident. Although the accident wasn't too serious I began having severe pain in my lower back and down my legs. So severe in fact that I often needed the help of one of my brothers to help me get in and out of the bathtub and to get dressed in the morning. At the suggestion of our family doctor I went to see an orthopedist.

Have you endured a physical injury?

Knowing that I had recently been in an accident the first thing the doctor did was to order up a full set of x-rays of my lower back. He then had me lie down on my back to determine my range of motion. As he bent my legs back the pain increased until it became excruciating. When his assistant brought in the x-rays he immediately put them on the light box to determine if the pain was caused by the bruising of the soft tissue or was it something more serious, like injury to the disc. I wasn't expecting what came next.

"You know, you're missing your fifth lumbar vertebrae in your lower back and the base of your spine curves to the right," he said. What? I'm missing part of my back? Where did it go? "No place," he responded, "you never had it. It's a congenital defect that we see now and then." What does that mean? "It means I have good news and bad news for you. The good news is this will probably keep you out of the Vietnam War. The bad news is you'll suffer from back problems all of your life." He was right on both.

Has your lack of physical ability or health revealed something about you?

My dad was 5"11". Both my brothers about 6'. I am 5'9½" tall. If I had my missing vertebrae I would have been closer in size to my dad and brothers. But it was the curvature of my spine that caused me the most pain. And not necessarily physical pain, but emotional pain. You see, the curving of my spine caused my right hip to be higher than my left hip, which in turn caused me to be less agile, and certainly not as fast a runner as my schoolmates. Earlier, I mentioned that I had to work three times as hard as the other kids just to be mediocre. I could have worked ten times harder and it still would not have made any difference. I was destined to suffer the verbal abuse and the humiliation of not being very good at sports my entire childhood. As an adult I had choices. And one of my choices was to not participate in sports. Any sports. For the fear and pain of being humiliated and laughed at was so ingrained in me that it could not be overcome. Nor did I even want to. So I just made up excuses to why I didn't play tennis, or golf, or softball, or water ski. Although I did take up snow skiing when I was between marriages (to meet the ladies) until I tore up my left knee. And when we owned our horse I'd saddle her up and ride into the foothills. I actually became a pretty good rider. No barrel racing or calf roping, but pretty good nonetheless.

On December 31, 1966 I received a letter from the U.S. Government Department of the Selective Service. It began, "Greeting: Uncle

Sam wants you," or something to that effect. I always wondered why Greeting: and not Greetings: I guess that the news was so bad for those of us receiving this letter that only one greeting would suffice. I was being drafted into the Army at a time when the war in Vietnam was escalating and 1 out of every 3 draftees was being sent to fight in a far off jungle to keep America and the world safe from Communism.

How do you feel when you get an official goverment letter?

My orthopedist gave me my x-rays and wrote a letter to my draft board describing my unique physical problems. In the fall of 1966 I was classified 1A. This meant they could call me up at any time. With my x-rays in hand and my doctor's letter I was able to get a meeting in front of the entire draft board. There was a doctor on this all volunteer board who read the letter and looked at the x-rays. I'll never forget what he said next, "Son, you mean they actually accepted you with this?" Yes sir they did, but at the time of my pre-induction physical I didn't know I had this problem. "I'll tell you what we're going to do," he said, "we will see that you get another pre-induction physical." Music to my ears. Oh the joy.

I waited three weeks to hear back from my draft board with notice of my second physical, instead I received another 1A draft card in the mail. What was going on? Where was the notice for another physical? I hopped into my car and drove to my Selective Service office on Devon and Clark streets. I bounded up the stairs to the second floor only to wait my turn to speak to a clerk. Finally my turn came. After explaining my predicament and the fact that the entire draft board had recommended me for a new pre-induction physical why was I still classified as 1A? That's when I heard the chilling news. Federal law stated that I was already given one pre-induction physical and

What "new year" do you remember as stressful?

that was it. One and no more. My next physical would be my induction physical, the one they give you right before they put you on a bus to some far away city to begin basic training.

In November of that year I met my future wife although at the time I wasn't sure if I had much future. The draft notice came on December 31, 1966 just in time to ruin my New Year's plans. Out of kindness, my folks didn't give me my Greeting: letter until January 2nd.

On a cold blustery January morning at 6:30 AM my dad drove me down to a non-descript Chicago building on Van Buren Street just west of downtown. With my three days clothes and one month's spending money my dad hugged and kissed me and with tears in both our eyes we said goodbye. As I rode the elevator to the 4th floor all I could think of was this was it. I'm going to Vietnam. As much as I detested the war and the politicians who sent us there, young boys like me would fight and die for the hubris of old men.

Have you ever felt like a number, not a person?

As memory serves me there were nineteen stations we had to wend our way through by following a 3 inch wide yellow line painted on the linoleum. There we were all of us in our t-shirts and boxers and briefs being poked at and prodded by both doctors and corpsman. At one point after reading my doctors letter, a doctor laid me back on an examining table and bent my legs back and forth to see how much range I had and how painful it was for me. I may have embellished the pain somewhat since I wasn't experiencing any major problems at the time. But when offered to view my x-rays I had brought with me just in case, he refused. From there it was just moving from one station to the next until we reached Station 18. We were almost to the finish line. We lined up outside this long open window where doctors sat at desks on the other side. As you moved forward you handed your file to the doctor, he would look at it, rubber stamp it with some government wording or just write in it and hand it back to you and guide you to where you needed to go next.

I was the third young man in my line so it was easy to hear what the doctor said to each of my future Army buddies as he made notations in their files and handed them back. The first boy handed the doctor his file and after briefly reading the results, the doctor took out one of his rubber stamps and stamped something in the file. As he handed the file back to the boy he told him to head on home. His bad knee prevented him from military service. You could see the joy on his face as he quickly ran to get dressed and leave the building. The next boy was told the same thing. Except there was no joy. He had enlisted. So number two went, if not as merrily as number one had, on his way.

Now came my turn. I handed my paperwork to the doctor expecting he'd pick-up one of those oversized rubber stamps, as he did twice before, but instead he just wrote something in my file, handed it back and told me to advance to the next station. What was the next station? Would some doctor there read my file and look at my x-rays and then send me home? I quickly got dressed and preceded to Station 19. As the yellow line turned a corner to the right my eyes looked up to the sign above the door. In big letters it read Station 19 INDUCTION. This is where they administer the oath and send you on your way. My future for the next 2 years was working for Uncle Sam. And the work could be hazardous to my health.

When have you felt you were in the wrong place at the wrong time?

As I entered the room there was a corpsman standing at the front collecting the individual files. As each new recruit handed in his file the corpsman would read the last doctor's comments and either tell the new recruit to take a seat or to go home. I handed him my file and in a rush of anger asked him why nobody had taken a look at my x-rays. While I was asking my anything but innocuous question he said something to me. Not having heard him I politely asked if he could repeat what he said. In a very condescending tone he repeated, "Go home. You're physically unfit for military service." What? You don't want me? I didn't have to be told twice. I ran across the hallway to the room that stored my winter jacket and my gym bag containing my 3 days' worth of fresh clothes. I grabbed my jacket and satchel in hand headed for the stairs, not wanting to waste any time waiting for the elevator. With my jacket still in my hand and the temperature in the teens I ran out onto the street to hail a taxi. By 10:30 I was home looking through the glass pane in our front door. With tears in her eyes I could see my mother vacuuming the hallway. My knock startled her but when she saw me through the glass her face turned from one of sadness to one of enormous joy. She ran to the door, threw it open and gave me a hug I'll never forget. Two weeks later I received my 1Y Selective Service Classification. Physical deferment. Can only be called up in a national emergency.

You know that old saying that God works in mysterious ways? I guess he does. I can't begin to tell how many times I was laughed at and humiliated in the school gym and on the field by my lack of athletic skills. How I wanted to be part of the popular group of kids. Those who were good at sports. And the girls who wanted to be friends with them. I can't begin to tell you of the fear I felt each day upon wakening and wondering what shame and embarrassment would befall me that day. And yet, here I was, safe from an unjust war and alive. My name was not on a black granite wall. Safe and secure because of the very things that caused me so much childhood pain. Thank you God.

When has something turned out to be a blessing in disguise?

CHAPTER 5

You see things; and you say, "Why?" But I dream things that never were; and I say, "Why not?"
— George Bernard Shaw

FROM OVERCAST TO SUNNY SKIES

From late 1971 until January of 1973 I had the best job in the world. I was one of five senior buyers for Toys R Us, and I worked with some of the best people in the toy industry. I had never wanted to be a buyer, preferring to be in front of the desk selling, rather than behind it buying. In addition, a number of buyers I knew who worked for national chains were not always on the up and up. Sometimes these buyers accepted large screen televisions and trips to exotic resorts to help them make the "right" buying decisions. This was a club that I

LUCKMAN'S LAWS
- Never ever walk into someone's office without knowing at least a little bit of the history of the company.
- It is absolutely amazing how many people and companies make money for quite a while before their lack of knowledge catches up with them.
- Be friendly to everyone. The guy in the corner pushing the broom today could be your buyer tomorrow.
- Life would be perfect if we could be like little children who naturally accept others regardless of race, culture or religion.

didn't want to be associated with. But buyers at Toys R Us were different. Before I could even go to work for them I had to submit to a polygraph test to ensure that I was an honest person and not prone to accepting kickbacks and bribes.

It was quite a change for me. Before taking this job I was a junior salesman for Milton Bradley Company, the number one manufacturer of board games and then Globe Wholesale, which was the largest and most progressive distributor of toys, school supplies and trim-a-tree products in the nation. In my four years selling in the toy industry I became friends with many of the salespeople I would later buy from. These were men and women in senior selling positions. I looked up to them and wanted to be like them. Most dressed well, drove fancy cars and had generous expense accounts. But it turns out the trapping of success did not mean they were good salespeople. Some used incentives or inducements that were out of bounds for a straight shooter like me.

What did you feel in your first big job?

I truly enjoyed being a buyer. And to be a buyer for the largest toy retailer in the world was certainly a feather in this young man's cap. I was responsible for not only buying the product but I had to give every item I bought a retail price at a profit margin that sustained the company. And it was here that I learned the discipline that would serve me well in everything I did later in life. Les Kempner and Ron Tuchman were my mentors and I can't ever thank them enough.

What was most interesting was dealing with the various salespeople who called on me, both in-house people and manufacturer's representatives. As you would expect, some were great salespeople and some were good salespeople. But there were many who were mediocre at best. For a buyer, what differentiates the great from the mediocre is the salesperson's knowledge. The great knew not only their line backwards and forwards, but they also knew all there was to know about their competitors' product lines. As an example, one category I

What criteria do you use to judge good versus bad sales people?

bought was microscopes and chemistry sets, an extremely confusing category to buy. The subtle differences in sets were not often easy to discern. And since we carried multiple sets at different price points I had to rely on the salesperson to help me put a program together. At the time there were two manufactures I bought from, Skillcraft and Gilbert. The Skillcraft rep was a blessing. He not only knew his line but he knew the Gilbert line just as well. He would often steer me to the best value, even if it meant not selling me his product. The Gilbert rep was totally opposite. When I would ask, "What's the difference between this microscope and that microscope?" He would take the catalog from me and read me the description. I could do that!

One of the first two things you learn when you become a buyer is, one, to read upside down. That's so you can see the rep's price sheet, and know if you are getting the best deal. And the second is to look through a manufacturer's catalog of products and their price lists and determine how they laid it out; alphabetically, numerically or by product category. I did not enjoy having to wait for a salesperson to take the catalog from me, fumble through it and then read me what it said. This type of salesperson always slowed me down. And

What were your goals when you decided you could sell for a living?

as most of you know time is your most precious commodity. Many times I would tell them to go get a cup of coffee and wait in the lobby. And when the purchase order was ready I'd send for them. I bought from these people not because I wanted to, but because I had to. I needed their products in my stores because my customers wanted these brands. But when it came to the lesser known product lines they carried and wanted to sell me, the answer was always NO!

I vowed that if I ever went back into sales I would be the type of rep I'd want calling on me. Reps who knew their product line, catalog and price list layout and knew their competitors' lines as well as their own. This type of rep is a Godsend to buyers. When I did get back into sales I think I succeeded in becoming that type of rep.

I cannot reflect on this time in my career without sharing a short story with you about ego and fear. Early in my tenure as a buyer I got a call from a manufacturer's rep who at the time represented a very hot line, Matchbox Cars. This rep made a lot of money with Matchbox and experienced what often happens to reps who sell a hot line; other hot lines come to them. They don't have to be good salespeople, in fact there were many times I would ask myself, did the rep make the line, or did the line make the rep? All too often mediocre salespeople made a lot of money in spite of their poor selling skills. That is until their hot line went cold.

Anyway back to my story. I knew who this rep was. I had met him numerous times and when I saw him I always made it a point to be friendly and say hello. But at the time, I was just a "junior" salesman at Milton Bradley and a "jobber" rep at Globe Wholesale. I was just a kid and no one he had to acknowledge. After all, he was a big time rep and I was small potatoes. Until I went to work for Toys R Us, that is. Within a week or two of starting at Toys R Us I got a call from him wanting to make an appointment to show me his various product lines other than Matchbox, because another buyer was already buying his hottest line. He began the conversation by stating, "Hi Mike. This is "super rep" and you don't know me but I represent Matchbox Cars and other lines and I'd like to set an appointment to show you what I have." It was at this point that I interrupted him and said, "I know who you are. I met you (and then related the various times that we had met)." On the other end of the phone line this guy started hemming and hawing like he was a teenager calling a girl for the first time. I rescued him by asking if he would call me back in another week after I had settled in to my new job. He never called me back. Fear, humiliation and ego prevented him from ever meeting with me while I bought for Toys R Us. I wonder what he told his manufacturers when they asked him why he never sold their products to the largest toy retailer in the world.

This might be a good time to talk about a major fear I had working as a buyer. And that was, am I buying the right quantity? We

Has anyone set a bad example in your career?

used to use a formula broken down by A, B and C stores. These were how we labeled our most productive to least productive stores. If I bought 72 pieces for an A store, then a B store might get 60 pieces and a C store 48 pieces, less any inventory we currently had on the counter. But even with a formula, when your pencil sits above a little box and you are committing your company's assets, doubt and fear tend to make you think twice. This is a good thing. But sometimes your doubts and fears run over work hours and you bring them home with you at night. Not a good thing. One day I brought this up with one of my colleagues, Phil Bloom. Phil was about five years older than me and an excellent buyer. Over lunch Phil gave me some excellent advice. He said, "Mike, (I went by Mike back then) accept the fact that no matter what quantity you put down you're never going to be right. You are either going to buy too much and have to carry it over and mark it down to get rid of it, or you're going to buy too little, disappoint your customers and miss sales. So just use your best judgment. That's what they pay you for." After that lunch I never worried about it again.

Are you afraid to make important decisions because you might make a mistake?

I have another story you may enjoy. One of the categories I purchased was sporting goods. Now at this time there were only a handful of free-standing big box discount sporting goods stores. So Toys R Us had a fairly good sized sporting goods department. We carried the traditional sporting goods products; baseball, football, basketball and lawn games. Plus I bought soccer, hockey and camping, and we bought them deep.

Now at that time I dealt with all the major brands; Wilson, Rawlings, Spalding and Mac-Gregor, plus at least 25 smaller companies. These old line sporting goods companies had a tradition of hiring ex-jocks. Since the bulk of their business came from small mom and pop sporting goods stores located in practically every town and hamlet in the country, this talent pool

Do you see people with less talent or knowledge getting ahead?

worked well for them. These mom and pop owners were enamored of these ex-jocks and often invited them home to have dinner with them, and then invite all their friends over to meet the receiver who caught the winning touchdown pass in the Cotton Bowl of whatever

How do you feel when someone tries to "big-time" you?

year. Now, I had a cousin my Dad's age, who had played professional football for the Chicago Bears by the name of Sid Luckman. Growing up, Sid would invite me to Bear's training and introduce me to the team. So meeting or knowing jocks was not a huge deal for me. Plus, I always perceived famous people as being just regular people with extraordinary talent.

One day I had a meeting with one of these major suppliers to set the program for that particular year. It might have been MacGregor. The receptionist called to say that "Biff Jones" (or so we'll call him) was here to see me. I told her to go ahead and send him back to my office. Within a minute there was this huge guy filling my doorway. With his beefy hand he shook mine and introduced himself as, "Biff Jones" Rose Bowl 1959.

After a little chit-chat we got to work. Now at the time we bought as a distributor and not as a retailer, since the quantities we purchased were huge and distributor pricing was cheaper than retail pricing. The first question "Biff" asked me was who was Tamaron Distributing? I explained that we were a toy and sporting goods wholesaler. His next question was who do we sell to? I told him that the bulk of our vast inventory went to our own stores. His next

Have you ever been disappointed by a prominent person?

question floored me because our offices happened to be in the same building and around the corner from one of our stores. He asked, which ones are your stores?

It was beyond belief that a major manufacturer could hand over one of their largest accounts, if not the largest account to one of their salespeople, and that person would have no idea who they were calling on. I know that there was no Internet then to do a little research. But come on. Ask your boss. Ask your colleagues. Go to the library. Or, just figure it out yourself - with our office entrance less than 20 feet east of a large Toys R Us sign. This certainly wasn't rocket science.

Unfortunately, the best job in the world would leave me all too soon. At the time, there were two divisions of Toys R Us. There was Children's Bargain Town headquartered in suburban Chicago where I worked, and Toys R Us out of Beltsville, MD. Both were owned by Interstate Stores, which also owned Topps Discount Stores located in the mid-west and eastern regions of the country, and White Front Stores located on the west coast. They also owned a number of department store chains scattered across the country. Since each division of Toys R Us was a duplicate of the other, Interstate Stores decided to merge the two buying groups and move them both to New Jersey.

If the best job you ever had was gone, where would you go?

Now I certainly had nothing against New Jersey, but if I were to move away from Chicago and my friends and family I was hoping the move would be to; San Francisco, Dallas or Atlanta. Someplace far away from the harsh winters of the Mid-West. I was probably the first of the buyers in our division to let management know that even if offered a position in New Jersey, I would turn it down. And so, I put out the word that I was looking for a position as either a buyer or seller and I'd be willing to move if offered a job in one of my three chosen locations.

Through the son of the toy buyer at Montgomery Ward's, who was also in the toy industry, word reached me that there was a man in San Jose, California who wanted to open up an up-scale chain of freestanding toy stores, and he was looking for someone with my background and experience. So on a beautiful mid-January Super Bowl VII weekend in 1973, I flew out to San Jose to interview for a position as Vice President of Merchandising for Magic Village Toys and Things.

Where is your ideal place, and why aren't you working there?

Having been to Los Angeles only once, and only for a few days, I had no idea where San Jose was. Dionne Warwick's song, *"Do You Know the Way to San Jose?"* didn't help either because it wasn't very specific. But a Texaco road-map placed it about 45 miles south of San Francisco. And oh what a thrill. If I took the job, my daughters would be California girls.

To those of us who grew up in Chicago in the late 1950's and early 1960's, California was the magic kingdom. It was definitely California dreaming with the Beach Boys, Jan and Dean, surfing, and even Dick Clark's *Bandstand*. And in 1973 it was Haight Ashbury and the sum-mer of love in San Francisco. What could be better?

I was offered the position and flew back to Chicago Sunday night. By Monday evening, after non-stop conversations with my wife Phyl-lis, we decided to accept the position. The decision to move was virtu-ally a no-brainer. My salary would be 20% higher than I was earning at Toys R Us. I would have a great title. I would get stock options. And best of all, we would be living in the Golden State.

The following weekend Phyllis and I flew back out to San Jose to look for a house. We expected this city, known then as the Valley of the Heart's Delight, to be just like the cities back east. The first ques-tion Phyllis asked my new boss, George Shahood, was where the Jewish neighborhood was. George was Lebanese and his wife German, and when he answered it was with a laugh in his voice. "There is none," he responded. "Just like there is no Ital-ian neighborhood or Irish neighborhood. People in San Jose just live where they choose." And so off we went to buy our dream house in what we soon discovered was a fully integrated neighborhood.

Do you expect people to be prejudiced?

In 1973 San Jose was growing by leaps and bounds. This sleepy little agricultural town established in 1776, always in the shadow of San Francisco and Oakland (and soon to be larger than both), was now growing silicon, the base material for semiconductor chips. In time San Jose would be known throughout the world as Silicon Valley. With all this growth came a huge selection of new homes to choose from. As you drove down the main thoroughfares you would see sign after sign advertising new housing developments. On Saturday we went from one development to another until we finally decided on one, Shadow Brook, in Almaden Valley. This was where we were going to buy. Growing up in Chicago we didn't have mountains. We didn't even have hills. But from the living room of our new home we would soon gaze upon a beautiful hill and from our back yard the lush Santa Cruz Mountains where lumberjacks still plied their trade. On Sunday we went back to the builder's offices and purchased our California dream home, a 5 bedroom, 3 bath, 2,600 square foot two story home on a cul-de-sac off another cul-de-sac, for a little over $50,000. The perfect home to raise our 2 and 4 year old daughters.

On March 17, 1973 we said good-bye to our friends and family and in typical mid-western fashion left Chicago during a snowstorm for the clear blue skies, sunshine and unbelievably green mountains of Northern California. We arrived in San Jose on Wednesday March 21st about noon and immediately found a hotel to rest before we set off to find a furnished apartment, since our new home would not be completed until June. With so many people moving to San Jose it wasn't difficult finding a furnished apartment, just difficult finding one that allowed children. After going from complex to complex we came across one that accepted families and as it turned out was within a mile of my new work. On Thursday we moved into a 2 bedroom 2 bath completely furnished apartment. With average high temperatures of 67 degrees in March it wasn't difficult to acclimate ourselves to California living.

When you left home, were you excited, sad or ?

Our first visit to our new home came on Friday. There wasn't much to see, just the forms for the foundation. But it was certainly a thrill. We walked around the foundation talking about which room was which and how we were going to decorate it. For the next three months we made our pilgrimage at least twice a week hardly containing our excitement as our dream home took shape. In mid-June we closed on the house and pulled our furnishings out of storage. It was everything we dreamed of and more, especially the fact that the girls each had their own rooms and could choose how they wanted to decorate them.

Within 30-45 days all of our neighbors had moved in and the great news was almost all of them had children for our daughters Melissa and Jennifer to play with. Weekends would find all of the families outside while dads cleared the ground of rocks and boulders to begin laying the sprinkler system for the sod and greenery to come.

Every home was occupied by a young couple with small children with the only difference being our ethnic backgrounds. From the

What did you notice about your new neighborhood?

cul-de-sac that led to our cul-de-sac, two houses backed up to our home. The first was owned by an African-American family with three children. Next door to them was a Chinese family with two kids. Then our house. Next door to us on the other side was an Italian family with one daughter and next to them an Irish family with three children.

Across the street we had a Japanese family with no children yet. Then a German family with two children the same ages as my two. Then another Japanese family expecting their first child and finally another Italian family with two children. This certainly was not like any Chicago neighborhood that I'd ever been in.

Phyllis grew up in Fargo, North Dakota. Growing up in her neighborhood there were just a handful of Jewish families. Her neighbors may not have been Jewish but they were certainly all white. On the other hand growing up on my block in Chicago everyone was Jewish and practically everyone in my grammar school was Jewish, including most of the teachers and the principal. To my wife and I living in San Jose was like living in the United Nations where all the inhabitants came from either some other country, or experienced an entirely different culture from the ones Phyllis and I did growing up.

Now, you probably think that I was very uncomfortable in these surroundings, considering how I was raised, but I was anything but. Yes, it was strange. I had never experienced anything like it. But in a way it was both stimulating and liberating. It challenged me to open up to new people and new ideas. It was like being set free, no longer was I insulated from the world around me. I grew to learn about others who were different from me. Those who were born into a different religion or those who grew up in a distant land that I'd only read about in textbooks. I shared with my new neighbors what it was like growing up in my home in Chicago, and they shared with me what it was like in theirs. And do you know something? Their dreams for themselves and their children were no different than my dreams for me and my children. And when you come down to it that's all that really matters.

Have you been defined by your race or religion?

Nothing brought me greater joy than seeing my daughters playing with their friends. Color of skin made no difference. Nor who went to religious services on Friday night and who went on Sunday morning. They were just kids having fun.

San Jose is the capital of Silicon Valley and it is what every American city should be like. Drive through any neighborhood or walk through any mall and you're going to see people from every nation on earth. The parents might still wear their traditional garb, but the kids all wear Gap, Disney and Nike. My grandchildren participate in their grammar school's yearly play and of course Papa and Nana Arleen have to be there to cheer them on. What's amazing is seeing all those brown, black and freckled faces all together. This is what America could be. This is what America should be.

What is your vision of the country?

CHAPTER 6

"I've been absolutely terrified every moment of my life --
and I've never let it keep me from doing a single
thing I wanted to do."

– Georgia O'Keeffe

ACCEPTING AN AWARD

On March 26, 1973 I went to work for George Shahood at Magic Village. George was a successful retailer. He owned a chain of television stores in Northern California called Continental TV that he grew from a single store. In those days there were no electronics superstores just smaller retailers offering televisions only.

George had several children living at home whom he adored. Especially his youngest daughter Sasha. There was a toy store directly

LUCKMAN'S LAWS

- When faced with the choice more people prefer death than public speaking. Luckily for them, they won't have to give the eulogy at their own funeral.
- When standing face-to-face with your greatest fear remember that the worst part is already over. It was the days and weeks of worry leading up to this moment that were excruciating. Now it's just a matter of doing it.

- Never be afraid to make mistakes. We're all human and that's how human beings learn.
- Fear is a lot like dark threatening rain clouds. From afar they look intimidating but up close they have the consistency of cotton candy.

across the street from his main San Jose store and George was in there several times a week buying presents for his children.

Starting in 1972 George began closing down most of his stores. But, not by his choice. The early seventies saw new lower prices for color television sets and George wanted to capture sales in as many metro markets as he could. The problem was his agreement with Sylvania Corporation, his main resource, limited his geographic market to just the San Francisco bay area. But 90 miles to the northeast was Sacramento, and George saw opportunity. He opened several stores in this

Have you witnessed a dying industry or business?

new market and stocked them with product from his bay area stores. That was until Sylvania found out. And, when they did they stopped selling to Continental TV. Without product there was nothing George could do but to close down his stores one-by-one and bring a federal lawsuit against Sylvania for restraint of trade.

With nothing really to do, George decided to open what he hoped would be a chain of very elaborate free-standing toy stores. What could be more fun than owning a toy store? His architect came from Las Vegas, and had recently designed Circus Circus. As Vice President of Merchandising and later President, my job was to buy all of the merchandise, retail price every item, layout the store, and choose the items we would advertise each week. To do all this I found myself working upwards of 100 hours a week, 7 days 6 nights. Lucky I was young.

The store was quite unique. It was triangular in shape with approximately 30,000 square feet, and three stories tall. Floor one was carpeted, unheard of in those days, and had a yellow brick tile road circling the selling floor. Floors two and three were mezzanines with the second floor used to display infant and children's products, and the third floor used for storage. Towards the back of the main floor we had a Big Rock Candy Mountain that hid a children's bookstore and stairs to the 2nd floor selling area. On the main floor we had a walk-in dollhouse with heart shaped windows and a full selection of upscale collector dolls inside. On the right as you walked in we had a zoo of stuffed animals with Plexiglas poles used as you would see metal bars on a cage. All in all it was a pretty impressive place. So impressive that we entered it into a yearly contest sponsored by Playthings Magazine, a leading toy trade periodical, in the main category of Best Toy Store Design. And we won.

What's the best work enviroment you've ever seen?

In early February 1974, during Toy Fair, the annual trade show where every manufacturer of toys displays their new products, Playthings held their awards ceremony. Since I was to be back for two weeks attending Toy Fair it was natural that I would attend the formal dinner at the 200 Fifth Ave. Club to accept our award. No problem, until I was told I had to give an acceptance speech. Public speaking scared the hell out of me. And I know I'm not alone. Studies have shown that more people fear speaking in public than fear dying. Go figure. I was OK talking to small groups but a ballroom full of toy industry leaders was out of the question. My mind raced to find a solution. I'd be back in New York for 2 weeks. Perhaps I could get sick. Maybe just laryngitis. Now, that might work. But everybody I asked for advice on finding a way out just told me to suck it up and just do it. OK, I'd find a way to do it.

How do you feel about public speaking?

The first thing I had to do was write my speech. I was told that the people in attendance wanted to know how the store came to be. What thought went into its unique design? Were more stores planned?

What would I add or do differently in the new stores? Obviously, I couldn't just say thank you. The people at Playthings suggested my speech should be about 15 to 20 minutes long. All I could think of was me saying thank you and then 15 minutes of dead silence while my mind went blank. This could be humiliating. This could be a disaster. I could almost see the next issue of Playthings Magazine with a picture of me and the caption, "Idiot accepts award for Best Toy Store Design. Gives 15 minute silent speech!"

So anyway, I wrote my speech and practiced it day and night. Fortunately, I'd have my notes in front of me when I delivered it to the audience. But that too caused me fear. What if I lost my place? Should I start over again? What would happen during the long pause while I hunted to find my

What are your coping strategies?

place? Would the audience start giggling and laughing like my classmates did in grammar school? Oh, woe is me.

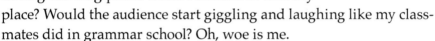

Finally, the evening arrived for the awards banquet. I was seated at the main table along with the other award recipients during dinner. They all looked so relaxed. Well sure. They didn't have to talk as long as I did. In fact all they had to do was say thank you and what a great honor this was. That was it. Me, I had to do a dissertation.

As each winner of the various categories, Best Toy Department, Best Toy Promotion, Best Doll Display, Best Whatever was called up to accept their award, my time of reckoning was coming. And then I heard the master of ceremonies say, "And now our top award for Best Toy Store Design goes to Magic Village in San Jose, CA. Accepting this award is Mike Luckman, Vice President of Merchandising." I was so scared as I walked to the stage that I thought my legs would give out from under me. But when I got to the podium an amazing thing happened. I knew that the worst was behind me. I knew I could do it. Yes, there was a quiver in my voice, at least to begin with. And yes, I could feel my heartbeat pulsing in my fingertips and when I looked down at my hands I fully expected to see the tip of my index finger glowing like E.T. in the movie. But as I went on things got better, not worse. I talked about a subject I was very familiar with. The words flowed along with the time, and before I knew it it was over and I could hear the applause. And the applause was for me. And, that felt so good. I had felt the fear but overpowered it.

The story could have ended there, but I never wanted to experience that utter feeling of fear and helplessness again. I was determined to do something about it. And that something lead me to the Dale Carnegie course upon my return home to San Jose.

Have you felt fear and overpowered in front of an audience?

For those readers who have never heard of Dale Carnegie let me introduce you. Dale Carnegie was born November 24, 1888 in Marysville, MO.

After college he went into sales, first for a company that sold correspondence courses to ranchers and later Armour and Company the huge meatpacking company where he grew his territory of South Omaha, Nebraska to #1 in the nation. With $500 saved he quit his job and moved to New York City to become a lecturer, but instead enrolled in the American Academy of Dramatic Arts. He tried out acting but soon gave it up and nearly broke, decided that he would teach public speaking. Living at the YMCA on 125th Street he convinced the management to allow him to teach a course in public speaking. Not having enough material for the time allotted he suggested to his students that they each come up to the front of the class and do a 2 minute impromptu speech on what made them angry. What followed was the beginning of the world famous Dale Carnegie Course. In 1937 Mr. Carnegie wrote a self-help book entitled How to Win Friends and Influence People. 73 years later this book is still in print and remains not only a best seller, but one that is on every CEOs bookshelf. And certainly, one that every salesperson should read.

What courses or groups could you join to overcome a fear of public speaking?

So, in March 1974 I signed up to take the basic Dale Carnegie Course. And, I've got to tell you I loved it. We met one evening a week for eight weeks. The three hour program was divided into three separate components. We would discuss the book How to Win Friends and Influence People, then move on to a discussion on another of Mr. Carnegie's books How to Stop Worrying and Start Living, and finally the part I grew to like the best, Effective Public Speaking. This part of the training was more experiential. Each week they would have each of us stand up in front of the class and give a 2-minute impromptu speech to the rest of the class. Scary! Huh?

I loved the procedure they used for choosing the topic. They would call us up one at a time and when the person before us started their 2 minute talk we picked a small folded piece of paper out of a basket. On that piece of paper was the subject of our speech. We now had less than 120 seconds to come up with what we wanted to talk about and put it into some type of order, and it had to last for the full two minutes. And believe me, those were long minutes.

Talk about tough. This was trial by fire. I remember the fear I felt in my gut each time I did it. What was comforting was knowing everyone in the class had to go through the very same thing, and I'm sure felt the same fear. But by the end of the 8 week course everyone in the class could get up and instantaneously talk for a full 2 minutes, on almost any subject.

Today I love getting up in front of groups and talking. Do I ever feel fear? Certainly. We never fully get over fear. What we want to learn is to walk through it. To overpower the fear. To not let it stop us. Feel it, acknowledge it, and then go ahead and do it anyway. What's the worst thing that's going to happen to you? Make a mis-  **Could you learn to love public speaking?** take? So what. That's what life is for. How else would we ever learn? How many times do babies pull themselves up only to lose their balance and fall down on their padded bottoms? If they gave up because of fear of failing the majority of the world would be crawling their way to work. Can you picture that? Only the fearless ones would be standing tall and walking. Which one are you?

CHAPTER 7

STAY IN ELECTRONICS OR GO BACK TO TOYS

Things did not work out as I had expected at Magic Village. George Shahood lost his lawsuit against Sylvania when the U.S. Supreme Court reversed a lower court's judgment in his favor. It was then that I realized that Magic Village was financed on a house of cards, borrowed money based on a lawsuit that went south. Large freestanding toy stores lose money nine months of the year. They break even in the tenth month and make all their profit in the last two months. With investors worried about their loans to the company, new funding looked questionable and without new funding it was only a matter of time until Magic Village collapsed.

In early December 1974 I was approached by National Semiconductor, a $250 million semiconductor manufacturer in Silicon Valley California. They had created a consumer products division several years prior by the name of Novus to manufacture calculators and

LUCKMAN'S LAWS
- Others may bully you and trash your ideas, but don't think you can out bully them.
- Examine your anger at others, especially when you feel like name-calling. Ask yourself, what in my background is handicapping me – and how can I choose another way.

- Arrogance has its roots in believing your own press or the stories you make up about yourself in order to feel more important or better than other people. It is then that you become a legend in your own mind.
- It has been said that people rise to their own level of incompetence. Don't let your competence in one area be undermined by your fear of taking steps to change your attitude or behavior.

LED watches and clocks. These two products lines were the first consumer electronic products in the marketplace. In 1974 these products were creating enormous profits for the three largest manufacturers: National Semiconductor, Bowman and Texas Instruments. Novus had an idea for a children's calculator toy and had no idea how to enter the toy market. So in late 1974 I was offered a position to be the new Marketing Manager for toys. I was to work alongside their two other Marketing Managers, one for calculators and one for watches and clocks.

Have you ever invented or launched a product? How does your story compare to mine?

The engineers at Novus had created a somewhat different calculator for children. Rather than an LED readout, like typical calculators, they instead had two colored LEDs, one red and one green. Prior to my arrival they had already decided upon using an owl overlay where the red and green LEDs became the owl's eyes.

One additional feature was a question mark key (?). The way this children's calculator worked was the child had to solve the math problem first, using basic arithmetic, then enter the problem into the calculator and press the equal's key (=) and then enter the answer. Once everything was entered the child could now press the question mark key (?). If they were correct the green LED would light up, and if they were wrong, the red one lit. We named the product the Quiz Kid.

My immediate role was twofold; I first had to create a business/marketing plan. How should we go to market? What retail stores would it be sold in? Who would sell it to those retailers? What should be the wholesale price? What type of advertising would it need to succeed? How many could we sell? Second, I needed to get the product ready for the retail world.

First, we needed a workbook for the math problems. Preferably games for the children to play. Second, we needed to create a package that would show the product well but protect it from being pilfered while on the retail counter. And third, we needed some accessories, a drawstring bag for kids to carry it around, and a sticker as an award. And we needed to do all of this in the first three months of 1975 if we expected to have an impact on Christmas toy sales.

I began with the workbook. Through the advice of educators we chose the University of Minnesota College of Education to develop a workbook for us. It was made up of numerous math games that children could play. Since they had to use their math skills to come up with the right answer, we felt we shouldn't have a problem with parents who otherwise might object to a calculator that could become a crutch, preventing their son or daughter from learning math (something we don't even consider today).

My next project was the package. I created a tag line for our toys: Novus – 21st Century Toys and Games. We brought in packaging people to create what we felt was the perfect retail package. On the front was a clear plastic window that showed off the Quiz Kid but prevented opening the package to steal the calculator. Also on the front was a picture of a young boy and girl playing with the Quiz Kid on the floor with the workbook open in front of them. On the back was a letter from me addressed to parents. My next project was defining the market: which retailers would carry the product and who should sell it to them?

The mid 1970's saw the emergence of a major market for electronic gadgetry. The four function calculators that originally sold for $350 were now dropping in price due to the increased yields experienced in the manufacture of semiconductors. As more chips proved viable on a disc, the price per unit dropped and so did the price of the finished product; calculators, watches and clocks.

In 1975 the major retail outlets for electronic products were department stores. Every department store chain across the country created an electronics department, usually on the main floor where foot traffic was the highest. Because electronic calculators and watches were in high demand these department store chains promoted and advertised these products heavily. It was not unusual to see full-page advertisements from the various department stores every Sunday in newspapers across the country.

To reach this market Novus employed approximately a dozen salespeople dedicated to working primarily with department store buyers and any other chain stores venturing into electronics. As marketing manager for toys it was my responsibility to not only define the market for electronic toys but also create the means to reach as many parents as possible who would buy their children a cutting edge product. Having been with a major toy manufacturer, then the largest toy distributor in the nation, and finally rounding out my resume as one of five senior buyers for Toys R Us and then Magic Village, I had a pretty good idea how to get the first electronic toy to market.

Other than the major toy manufacturers: Mattel, Hasbro, Kenner, Topper, Ideal and others who had their own dedicated sales force, most toy manufacturers used the services of independent manufacturers' representatives. These reps were paid a fixed commission on everything they sold that was eventually shipped. As a buyer, the majority of salespeople I worked with were manufacturers' representatives, and I liked the fact that they were usually attentive to buyers' needs and knew the competition. Hence, it was through manufacturers' reps that I wanted to bring the Quiz Kid to market. You see, even though electronic gadgets were for the most part being sold in department stores, I believed the Quiz Kid was a toy, albeit different because of its electronics, but still a toy. And toys were sold in toy stores and toy departments in both department and discount stores. And this is where my troubles began.

Novus had a sales force that was responsible for calculators and watches and clocks. They reported to my boss, Scott Brown, who was Vice President of Sales and Marketing. His background was as a semiconductor salesman, in a business-to-business selling environment. He had no experience marketing consumer products. However, he did have experience as a consumer, which he thought would be sufficient for directing how the Quiz Kid should be marketed and sold. At the time I was working with him my perspective was that he was very much the wrong man for that part of his job. Frankly, I had almost nothing but disdain for him. Why? First, Scott believed that consumer products should be marketed like semiconductors; the higher the yield the lower the price. But lowering the retail price of a consumer product doesn't necessarily gain you greater market share. And two, his belief that electronic toys should be sold in the electronics department right next to calculators, watches and clocks. While, I on the other hand, believed it was a toy and needed to be sold by toy reps who knew toy buyers, in their individual markets and accounts.

Can you see a problem brewing here?

I did not at the time. At least, I did not see the real problem until recently when I thought about what I would have done then, given what I know now.

Have you ever been so enthusiatic you're blind to real danger?

Like most young people or experts in one particular area, I believed wholeheartedly in my own opinion. I invested 100% of my trust in myself, above anyone else's judgment or ability to comprehend the forces that were affecting the situation.

I thought the company should do things my way, when it came to the products I was responsible for.

I was a toy marketer brought into an electronics giant that was about to launch electronic toys. It should have been an ideal fit. But, I was missing a key insight about who I was based upon the ecosystem I had landed in. When you are new to a company – or you get a new manager or a new client, you must have a great deal of respect, tact, diplomatic skills, charm, and patience in order to be valuable to the company. Because it's not great ideas that make a career or a company – my life proved that. It's the ability to get along well with other people, especially when you have a difference of opinion with those who outrank you. And, that takes a great deal of self-control and empathy for many of us. Something I was short of while working at National.

I also failed to recognize that as an outsider I did not have the necessary equity or trust built up to help people see that even if they didn't understand what I was doing or agree with me, they should still take a risk on doing things my way. Yes, I knew toys and consumer product marketing, but I didn't "grow up" in the electronics business. I didn't understand the company culture, and even worse, I did not respect it. And, like a bull in a china shop, my actions made clear that I did not respect their authority, their systems or them.

Do you fail to woo people whose help and support you need?

And, so you can imagine what happened with "my" products and my career.

I was begrudgingly given the authorization to go ahead and hire toy reps to cover the nation, but it was a constant fight between my reps and the Novus' salespeople. The same thing for marketing. I developed what I believed was a solid plan that included placing the Quiz Kid on TV for a minimum four week advertising campaign in the top 15 television markets in the country. Even though my superiors did not believe in what I was doing they did allow me enough rope to hang myself. And I used every inch of it.

One of the first things I did once the Quiz Kid was ready to go into production at our Salt Lake City, Utah factory was give the Quiz Kid a partner. If we could sell the parents one item why not try for two. In comes the Whiz Kid. The difference between the two toys was that the Whiz Kid was actually a full four function calculator for children. The University of Minnesota College of Education also wrote the workbook for this item and the packaging was very similar, again with a

Have you discounted the concerns and experience of your boss or colleagues?

letter to the parents on the back from me. It was easy to expand the category with a second product and capture additional revenue.

When I wasn't flying across the country visiting potential customers or working with my reps, I was working with the engineers in creating additional products. I was fortunate to work with the head of Novus engineering, a great guy by the name of Stu Weiss. Even though Stu was also only a "consumer" and not a marketing expert, I didn't deride his skill sets because he did what I wanted him to do – respect me and collaborate with me. I considered him one of the few engineers who truly did understand consumer product marketing. I imagined he must have come from a family of merchants because in my limited experience, I found that most engineers detested marketing people. We are always asking them to do something for us, add a feature to the product or tweak a feature to add additional benefits. Often what we ask for is so outside the norm, it seems nearly impossible. So when asked, their initial response would usually be, "can't be done." Actually, if I weren't so arrogant, I would have realized that makes perfect sense. Ask someone to do something near impossible, what else would they say?

But I found if I continued to ask, very much like a child shopping with his mother who wants a new cereal and won't give up, please mom, please, I could eventually convince them that they could do it and get what I wanted. Again, this would not be what I would do now – considering this begging and whining is so demoralizing to myself and insulting to the other party.

When I was in that mindset, I could point to what I thought was the best example of this animosity between engineers and marketing people. It was a cartoon that many of the engineers put up in their cubicles. It showed a beautiful mansion on a hill with big luxury cars out in front and a sign that read Marketing. At the base of a winding road down the hill from the marketing mansion was a small ramshackle wooden structure with a crooked handwritten sign that read, Engineering.

Even before the Quiz and Whiz Kids hit the store shelves we were working on another project, a video game system. In 1975 the first home video game came to market. It was a home version of the incredibly popular arcade game made by Atari, by the name of Pong. Atari came out with a black and white home version that connected to the back of the TV through the antennae connectors. It retailed for about $50. At the same time other toy manufacturers were bringing to market black and white versions of other video games, most not too sophisticated, but all retailing for about $50.

About this time a developer came to Novus with a more advanced video game, more exciting than anything that was out there, and in full color. It was a moon landing game and would have blown all the other games currently in the marketplace out of the water. But looking at the market for video games I believed that consumers would grow weary of buying a new game and then having to move the television away from the wall so that dad could unscrew the wires, remove the current game, attach the new one to the antennae connectors and then move the TV back against the wall.

Now I am not an electrical engineer. I know virtually nothing about semiconductors or electronics. So, I went to Stu. I asked him, "Is there any way that we could put the technology that puts the signal on the TV into a permanent platform, and then put the game technology into a cartridge that we could patent, so that only our cartridge design would fit the unit?" "Sort of like the razor razorblade concept," he responded. "Exactly." As I told you earlier, Stu Weiss was one of the few engineers that I have worked with who had a firm grasp of the consumer marketplace.

My goal was to design a video game system that once attached to the television set, would never have to be removed. When they wanted to change games all the player(s) would have to do would be to remove one game cartridge and insert another. Additionally, I saw a huge revenue opportunity for Novus. Because only our patented cartridge would fit our system we could then not only create our own games, but also license other game manufacturers to design and sell their games, and pay us a royalty.

Stu and the other engineers bought into this concept and a revolutionary product was born. While the engineers were working on how to design our video game system I created a marketing and business plan. Within several months we had a working mock-up of the unit, and let me tell you, it looked great. Although it was made of plastic it had the same wood grained look as a television. The top, where the cartridge would fit, was made of a smoky plastic that gave it the overall look of quality. The business and marketing plan was quite comprehensive but yet, pretty straightforward. The product would be sold through toy stores and the toy departments in all department and discount stores. We would roll out the system in Spring 1976 using our current toy manufacturer's representatives.

I envisioned a television commercial that began by showing a family sitting on a couch facing their TV. As the camera moves in from behind we see that they're playing this exciting video game. We overhear them laughing and congratulating each other. The camera then continues past them to the TV. Our TV screen is now filled with the game as if we were playing it at home on our own TV. The announcer's voiceover would then describe the game and where it could be purchased.

We decided on a wholesale price of $65 FOB our west coast factory with a suggested retail selling price of $100. The gross profit margin for the retailer was 35%. We would hold to that price rather than seeing the item discounted and retailed for as low as $64.99. That's right! In the toy industry the practice has always been to take the most advertised and hottest toys and sell them either at cost or below. These items are used as loss leaders to entice people into the store with the hope that they'll buy other products that offer a full retail margin that could range from 30% to 70%.

Everything was in place and ready to go into production with my bosses in agreement, or so I thought. But then it happened. Word came down to me that Charlie Sporck, CEO of National Semiconductor, wanted to see me. Charlie had come from Fairchild Camera and Instruments and joined National when it was still a small struggling company facing bankruptcy. He built it into a Silicon Valley powerhouse and when I joined the company in late 1974, its revenues were approximately $250 million. Charlie was a legend in the valley. As much for his semiconductor manufacturing genius, as for his autocratic style of management. Charlie was tough. It was usually his way or the

Have you ever felt much smarter than your boss? Did you let it show?

highway. You didn't win many arguments with Charlie Sporck.

Charlie, like my direct boss Scott Brown, believed you could market consumer products the same way you marketed semiconductors, on price. As the yields improved (the number of viable chips on a silicon wafer) the price per chip dropped. The lower the cost of the chip the lower the retail price of the item the chip went into. As an example, a four function calculator when first introduced to the marketplace had an approximate retail price point of $350. But as the yields increased the prices dropped dramatically. Today you can find four function calculators as low as $1.99. Consequently price was uppermost on Charlie's mind.

So here I was, a 30-year-old marketing manager summoned to Charlie Sporck's cubicle in the main campus building on Kifer Road in Santa Clara. Am I to be praised for all the good work I was doing, or was something about to hit the fan? I was not confident. In fact, anything but. I was scared. Waiting outside his cubicle gave me even more time to create these fear-ridden thoughts about what was about to transpire.

Finally, I was ushered into his, larger than most, cubicle. And there he was, this mythic Silicon Valley figure behind his desk puffing on a big Churchill cigar. He shook my hand, gestured to a chair for me to sit down and then sat back, put his feet up on his desk and began. "Luckman, I'm shutting down the video game project," he barked. I was in total shock. "But why?" I countered.

He responded. "It's all here in your business plan." What? What could possibly be in my business plan that could make someone decide to kill off what could become a huge revenue generator for the company? Of course, now I see what "could become a huge revenue generator," I wasn't exactly holding the goose that lays the golden eggs. "Could" means "might" not "will." And, while the idea was a huge winner for another company later on, is it possible that this was not the right time or the right company? That's exactly what history shows.

"Luckman, you stated right here, that everyone in the market right now with a video game was selling it at around $50. This cartridge system is $100 and nobody is going to spend $100 for a video game when all the others are half the price." And that was it. There was no room for argument. I was scared before I came in and now my fear had risen to a critical level. His word was law. He was either right and my confidence in myself was shattered, or I was right and someone would come out with this product and I'd be vindicated. Either way I lost my baby.

It's interesting to note, that recently another person – an engineer – was credited in my local paper the San Jose Mercury News for inventing the video game system that I had envisioned. The difference between us is this engineer was involved in the successful launch of an incredible product, and I was not. In trying to set the record straight with the story's reporter, I dug through the Smithsonian records to send him an old Silicon Valley newsletter, Microelectronic News, from January 29, 1977 that stated, "Of course you know that Fairchild's tape-cassette-programmed video game is the hottest thing in the industry, but did you know that it originated at National? It was the brainchild of Mike Luckman, but National nickel-and-dimed it to death. So a disgusted ex-manager from National, later a consultant, peddled the idea to Fairchild." That quote and $2.00 will get me on the bus in most major cities. Yes, the video game system had to be marketed at another company. Novus couldn't do it. But now and then, I wonder if I could have managed myself differently and had a different story to tell about my role in this revolutionary product.

How have you felt when a dream was snatched away from you?

While we were working to get the Quiz Kid and Whiz Kid into production, and working on the video game console, Stu came to me with a question. Engineering had recently perfected sound on a chip. The ability to actually put the music scale on a semiconductor. Was there a viable consumer product we could create using this chip? As I mentioned before, I'm not an engineer, nor am I musically inclined. I don't play an instrument, I have a tin ear and I can't sing. But I do know a good idea for a consumer product when I hear one. So I bombarded Stu with questions. Could it sound like a piano? "Yes, it could." Could it sound like an organ? Once again, "yes, it could." Could it sound like percussion instruments? "Yes, yes and yes." All this from a little chip the size of your fingernail.

By now, using the above clues, you've probably guessed what consumer product I dreamed up using this new technology. Yes, that's right, an electronic keyboard. With this new semiconductor we could design a full piano-sized keyboard that would sit on any flat surface, a table or a stand. This keyboard would replicate the sound of a piano or an organ. Up until this time if you wanted a piano or organ you had to invest a lot of money and the space necessary to fit in a piece of furniture. Now you could have an incredible musical instrument sitting on your kitchen table.

Once again, I took off like a heat seeking missile, on what turned out to be another rogue mission. After a lot of thought and research, about the market and the size of the market, I was ready to write a business/marketing plan for an electronic keyboard. I learned how many Americans owned pianos. How many owned organs. How many of each were sold every year. What was the average retail price. How many people enrolled in music lessons each year. How many grade schools, middle schools and high schools offered students music lessons. I was loaded with the knowledge I'd need to write a plan that would become a roadmap for entering the market with another revolutionary product.

I forwarded my plan to my boss Scott Brown, and waited. Within a week I had my answer. Once again I was summoned to Kifer Road in Santa Clara. This time I was prepared to argue my case. Argue I did, although I wouldn't recommend that to anyone trying to do anything in a big company, unless you own it. The points I made? A keyboard was totally revolutionary. No one else had one. We would capture a huge percentage of the market before any competitors could even challenge us. We had the name recognition because of calculators and watches. We had a solid customer base. We had a direct sales force already in place as well as our toy reps. Everything was in place ready to begin designing our products. It was a win-win-win proposition. What could possibly go wrong?

So here I was again, on high, meeting with a true legend of Silicon Valley. Surely, Charlie Sporck, brilliant man that he was, would see the market opportunities for an electronic keyboard. Why I thought that, given his lack of understanding of the retail marketplace, I can only attribute to my enthusiasm, intelligence about the market and resistance to understanding the ecosystem I worked in. What my head wouldn't allow me to integrate, my gut clearly knew. His assistant ushered me into his office-cubicle telling me Mr. Sporck would be in momentarily. Nervously I waited. My mouth dry and my stomach churning. What seemed like an eternity but less than 10 minutes later, Charlie entered his office, once again puffing on his cigar, sat down behind his desk and picked up my business plan. In only a matter of minutes he would tell me what a brilliant idea I had. How it would revolutionize the musical instrument market and add hundreds of millions of top line revenue to National Semiconductor. I would be praised for my business acumen and my marketing genius. I'd be famous. These were almost delusional thoughts.

Waving my business plan in the air, Sporck looked at me directly, and said these words I'll never forget, "Luckman, don't you know that when people want a piano or an organ they want a piece of furniture. They don't want a plastic keyboard. They want a Steinway piano or a Hammond organ," referring to the premier manufacturers of pianos and organs. "They want it in black, or maple, or oak, to go with their living or family room furniture. This is not a business we want to be in," he concluded. And that was that. By the early 1980's Casio and Yamaha, both major Japanese electronics firms, had entered the marketplace and today dominate the world's market for electronic keyboards.

When has your brain told you something different than what your gut felt?

By the late fall of 1975 the Quiz Kid and Whiz Kid were on retailer's shelves across the country retailing for about $14.99. They were selling, but not in any great quantities. We planned a 4-week television advertising campaign in the 15 major markets, to begin the week of November 10th. Typically, it takes at least 2-weeks before you'll see much activity at the retail level. And even then, you're still hoping that your product will take off. Aha! Now that's the truth about the risk of "could generate revenue." Yet I had worked myself into a frenzy about how right I was nearly every time I envisioned, researched and wrote a business plan for a product.

For most of the year I was at National it was a constant battle with my bosses. As I mentioned earlier, I had very little respect for them and it showed. I told myself all kinds of things for years as a way to soothe my ego. Some of these things make some sense and some make almost none. For example, I looked at my adversaries and thought they were all engineers, with little or no knowledge of the consumer marketplace. I was only 30 years old at the time but I had a lot of experience in multiple channels of distribution. I worked for 6 years in retail selling men's clothing. I worked for Milton Bradley Company, the leading board game manufacturer and Playskool toys when Milton Bradley purchased them in 1967. From there I worked for Globe Wholesale in Chicago, then the largest toy wholesaler in the country. Then as one of five senior buyers for Toys R Us, at the time the number one toy retailer in the world, and finally Magic Village before going to work for Novus, the consumer products division of National Semiconductor. I had channel marketing down pat. From manufacturer to distributor to retailer, and all were leaders in their field.

When have you overstepped your boundaries?

Can you imagine how ego works against clear thinking? I counted my experience selling suits, shirts and ties for 6 years in retail stores as part of the evidence as to why a semiconductor company should spend millions of dollars at my direction. Of course, some of my experience bore some weight – but looking back now, it makes perfect sense why management would push back. My plans were excellent,

When have you convinced yourself you knew more than you actually did?

but plans are just that. No one has ever written a business plan that ends, "and in year five we go broke." Yet, a good many new products and companies do fail. At the time, I didn't see that perspective and couldn't comprehend the validity of it.

My fights at Novus were legendary. I saw what I thought to be the future. Not just electronic calculators for children, but vast numbers of toys using modern technology to increase a toy's play value. And then, of course, the learning potential that electronics brought to the toy industry. And, I still believed there was a market for the cartridge video game system and electronic keyboards.

Monday of Thanksgiving week, November 24, 1975 started off like any other weekday in Northern California. Winter weather had not yet started and although the overnight temperatures were dropping the daytime highs were in the 60s. At about 10:30 my boss, Scott Brown, called me into his office. He began our meeting by describing in great detail, as most engineers do, all of the arguments we had over the past year. Can you imagine the irritated feelings I engendered and the damage to my reputation I did? So much so that the details of each argument could be recounted? If I had an employee constantly fighting for his way and no other way, my memory would probably be just as good and my fuse equally short.

Scott Brown felt electronic toys would be sold in the electronics department, I in toy stores and toy departments. He believed that his direct salespeople would be best to sell our two toy items; I believed that toy reps would be the better way to go. His opinion was that the 2-weeks' worth of television advertising was a complete waste of money and the second 2-weeks should be canceled. My opinion was that it was only 2-weeks into a 4-week campaign and we'd see results by Friday of that week, the day after Thanksgiving. He also believed I had wasted a considerable amount of time and company resources on the video game system and the electronic keyboard.

Have you been fired? How did it feel?

All in all he made a pretty good case as to why I should be fired. And that's exactly what he did. I was fired. As the words sank in it felt like a horse had kicked me in the chest. I couldn't seem to breathe as fear gripped every cell within my body. It was as if my world had stopped. I couldn't believe they were doing this. It shook my confidence to the marrow. And yet, I still believed I was right. That the Quiz Kid and Whiz Kid would take off and that someday a more progressive company would bring to market a video game system like I envisioned, and electronic keyboards would be found on everyone's kitchen table. But for now, I was a member of the unemployed. What would I do next?

I'm sure I don't have to tell you that Thanksgiving 1975 was not a happy occasion in the Luckman household. I sat starring at the turkey in stunned disbelief. And all I could think of was I'll show them. But how? And then again, maybe they were right. Maybe I wasn't as smart as I thought I was. But then again, I never thought of myself as being overly smart – and yet I acted as if I was smarter than everyone at that company. And, that attitude robbed me of the chance to show them what contributions I could make – and it robbed me of the confidence I needed to move on with the ideas myself. You need a lot of guts to create a start-up company, find venture capital to fund it and run with your own ideas. It's easy to demand from others what you will not demand from yourself.

What holiday did you suffer through?

Friday, Black Friday, the day after Thanksgiving, is the busiest shopping day of the year. And busy it was in the 15 TV markets the Quiz Kid was advertised in. In those 15 major markets every Quiz Kid disappeared off the shelves within minutes of the store's opening. My friends inside Novus told me that National went to 3 shifts in their Salt Lake City manufacturing plant and were now making them in Malaysia, and flying them in. I was right. I was vindicated. And, I was still unemployed.

You would probably like to know what happened in the marketplace for the video game system I developed. Does the name Atari mean anything to you? Scott Brown's boss was Gene Landrum, General Manager at Novus. Gene was fired several months before I was.

His next position was as a consultant with Fairchild Semiconductor where they developed their version of the cartridge video system called Channel F, but abandoned consumer products prior to making the Channel F a household name. Gene's next position was at Atari where they did come out with a cartridge video game system. It was their model 2600 system that retailed not for $100 like I had suggested, but for $250. Two and one-half times the amount. That system and the royalties paid to Atari by other game manufacturers propelled Atari into a billion dollar company. National Semiconductor reached revenues of a billion dollars a year. But could have enjoyed revenues of two and even three billion dollars if they had only listened to some 30 year old kid with a few crazy ideas. Thinking back, I wonder how many elements of the situation would have had to be different in order for National to do what it did not – and how I could have played a role in that.

When have you stared the future in the face, alone and overwhelmed?

I wish I could say that at this point the world was my oyster. I could name my own ticket. I was a hot property. Wrong. I hadn't accomplished anything that anyone in the industry would recognize. Remember, the only real success I had at that point was the Quiz Kid. And I was fired before it took off. Other than my letter to the parents on the back of each product no one really knew who created this number one toy. Atari would not come out with their 2600 video game system until October 1977. The early 1980s for the electronic keyboard. What I know now that I did not know then: patience even more than genius or hard work is often the key behind success. An idea you come up with today may not be marketable for years – that's one of the benefits that seasoned marketers and managers have over wunderkinds.

As December came I needed to decide my future. Should I stay in electronics? Should I stay in toys? I was scared and I was confused. What should I do?

When you're scared and feel all alone you gravitate away from your fear in hopes that you'll reach some sort of comfort zone. My comfort zone was the toy industry where I knew the business and the players, and I had been in it long enough to where I was pretty well known. But, I really wanted to stay in electronics. This was the future. The problem was I really didn't know the industry, which should have occurred to me during all the fights I was having at Novus. That's what my bosses were thinking. If I had admitted that to myself and to them at the time, I would have had a very different attitude and likely a very different trajectory. I might have gone up the company ladder instead of out the company door.

In 1975 there were very few electronic products on the market except calculators, watches and a few clocks. There were no electronics retailers the likes of Best Buy and Fry's. I knew consumer products. I knew nothing of semiconductors, resistors, transistors, microprocessors and circuit boards. I was a good three to five years ahead of my time and I had a wife, two beautiful daughters and a mortgage.

And so, I gave in to the reality of my situation as well as my fear about trying to make my case to anyone who might have been willing to take a chance on me in electronics. Instead, I stayed in the toy industry. Many of my friends in toys suggested that I become an independent manufacturer's representative. Start my own company. Find companies to represent and just sell. Since I loved to sell this seemed like the wisest choice for

Are you creating regrets?

me. It's now 35 years later and as I look back on that decision I'm still not sure that I made the right choice. Yes, I was successful as a rep. I built my one person organization into a powerhouse. At one time I had 15 people selling for me. But now and then I think about what could have been. Maybe, if I had spent more time researching I would have found other companies, similar to National Semiconductor that may have wanted to get into toys or other consumer electronic items. Or maybe, work for a company that wanted to sell chips to the Mattels and Hasbros of the world. Unfortunately, I was young, shell-shocked and didn't have the self-confidence to make my case to a company that would have let me stay in electronics.

WHAT I KNOW NOW THAT I WISH I KNEW THEN:

I don't think anything shakes your confidence in yourself more than being fired from a job. For as long as I held my position at Novus I felt I was doing a good job. I just ignored some of the facets that would have taken it from good to great. Sure I felt I was doing what needed to be done to commercialize electronic toys. This is what I was hired to do. This was my background. Unfortunately, working for a large international corporation, or any size company for that matter, requires a lot of maturity, diplomacy and honesty about your own shortcomings and those of the people working at your company. I didn't face those shortcomings until essentially, I fired myself from the electronic toy industry. I looked at my resume, my short tenure at Novus, measured my self-confidence, and a future in electronics didn't make sense to me.

For the majority of our lives, at least from preschool on, we experience living with bullies. These are the people with enormous egos who make our lives miserable. Starting in grade school they and their friends beat up on others that **Have you been bullied? Have you acted like a bully?** they perceive as inferior to them. They do it both verbally and physically. If we don't meet their standards they certainly let us know. They are cruel and totally insensitive to others. Their worlds revolve around themselves. And we hate them. We hate them with a passion. It's easy for me to see other people who are bullies. But it's hard to see myself as a bully. I was a bully for my point of view. I disrespected those around me. I denigrated them, maybe not to their faces, but I dismissed them. I perceived all those people as inferior to me. And, they returned the favor. Finally, I became a bully to myself. I let fear overpower the opportunity to gain clarity about what I could do better next time.

I guess there is something in my makeup, that when given an assignment, I take the most efficient and expeditious route to get there, often without thinking of the people who might need to be brought along or shown respect as part of the decision-making process. I have failed in large part because I misunderstood that being given an assignment doesn't make me the big cheese. It can't be my way or the highway. To protect my ego, I have told myself a lot of things that aren't true and in some ways crippled me. This includes; if you don't play the game you'll have every one of your fellow employees cheering you on. Yes, they'll be rooting for you. Rooting for your failure. Waiting for your comeuppance. And when you fail they will rejoice. Because it was their toes you stepped on in your quest to do the right thing.

Can you imagine succeeding in a company when that's what you believe is going on around you?

What I wish I knew then that I know now is that you're going to meet many bullies in your life, and one of those bullies may be yourself, as it was for me. Bullies beat us up. They put us down. They make us doubt ourselves. For whatever reason they must inflate themselves by deflating us. There are times their words and deeds seem to suck the life out of us. I wish I knew that back then, I was good enough but I needed a lot of work on my interpersonal skills and maybe my character. I needed to examine how from an early age I developed revenge fantasies when an authority figure went against me. I needed to develop more functional strategies to deal with my rage and sense of inadequacies. I needed to know that I wasn't on a pedestal – that I didn't have to hide the simple truth about myself. And, that if I saw the real me, then I could understand how other people were likely seeing me. And, that would be good for everyone.

What beliefs about other people are hurting you?

Even though I never got credit for the success of electronic toys, the cartridge video game system and the electronic keyboard, I was smart enough to actually think of those inventions and went a long way toward shaping them as products. I was good enough to do that, and more.

CHAPTER 8

FROM OUT OF NOWHERE

By 1980 things were looking pretty good for the Luckman family. Melissa was 11 years old and Jennifer was 9. My repping business was going well and we had just moved into our first showroom in downtown Los Angeles. Many of our friends were moving from our sub-division in Almaden Valley in San Jose to larger more luxurious homes in places like Monte Serrano and Saratoga. And, it wasn't too long before my wife Phyllis was anxious to move out of our five bedroom, three bath, 2,600 square foot house into something a bit larger. Her reasoning was my business was successful, so why not? I liked our home, but as many of you have probably experienced, when your spouse makes up his or her mind there's no getting around it.

LUCKMAN'S LAWS
- Life is so very fragile. One day you're king of the world. The next day you're following the elephants with a shovel in your hand.
- If you believe that things never happen to you, but only to people like "George," be careful and count your blessings. For someday you may wake up and be George.

- When we screw-up it's bad. When a doctor screws-up it can be catastrophic.
- You are never alone. Wherever you are God is right there with you.
- No matter how bad things may seem, there are good people out there ready and willing to help.

I finally agreed, but with one stipulation, I wanted this house on a piece of land. We had recently bought the girls a horse we were boarding in Almaden and although Jennifer soon got bored of the whole horse thing, Melissa was loving it. We decided on a custom house on 2½ acres in a small town just south of San Jose called Morgan Hill. This 3,800 square foot house was being built just for us. Phyllis and I would sit up every night in bed with the plans spread out on the covers, talking about what we wanted to do in every room, and where we would build the stables and riding arena. These were happy times filled with a lot of hope for the future.

Have you ever let someone else make up your mind?

We moved in that spring and by summer we were well on our way to creating the perfect home. Both Phyllis' and my parents had retired to Sun City, AZ just outside of Phoenix, so it was decided that we'd take a little vacation and visit them. While there Phyllis' mother commented on how much time Melissa was spending in the bathroom and it looked like she'd lost some weight. With everything that was going on in our lives, and the fact that the girls had their own bathroom, we didn't really pay that close of attention. But it did look like she had lost some weight.

Upon our return to San Jose Phyllis brought Melissa in to our pediatrician who examined her. His diagnosis was that it was probably some stomach bug and to give her some Kaopectate for the diarrhea and not to worry. So we didn't. But within a week her symptoms grew worse. She was now, along with the diarrhea, suffering from some very high fevers and severe stomach cramping. Plus she was now losing a lot of weight. We brought her back to our pediatrician who immediately checked her in to Good Samaritan Hospital for tests to determine what was wrong. As you can probably imagine, both Phyllis and I were scared to death of what they'd find.

They began with the basics, upper and lower GI and blood tests. But nothing out of the ordinary was found. From there the tests became more and more sophisticated as they looked for one disease after another. But all proved negative. At first, when the results came in we prayed that she wouldn't have that particular illness. But when they started with the spinal taps we wished she had been diagnosed with one of the simpler illnesses, which had known cures. We were now in the God forbid stage. All the great doctors, nurses and technicians at Good Sam could not put a name to what Melissa was suffering from. They suggested that we take her to Children's Hospital at Stanford University.

Has a loved one's illness changed your life?

Stanford is one of the foremost teaching hospitals in the world. To be a doctor or researcher associated with Stanford meant that you were at the pinnacle of your career. Certainly they would know what was wrong with Melissa and through their brilliance would make her well.

Within a few days we had an appointment with a pediatric gastroenterologist at Stanford. He too wasn't sure what Melissa was suffering from but felt it was certainly within his area of expertise. It definitely had to do with her digestive system. But exactly what, nobody knew. By now Melissa looked like she had just been released from a concentration camp. Each rib stood out on her skinny chest. On her back you could count her vertebrae from top to bottom. And, her thighs were hardly bigger than her calves, with her knees bigger than both.

How do you cope when no one knows what is wrong?

If you have ever had a sick child then you know what Phyllis and

I were going through. Besides the constant fear your mind runs wild with one delusional thought after another. Is what she has fatal? Will we lose her? Can she be cured? Will she require surgery? What's the rest of her life going to be like? And then comes the guilt. Did we as parents cause this in some way? Did we pass on some unknown disease? Was it in our genes? Would Jennifer come down with the same thing? It became all consuming.

Within an hour of her initial consultation with the pediatric gastroenterologist we checked Melissa into Children's Hospital. For the next week Melissa was put through a battery of tests, and finally her doctors had a name for what Melissa was suffering from. She had Crohn's Disease. We had never heard of this disease. It certainly was not one of those diseases that they hold telethons for. Crohn's Disease and its related disease Ulcerative Colitis are inflammatory bowel diseases (IBD) where the patient's immune system is falsely told that foreign microbes are invading the digestive track and so the body's defense mechanisms attack the invader. The problem is, there are no foreign bodies and the immune system attacks its own tissue causing it to ulcerate and bleed. Because of the tremendous abdominal cramps, bloody stools and pain this causes the last thing the patient wants to do is eat food. And of course, this leads to extreme weight loss. To begin her healing Melissa was put on a very high dosage of Prednisone, an anti-inflammatory steroid that has its own devastating side effects. Melissa was taken off all food and for 8 weeks received all her nourishment through an IV tube.

Where is God when someone you love suffers?

Melissa shared a room with three other girls. It was not like Good Sam where the children were recovering from accidents or broken bones, or flus and viruses. Here the children were suffering from cancer, cystic fibrosis, and other catastrophic illnesses. During one particular stay Melissa lost a roommate who passed away during the night. Children should never have to experience this. But yet, this is life. From out of nowhere our lives turned upside down.

Phyllis visited during the day while I spent the evenings with Melissa. Every night I had dinner in the cafeteria. And every time I left her to return home I got into my car and cried. There were many times, through my tears, I screamed at God. How could he let someone so young, so beautiful, so precious, suffer like this? And yet it was my strong belief in God that sustained me during this and subsequent crises in my life. I remember being in Chicago on a business trip and having dinner with some old friends. They asked me how I was able to cope with all that was going on in my life. And without a moment's hesitation I replied, that every time I came to the end of my rope, God gave me a little more rope.

This eight week hospitalization at Stanford Children's was the first of many for Melissa. Every time she had a flare up it meant another seven to eight week stay. Crohn's Disease had no cure then, and 30 years later there still is no cure.

At one time Melissa was experiencing what seemed like a very severe flare- up. Instead of her pain being localized to the right side of her abdomen where she had always experienced it, it now stretched from one side of her abdomen to the other. Her gastroenterologist Dr. John Kerner believed that since the pain was not localized to one side, it was not a flare-up but a psychosomatic manifestation. We thought he was brilliant - how could he not be? He was head of pediatric gastroenterology at Stanford. So we believed him, at first.

He admitted her to the psychiatric side of Children's Hospital. This again was a long-term hospitalization, except this time Melissa had to meet regularly with psychiatrists who tried to make her understand that the pain was all in her head. Phyllis, Jennifer, Melissa and I also had to meet with a family psychiatrist to work out what he considered our dysfunctional family problems. The goal was once we transcended our family dynamics, Melissa's pain would disappear.

This was probably the most excruciating hospital stay for Melissa. Not only was she in constant pain, but everyone thought she was crazy. They didn't believe her agony was coming from a physical problem. They didn't believe her pain was real. In addition, the psychiatric side of the hospital was often shunned by various celebrities who would visit kids with chronic or fatal diseases, but very seldom visit the kids hospitalized for mental illness issues. I'm not sure if even Santa Claus made it to the psychiatric side that year.

After approximately five weeks of getting nowhere and having constant arguments with her doctor, we were exasperated, and he was incensed that we no longer believed in his diagnosis or treatment plan. Dr. Kerner finally said, if we didn't believe him we were more than welcome to take her to the University of California San Francisco Medical Center and have them take a look at her. Within days Phyllis had Melissa up at UCSF where two gastroenterologists examined her. Their opinions? Her Crohn's Disease was running rampant, and the reason the pain covered her entire abdomen was that the disease was no longer localized to the right side. They said she needed to have a bowel resection to cut out the diseased portion of her small intestine. The question was, should we have the surgery done at UCSF or Stanford? Since Stanford was considerably closer to where we lived, we decided to bring her back there, except this time she would be in the medical-surgical side of the hospital, and we would have nothing more to do with Dr. John Kerner.

When you've not seeing progress, how do you take action?

Melissa's surgery was scheduled for early on a Monday morning. Her surgeon was great. A very likeable doctor by the name of Harry Oberhelman who was easy to talk to, and he understood our concerns. He explained exactly what he was going to do and did his best to dispel our fears. Phyllis and I were there with Melissa as they prepped her for her surgery. It was now time for the orderlies to wheel her into surgery. As they wheeled her down the hallway to the operating room, Phyllis holding one hand and I the other, it was difficult not to cry. For Melissa's sake we held back the tears but it was impossible not to feel the fear. It cloaked us like a heavy dark gray overcoat from head to toe. Would something go wrong? Would she die on the operating table? We could not stop the worried, doubting and ultimately delusional thoughts. And with every thought came a new fear.

AN END TO LIFE AS WE KNEW IT

I was told by a mother I had met at Ronald McDonald House, whose son was suffering from cancer that 85% of marriages that have a child with a catastrophic illness end in divorce. My marriage to Phyllis was not strong to begin with, and it was heading down that track. By the time of this first surgery we had already been separated for about a year. The stress one feels each and every day is unbelievable. You forget what normal is.

With Melissa's illness and our pending divorce, our lives turned upside down. Jennifer, 22 months younger than Melissa, tried so very hard to be as accommodating as she could. But her life was very difficult. When friends and family called they often forgot to ask her how she was doing and how she was, but instead would immediately ask her how Melissa was doing. Jennifer's life, her dreams, her needs, and her wants were overlooked and on hold. She suffered on her own as we navigated our crises.

Who gets overlooked when one family member is in crisis?

Three hours after wheeling Melissa into surgery her doctor came out to the waiting room to brief us on how the surgery went. Dr. Kerner, who always believed that her inflammation was no more than a couple inches in length, and now was actually in her head, was off by 16 inches. The surgeon had removed 18 inches of her small intestine. The surgery was called a resection where they take out the diseased portion and then sew the two open ends together. As Phyllis and I walked into the recovery room it was hard to hold back the tears at seeing our precious child with all these tubes going in and out of her, hooked up to multiple machines, each one beeping a different beep. We were of course scared that at any minute one would go off signaling our greatest fear had come to pass.

Melissa slept most of Monday but when she did awake she complained of severe pain. This we were told was to be expected. On

Tuesday Melissa was up and walking, dragging her IVs with her, but the severe pain was still with her. On Wednesday she had a fever and now the pain was so severe she didn't want to get out of bed. With her temperature spiking, her doctors believed she had some sort of infection in her system, so started her on antibiotics. Thursday was about the same. Whenever the bowel is touched, as in a surgery, it shuts down. About this time she should be hearing some rumblings in her bowels announcing that they were starting up again. But nothing was happening. On Friday, Phyllis brought Jennifer to visit. As a family we stood by Melissa's bedside each saying a silent prayer for her recovery.

That night Phyllis and Jennifer left about 8:00 PM, but just before they did her surgeon came in and said he wanted to send her down for x-rays to see if they could determine why she wasn't responding. I told Phyllis to go ahead and leave and I'd stay with Melissa. At about 9:15 they wheeled her down for the x-rays. At 10:00 PM she returned followed shortly by Dr. Oberhelman. He asked me to follow him to the waiting area down the hall from Melissa's room. As we sat down I could see by his face that things were not good. He proceeded to

Have you ever experienced a crisis that seemed to only get worse?

explain that as a result of the Prednisone she had been taking for so long the two ends of her intestine were not growing back together. This in turn was causing the extreme pain, fever and bloating she had been experiencing. I asked what the solution was and he said they needed to go back in and correct the situation. When, I asked? "Now," he replied. I guess he could see the fear flash across my face for he quickly added, "Don't worry. She's going to be OK once we do the surgery. She isn't going to die."

I immediately called Phyllis to apprise her of the situation. After finding a neighbor to watch Jennifer, she was in her car on her way back to Stanford. At 12:45 AM Saturday morning Dr. Oberhelman came out of the operating room and sat down to explain exactly what he found when he opened her up. It was as he suspected. Her tissue had been severely weakened by steroids. He stitched the two ends back together but wanted to relieve the strain on her gut, so he gave her a temporary ileostomy. At the point where the stomach enters the small intestine he created an artificial opening so that Melissa's waste matter would now empty into an external bag, taped to her abdomen. His plan was to leave it like this and then reverse it in one year.

As a kid I heard about someone whose colon was removed and had to have a colostomy. For the rest of their life they had to wear a bag to evacuate into. To a young child this seemed a very scary thing.

Have you seen something you feared materialized?

In the back of my mind I always worried that maybe I'd have to have one of these someday. It's ironic that one of my greatest fears would be visited on my oldest child.

A year later Melissa had her third surgery to reverse the ostomy. To date Melissa has had 12 surgeries, some requiring additional resections, and has very little of her small intestine left. She still has flare-ups and she still suffers from this devastating disease. I've since lost count of the exact number of her hospitalizations. She is a remarkable person. Although only 4′10″ (the disease affected her growth because she came down with it before puberty) she is tough, smart, beautiful and an amazing mother to my five year old granddaughter.

She is a shining example of a person who lives away from fear and isn't defined by circumstances. Her sister Jennifer is another shining example. She has also created a wonderful family life with her husband and children.

When have you felt alone in a crisis?

They say that time heals all wounds. And it's true. No matter how difficult the situation you're going through. No matter how hard the journey. You are not alone. Others have walked the path before you. And God walks with you. Sometimes he even carries you when the burden on your shoulders is just too much.

I mentioned earlier that I would leave my visit with Melissa and get in my car and rage. I'd yell at God. No, I'd scream at him. How

could you let someone so young, so magnificent suffer li
when the tears stopped flowing and I'd be on my drive h
ogize to God for my anger, and an incredible peace wou
me. It was like he knew I was angry. He knew I was frustrated, and
yet it was OK with him that I raged. He loved me no matter what!

During this time, with all that was going on in my life, I grew
very spiritual. Now I want to make sure we're on the same page. I am
very spiritual, but not very religious. At about 12
years old I began to see the hypocrisy of organized
religion. What was with all the rules? And why an **How have**
angry, vengeful God? Why not a loving beneficent **you felt about**
God during
God? If God were so loving why would he draw **various times**
a line in the sand and smite us if we crossed it? If **in your life?**
we truly are God's greatest miracle and he gave us
our bodies and all those pleasurable sensations, then why does he get
angry when we experience pleasure? Why do I need an intermediary
like a priest, minister or rabbi, can't I just sit down and talk to God?

This was pretty heady stuff for a 12 year old. And yet, I believe it
even more today than I did back in 1957. My belief in God sustained
me through many, many difficult times in my life. I see God as my
friend. He is the universe. He is all there is. I believe there is but one
mind, the mind of God, and we all place our thoughts into this mind
and expand the knowledge that is available to all of us, God's children. This Universal Mind is very much like a bank, we deposit our
thoughts in this mind, and we then make withdrawals of knowledge
whenever we need them.

Have you ever been weighed down with a
problem you could not solve until finally you gave **Have you**
up and let go, and then the most perfect answer **leaned on**
God to solve
popped into your mind? That answer came from **problems?**
God. In U.S. Andersen's wonderful book, *Three
Magic Words* in the fifth meditation he says of God,
"The answer comes with the question; the path is lighted with the first
step; the way is cleared with the looking; the goal is in sight with the
desire. I know that I am fulfilling the fondest wish of God, for I place

myself in His hands, taking each step of my life boldly and strongly, for it is God who prompts me, and God moves with sureness."

What I know now that I didn't understand then when Melissa was so sick, was that my friend was always there for me. Wherever I was I was always in the right place at the right time. For that is where God wanted me to be. I will never know why He wanted me to experience the things I lived through in my life. Nor do I really care. What I do know is that my will, is God's will for me. Whatever the path I walk it's where God wants me to be.

THE WORST DAY OF MY LIFE

When Melissa was about 17 years old, and still suffering from her Crohn's Disease, she became both anorexic and severely depressed. Anorexia nervosa typically affects teenage girls and young adults who see themselves as fat and literally starve themselves. All too often to death. Tell them they look great and they'll think you're lying to them. They don't see their bodies as they really are. Melissa's anorexia started because of the Crohn's. To her eating was associated with pain. So to avoid pain she stopped eating.

Do you feel or see that you've somehow caused others' pain?

Her depression was another story. They say depression runs in the family and both Phyllis and I have had our struggles with depression. And both our mothers were depressive. But the combination of her disease, the anorexia and the depression had created a severe downward spiral for Melissa. Plus, I had recently remarried and both my daughters felt uncomfortable with my new wife and her young daughter. They sensed that she was jealous of the time I spent with them. And they were right. But unfortunately, I didn't realize this until years later. We certainly had our problems.

Melissa was seeing a child psychologist by the name of Rod Dendulk in San Jose for the depression and anorexia. But the twice weekly therapy sessions weren't working. Her therapist felt that we needed an intervention or she would die. He knew of an inpatient hospital connected with a school in Provo, Utah. He had sent other patients there and all had made miraculous recoveries. He felt positive that it would benefit Melissa too.

It was decided that I would accompany Melissa to Utah. I purchased one round trip ticket and one one-way ticket to Salt Lake City. At a prearranged time I was to meet up with everyone at the therapist's office and then we would immediately drive to the airport, and be on our way.

When Melissa first saw me she shouted out, "What's Dad doing here?" The psychologist then explained what we were going to be doing. Melissa became hysterical. Crying and screaming that she didn't want to go. Emphatic that she wouldn't go. With difficulty we got her into the car and to the airport as she alternated between rage and sullenness. Through the entire 1½ hour flight Melissa sat in the window seat, crying but not saying a word. We were met in Salt Lake City by the director of the behavioral clinic at the hospital. A really pleasant man who soon put my concerns to rest. For Melissa it was another story.

Within an hour we were pulling into the hospital parking lot. A few minutes later we were passing through the locked doors of the behavioral unit. We were given a tour and I was impressed. The kids were friendly and reached out to Melissa who wanted nothing to do with them. She stood silent and sullen behind me. And then it was time for me to go. As I write these words my eyes fill with tears and the sobbing begins. I will never forget what happened next. When Melissa realized that I was leaving her there she threw her little body into mine, wrapped her skinny legs around me, and began to plead. "Daddy, don't leave me here. Daddy, don't go. Daddy, don't go." With whatever strength that was left in her she held tightly to me, until the nurses separated us. I was immediately led out the door and down the hallway still hearing her cries behind the locked doors. This was the worst moment in my life.

What is the hardest thing you've ever done?

87

CHAPTER 9

"Our greatest glory is not in never failing,
but in rising up every time we fail.
– Ralph Waldo Emerson

GOOD DAD, BAD DAD: YOU DECIDE

When Phyllis and I separated after 14 years of marriage I was angry about what had happened to the family life I had tried to create. At the time, I wasn't smart enough to be angry at myself or see the role my choices had played in our lives turning upside down. Instead, I was angry that Melissa was sick. Angry at God for letting it happen. Angry that our lives turned upside down. Angry at Phyllis for neglecting my needs in our marriage. Angry that I was forced to live alone in our home in Morgan Hill while I waited for it to sell. Angry at my mother, who rather than give words of comfort to me during Melissa's flare ups, spent our conversations telling me that a friend of hers next door neighbor's cousin's roommate's brother knew someone who had something similar, and I should tell Melissa's doctor at

LUCKMAN'S LAWS
- Parenthood should come with an instruction manual. Nobody ever showed me what a good dad was like.
- Anger, resentment and parenting don't mix.
- Children should be seen, listened to and loved unconditionally.

- We cannot always depend on someone to love us unconditionally. In its absence we need to accept ourselves and love ourselves unconditionally.
- Everyone should have friends they can confide in. If they did the world wouldn't be such a lonely place.
- Much of life is a balancing act. It works better when you have a trustworthy partner to help maintain your equilibrium.
- Life itself can be exhilarating when you learn how to truly live it.

Stanford about it. Angry that Phyllis and the girls were a family and I was the odd man out. And angry at the girls for their close relationhship with Phyllis.

In my usual sarcastic fashion, I always used to joke about Phyllis' and my marriage. I called it trickle down happiness. Similar to Ronald Reagan's economic policy that was popular at the time. In trickle down happiness if Phyllis did something or bought something and it made her happy, that was fine. If what she did or bought

Have you used sarcasm to avoid meaningful conversation?

then trickled down to the girls and made them happy, that too was fine. And if it trickled down further and made me happy, again that was fine, but it wasn't the real intent. This kind of sarcastic humor did not make matters better.

I always wanted to think I was this great dad, but in my heart I knew it wasn't true. I was the same dad to my girls that my dad was to me and my siblings. We knew he loved us and provided a good home, but he wasn't ever really engaged with us. I used to be envious of my friends whose dads would take them fishing and camping. The only time I could get some one-on-one time with Dad was when I would accompany

What is your idealized image of your role within a family?

him to his work. I don't ever remember sitting down with him and just talking about my life or my dreams. Or even what his dreams were as a young man. We didn't share a lot with each other, and looking back on it now I really think that I missed that in my life. I had no one to be my mentor. Even in his last year as the cancer was ravishing his body, we didn't have anything but surface conversations. There was so much more I wish we could have said to one another.

I was raised to be a good Jewish husband. Although I was never told what specifically that meant, it was a given that you would put the women in your life up on pedestals and provide them with anything they desired. My happiness was supposed to come from seeing how well I provided for my wife and children. It did not.

What mistakes made by your parents have you repeated?

Just prior to Melissa getting sick we moved into our dream home in Morgan Hill. We went from a 2,600 sq. ft. home that I really enjoyed to a 3,800 sq. ft. custom home on 2½ acres. I went from a $225 a month mortgage payment to a $2,225 a month mortgage payment. Why? Because all our friends were moving from their tract homes into McMansions and that's what Phyllis wanted. So I gave her and the girls what they wanted. I'm not saying I wasn't happy with our new home and that I didn't feel the pride of ownership, or the fact that I could afford to spend that much on a house. But if Phyllis hadn't pushed me to move up, I was happy to stay where we were. I guess my dreams were smaller than hers, or perhaps I was less optimistic. By the end of our marriage, I had proved myself right.

So here I am angry at the world and resentful that I'm the odd man out. And, I was resentful of my daughters. When it was my weekend with the girls, they expected we would go out and do something fun together. It seems crazy to think that annoyed me, given what we had all gone through. If I just wanted to stay home and watch TV or get some housework done, they would decline to come over. They also complained that I never bought them anything. They would compare me to my friend Mike Applebaum who was also divorced and had three daughters. "When Mike Applebaum is with his daughters he takes them out and buys them things," they insisted. This made me feel small and angry.

At the time I was paying $1,000 per month in child support for two children, and with all my other expenses I simply didn't have a lot more disposable income. Now I see it would not have been so difficult to be more proactive and creative in finding ing activities we could do together. I missed the chance to show them a lot of love, and fun, too.

Have you ever used money of a lack of it as an excuse for not acting better?

About the time both girls reached high school, I remarried. My new wife Susan was a very attractive redhead about 5'1" tall. A truly excellent 3rd grade teacher with a beautiful and talented daughter named Tracey whom I helped raise from the time she was four until about thirteen years old. Susan had one major flaw; she was a full blown alcoholic. She would never drink before 6 PM. But by 6:15 she would be on her second drink and then continue unabated until she went to bed. Often she'd have blackouts, where she couldn't remember what had happened the night before, nor what she even said to others. Growing up I had no exposure to alcoholics. No one in my family was one and none of my friend's parents were, although there were some rumors about the guy at the end of our block. Now it seems ridiculous that I could hold onto the illusion that I didn't know what I was dealing with. Clearly someone who drinks and blacks out is an alcoholic, and that's a terrible influence to bring into my children's lives.

When have you ignored a problem negatively effecting your family?

In my conversations with the girls we'd often get into fights. They, because we were living apart, didn't feel that I had a right to any say in what they did in their lives. They would only listen to what their mother said. A typical retort from one or both would be, "Dad, you just don't "understand!" "Understand" of course meant agreeing with them. Now, I will admit that I was still under the delusion that children should fear their father and at this time I still raged, so they certainly had a valid reason for us to argue and fight. I think I still wanted to believe I was a major part of their lives.

I wish my family situation could be easily and comfortingly explained by Mark Twain's quote about his father, "When I was fourteen, my father was so ignorant I could hardly stand to have him around. When I got to be twenty-one, I was astonished at how much he had learned in seven years."

The underlying problem was much greater and wasn't about my daughters' misimpression of me. The real problem was what I refused to recognize about my marriage to Susan. Whenever I would have these fights with the girls, Susan would always take my side, telling me I was a good father, that the girls were so ungrateful and to not to give in to them. She fueled my ego and my rage. What I didn't realize was all these self-serving comments were meant to drive a wedge between my daughters and me. Susan was jealous. No, Susan was doubly jealous. She was jealous for Tracey. That I was taking time away from her daughter, when I'd see Jennifer and Melissa. Time that I could be spending with the two of them. But even more insidious she was jealous for herself. She resented the girls for the time, money and love I gave them. She was competing with them for my affection. But, at the time, I was too blind and ignorant to see this.

Who is "egging you on," attempting to persude you to go against your better judgement?

What led to our divorce was her drinking. She tried numerous times to stop, but it never worked. Alcoholism is a progressive disease. And finally, one day, I just woke up and said to myself "This day is the best it's going to be and I know that tomorrow will be worse than today." And that was the end of our marriage. It saddened me that we couldn't make it better. But I was fighting something I could not battle and win, even though I had read several books on alcoholism. It was bigger than me. It was bigger than both of us. When Susan and I split it was a do-over of my separation from Phyllis. Susan and Tracey moved out to a rental and I stayed behind to sell the house we were living in in Blackhawk, a community in Danville, California. Once again, we picked the worst time to sell a property. Prices were drop-

Has substance abuse or addiction affected you?

ping and like in Morgan Hill it would take 18 months to sell. This was also about the time when I was losing my business, Michael Luckman and Associates, because of conflicts with one of the major companies my firm represented. When it rained, it poured during those years.

During this stressful time, I was very fortunate to be a part of a men's group that met weekly to discuss the various issues effecting each of us. Even though we came from different backgrounds, the ten members of the group were all close in age, born in the 1940's, raised during the 1950's and coming of age in the 1960's. As a group we chose a unique approach to personal development. We would go out and find psychologists or psychiatrists to facilitate our group. During this time we were fortunate to have a psychiatrist leading the group by the name of Ernie Pesci. Not only was he a capable leader, helping us to understand why we were the way we were, and acted the way we did, he also introduced us to spirituality.

Have you ever reached out and found others facing similar issues?

I sincerely liked Ernie and felt that he could help me through these trying times, and so I decided to see him privately on a weekly basis. As the weeks passed I grew to really look forward to our times together. Ernie, more than anybody, helped me see who I truly was and why I acted and responded the way I did to the people in my life. I learned to forgive those who hurt me and to seek forgiveness of those I hurt. I forgave my parents for how I was raised, but it still took me another 15 years to truly and completely forgive my mother for how my upbringing impacted my adult life.

What I wanted from my mother? What I was desperately seeking from her, was unconditional love. Our relationship from my earliest memories was based on my being perfect, or being perfected. The more praise she received about me from others, the more love was shown me. I bartered

Are unresolved hurts from childhood effecting your life today? How?

for what in a healthier family, would have been given to me naturally and unconditionally. Now I know that many who will read these words will think, "What an ungrateful son." But it doesn't alter the fact that for me there was a tremendous emptiness deep within me, and that effected my choices in marriage.

Do you have regrets about how you acted in the past? How can you make amends?

But the most important thing I learned from Ernie was how the pain I was carrying with me affected my relationship with my daughters. I realized that I was not the father I thought I was. That as much hurt as I was experiencing in my life, they too were hurting. At the time they needed me most I was not there for them. Melissa, who not only was experiencing repeated flare-ups of her Crohn's Disease along with weeks spent in the hospital, was also going through her high school years, which in itself is difficult for most teenagers. Jennifer was the child who faded into the background. She missed out on what was rightfully hers: a father who was there for her always. A father who would patiently listen and counsel her. A father who would shower her with unconditional love. Both my daughters deserved this. All children deserve this. I didn't get it as a child, and I didn't give it as a parent.

I'll never forget the day I returned home after a session with Ernie Pesci where we discussed this very topic. The pain of realizing how much I had hurt my daughters was overwhelming. As I entered my empty house I couldn't hold it back any longer. I collapsed to the floor and curled up in a fetal position and I cried. I cried for all the pain I had caused my children. I cried for my selfishness. I cried for my weaknesses. I cried for my anger. And I cried for the little boy who just wanted to love and be loved.

Can you visualize a positive, happy future with loved ones?

Today my daughters are grown women with children of their own, and I am so very proud of them. I am also happy to say that we enjoy a great relationship. Both married wonderful men who love them and cherish them. Both are amazing mothers. Melissa and her husband Hans have a precious 5 year old daughter, McKenna. Jennifer and her husband Mike have an incredible son P.J. who is 14 and a beautiful and talented daughter Teagan who is 10.

CHAPTER 10

LOSING MICHAEL LUCKMAN AND ASSOCIATES

My advice to everyone who reads this, think twice before you put your name in the name of your company. My manufacturer's representative firm was Michael Luckman and Associates. Of course, when I started it, there were no associates. Only me and my belief that I would succeed. The reason you don't want to use your name is the very thing David Sandler talks about in his highly effective and successful sales training program, Sandler® Training.

David Sandler talks about the "I" and the "R" and how you should never let one negatively affect the other. The "I" is your identity. This is who you really are. The absolutely beautiful, magnificent and perfect child of God. On a scale of 1 to 10 your identity should always be a 10. A perfect 10. You were born a 10 and you will always be a 10. For God does not create anything less than perfection.

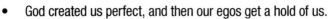

LUCKMAN'S LAWS
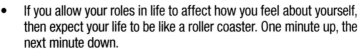
- God created us perfect, and then our egos get a hold of us.
- If you allow your roles in life to affect how you feel about yourself, then expect your life to be like a roller coaster. One minute up, the next minute down.
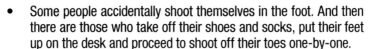
- Some people accidentally shoot themselves in the foot. And then there are those who take off their shoes and socks, put their feet up on the desk and proceed to shoot off their toes one-by-one.

- A company's salespeople should always be seated in the front seats on the bus. They, more than anyone, need to see what's coming down the road.
- Once, a very smart man told me, "If you want to get even with a prospect…let them buy from you!"
- Treat your boss like a prospect.
- The truly amazing thing is that we as humans are capable of doing and being so much more than we are. A whole world opens up when you release the brakes of fear, uncertainty and doubt.
- The success you never achieve is typically waiting in the moment after you accept the belief that you cannot go on anymore and quit.

The "R" represents your role or roles in life. When you were born your role was very simple, you were an infant. A beautiful little baby. You didn't have to do too much in this role. Just eat, sleep, tinkle and poop and give an occasional gurgle and smile. But as you grew older your role became a little more complicated. When you learned to crawl it was awfully cute. Everyone enjoyed watching you as you learned to crawl and then scamper along the floor. But then something changed. As your little legs got stronger you were able to pull yourself up to a wobbly standing position. My God! What magnificent vistas opened up for you. You could see all the little knick knacks laid out on the table. The magazine or book, the coasters, even the glass filled with liquid. All were new to you. And you wanted to touch these things. So you reached out with chubby fingers to grasp on to these wondrous new items. And then it happened. You heard for the first time the word that would haunt you all the days of your life. You heard the word NO!. No? What does "no" mean? But wait. When you first heard "no," it sounded different from all the other words you were learning. This word sounded harsher than the others. There didn't seem to be

When did you first hear "No!" How did you feel?

any love in it. You were on notice that you were no longer in charge of what you did.

That word scared me and I'm sure it scared you too – as it was meant to do. We were probably being protected from some unknown harm, but it did not feel good. With that single admonition, the momentary feelings of triumph over our little worlds changed forever. Now there were limits being put on what we could do. We were entering the world of judgment. We were being graded on behavior, which felt bad – even if "no" was said for our own good. For me, the word

Can you count the number of times you've heard theword "no?"

"no," made me feel like I was rejected and my ideas were worth nothing. For most of my career, it made me angry. I derided people who told me I could not do what I wanted to do. But, now I know that "no" is often a way station – a place along the road to getting a yes, perhaps making a better decision than my initial plan, being more inclusive and therefore more apt to be successful in a group. Unfortunately, as a grown up, I often acted like a child and threw some version of a tantrum when the world did not go as I demanded it should.

Shad Helmstetter, in his excellent book *What to Say When You Talk to Your Self,* stated that by the time the average person reaches their eighteenth birthday they have heard the word "no" a whopping 148,000 times. And that's in a fairly average positive home. What about those amongst us whose childhoods were far from idyllic? How many times did we hear "no" in our young lives?

How does that compare to the number of times you heard "yes?"

As far as I can tell, from the moment of my first "no," I chafed at the idea that someone was measuring me in a way that I did not determine or control. And yet at every stage of my life, it seems someone was either applauding or giving me a thumbs-down. As I grew from toddler to preschooler, people started to comment on how bright I was. How creative or talented. And I also heard about it when I didn't play well with others. That would haunt me throughout my life.

With every role you or I take on: student, athlete, boyfriend,

What leads to your feeling confident and optimistic? What deflates you?

girlfriend, employee, wife, husband or salesperson, someone is ready to give us a grade. Someone wants to say how good we are; or how poorly we did something. At some point, we don't need someone to tell us these things. We judge and grade ourselves. We become our harshest critics. We don't need anyone to tell us when we screwed up. We do one helluva job beating our own selves up.

Having my own company for 16 years and having as its name my name, life became something of a roller coaster. When Michael Luckman and Associates was doing well, so was Michael Luckman. But when Michael Luckman and Associates was struggling, so was Michael Luckman. You see I never learned how to keep my "I" separate from my "R." When my role as a business owner

How would you get started in a business that depended on your performance?

felt like I was a 10, my Identity also rose to a 10. I felt good about myself. I felt confident. In fact I had a lot of self-confidence, "I could rule the world!" But when I saw my Role as business owner, employer, and sales rep dropped to less than a 10, my feelings about myself plummeted. My confidence left me. And fear filled the vacuum. That's what happened to me in 1991 when I lost Michael Luckman and Associates.

As I mentioned, I started my rep company in December of 1975 as a one-man band. No associates selling, just me. But I had ambitions. Like all new manufacturers' representatives, the first thing I had to do was find manufacturers to represent. In my case, companies that manufactured toy products but did not already have representatives selling for them on the West Coast. Not a very easy task. Like anything else in life when you're late to the table, pickings are slim.

The first company that agreed to let me represent them was a stuffed animal manufacturer by the name of Gund. Originally founded in 1898 by Adolph Gund, a German immigrant, the company was now owned by Herb and Rita Raiffe. Rita was the daughter of Jacob Swedlin who bought the company from Adolph Gund in the early 1920's. At one time Gund was the leading stuffed animal manufacturer in the United States, but by the time I joined them in January 1976 they had just about reached the bottom. And in the stuffed animal business the bottom was carny plush. The cheap straw filled stuffed animals that you win at carnivals and beach boardwalks. This was a long way from the 1930's, 40's and 50's when Gund was the line to beat. At that time, they had just about every licensed movie and cartoon character, and their quality was excellent. But, the first line I sold for Gund was Easter 1976. They had standing Easter bunnies that when held up to your ear and squeezed, you'd hear the stuffing go crunch. Certainly not the softness they were later known for. But then something happened. And that something was Rita Raiffe.

Have you met an individual who dramatically changed a company?

Rita joined the company in the early 1970's and by fall 1975 had totally redesigned the product line. Gone was the carny plush, replaced by softer more cuddly animals. But what really made the difference was a bear that they were manufacturing in Japan. This bear was so soft and so cuddly that it made every other stuffed animal, in anyone's product line, feel hard by comparison.

Prior to becoming a rep I had no selling experience in California. At Magic Village I was a buyer. At National Semiconductor I was responsible for all sales and marketing activities nationwide. So as a new rep in California I didn't really know my prospective customers. I needed the help of other reps, reps whom I bought from and considered friends, to guide me to the various wholesale and retail accounts in my territory of California and Hawaii. My goal was to get to know these buyers and set meetings with them to present my lines from the manufacturers I represented. That meant cold calling all the buyers in my territory.

How do you feel approaching someone new and asking for help?

I'll be straight with you; I hate making cold calls. I was never comfortable on the phone. Even now I would prefer a face-to-face meeting to a phone conversation any day. I teach cold calling to salespeople and I believe in cold calling, as a difficult, but viable prospecting activity. Today, I'm very successful on the phone, getting past gatekeepers and setting meetings with C level managers. But I still hate the phone. How do you think I felt as a newly minted rep in a territory where I knew only a handful of my prospects? I was scared to death. I would start off making my cold calls with a list of prospects, an empty ashtray and a mug of black coffee. By the time I was finished I'd gone through 3-4 mugs of coffee and filled an ashtray full of cigarette butts.

What do you do under severe stress?

With my heart pounding in my chest and a freshly lit cigarette in my mouth, I would pick–up the fifty pound phone with a sweaty hand and dial the number. When a receptionist answered the phone, I could barely control the urge to hang up. With a tremor in my voice I would ask for the buyer that I wanted to speak with. The receptionist would transfer the call and as the phone would ring, I'd secretly pray it wouldn't be answered. But, as luck would have it, it often was. Here is an example of what those January 1976 phone calls sounded like:

Me: Hi this is Mike Luckman. I'm a new rep in this area and I would like to talk to you about some of the products I'm representing.
Prospect: Mike Gluckman? (The added "G" is the reason I started calling myself Michael instead of Mike). I don't think I know you. What are you selling?
Me: It's Michael Luckman and I represent Gund.
Prospect: We don't carry guns.
Me: No, not guns. Gund stuffed animals.
Prospect: Gund animals? We don't want that crap. If that's all you got we're not interested. Call me when you've got something I may be interested in.

I'm not saying that every call sounded like this. Just most of them. Gund had dropped to such a lowly status, that nobody, wholesaler or retailer, wanted to even take a look. Now I had also picked up some other manufacturers lines to represent so I wasn't completely shut out of meeting with the major buyers in my territory. But Gund was difficult. And a very difficult sell for some very stupid reasons.

Remember, I still carried quite a chip on my shoulder when it came to dealing with authority.

While I thought Rita Raiffe did a great job of designing for Gund, my feelings were very different when it came to Rita's husband Herb, the president of Gund. Herb was a big man, both in size and ego. Although I pursued his company and won the right to represent it, I didn't particularly like him. I didn't think he was smart. I gave him very little credit for what he had achieved. I mocked him and I certainly didn't respect him or his sensitivities, among them his pride.

How much respect and regard do you feel for your boss, clients and co-workers?

I once introduced him to a very large customer of mine who had never bought Gund before. He was the toy buyer for The Broadway, the largest department store chain in Los Angeles and his opening orders would be between $500,000 and $600,000. The buyer had a biting, sarcastic sense of humor, which I failed to mention to Herb. At that time, I would have said Herb was the kind of guy who would cut off his nose to spite his face, but I realize now that I may have done the same by reveling in Herb being put down by my buyer.

Upon introduction, Herb asked the buyer why he had never bought Gund before. The buyer replied, "I go to Asia myself and I knock you off and Dakin and other plush manufacturers with my own product." What the buyer was saying is that he goes to Asia to work with the very same resources as Gund and Dakin (another large stuffed animal manufacturer at the time) and he copies our designs for his own private branded products.

Have you failed to prepare a boss or colleague?

Of course this was all a bad joke, although it preyed on every manufacturer's fear: having their designs and suppliers stolen from them. If you knew the buyer and his unique sense of humor you would have known that this was meant to be a ribbing. But not Herb, who had just met him without being properly briefed by me. Herb believed him. After the buyer left our New York showroom, Herb came over to me and said, "We're not selling him!" "What?" I said. "You heard me, we're not selling him." I nearly begged, "But Herb, he's giving us over half a million dollars the first go round." Herb replied, "I don't care, we are not selling him." And we didn't. Broadway was the only department store chain in my territory that never carried a piece of Gund. Herb Raiffe's ego got bent out of shape, and I was out between $30,000 and $50,000 in commissions.

Herb had other ways to make selling Gund very difficult, at least in my eyes at the time. When a store bought from our competition, the minimum order would be as low as $100. Not at Gund. Our minimum order was $600. Another hurdle was the minimum quantity of each item purchased. Other manufacturers were usually 1 to 3 pieces. Gund 6, 12 and 24 pieces. Although I could easily get an order up to and over these minimums once I started working with a buyer, I couldn't get buyers to commit to meeting with me if they knew where our minimums were set.

Do you secretly mock or denigrate others? Do you suspect they know?

I thought Herb set these rules arbitrarily because he wanted us to work for our commission (which is actually a pretty fair thing to ask of salespeople now that I think about it). My other gripe was Herb flat out disliked salespeople. He disliked any salesperson, no matter the company – he even disliked his own salespeople. He felt we were just a bunch of lazy men and women who didn't bring very much to the table. We should all be grateful to him because we were selling a product that sold itself.

I also thought Gund and the Raiffe's were truly blessed. And as I would snidely put it, they made a lot of money in spite of their programs and policies. Rita's wonderful designs and the superb product she created were obviously fundamental, but it was their sales force that got them into retailers. Between 1976 and 1980 they put together a group of independent reps across the country that lived and breathed

Gund. I believed they prospered largely because I, along with other top reps, helped Gund build the best sales force of any company I had ever been associated with.

Are you only comfortable talking or selling to lower level staff?

In my larger retail accounts I was comfortable selling to buyers and their immediate bosses the Merchandise Manager– the people who placed the orders. However, I was not reaching out to the vice-presidents who selected the vendors that would own real estate on their selling floor–dedicated floor space to a particular brand - in the various departments. At that point in my career, I didn't have the confidence or experience of being able to sell at the top. And yet, through the stint of very hard work at a lower level, I was successful for myself, my firm and Gund.

Having a great sales force is a tremendous asset to most companies, if they take advantage of it. A hungry and highly trained sales force is a company's eyes and ears in the marketplace. They can provide their marketing departments with valuable information about market trends, competition, programs and what the buyers really want.

Do you have great ideas but regularly get shut down? Why is that?

Unfortunately many companies don't listen to their salespeople. Of course, I wasn't always the ideal person to try to persuade Gund management, because of my arrogance stance as reps we knew what would "work best" to get Gund into more and more retail stores.

Let me share with you a teddy bear story. In the mid-1980's Gund came out with a stuffed teddy bear modeled after a 1907 Steiff bear featured each year in the Teddy Bear calendar published by Workman Publishing. The teddy bear was named Bialosky after Alan and Peggy Bialosky who owned the original Steiff bear. They also wrote the definitive book on teddy bears, The Teddy Bear Catalog, also published by Workman.

Bialosky bear came in three sizes and was dressed in the identical outfit as the bear on the cover of the calendar. In a sales meeting prior to the opening of Toy Fair that year, I suggested to Rita that we were missing a wonderful opportunity for add on business. We should consider coming out with a line of clothing and accessories for the Bialosky bears. As was her way, Rita looked over at me with her head tilted down so she could look over her half frame reading glasses, and replied, "But Michael, you know we are in the stuffed animal business, not in the clothing business!" And all further conversation ended. I could not believe how blind she was to the opportunity staring her in the face.

When has your good idea been copied or stolen? How did you feel?

Within a year of the Bialosky bear's introduction another stuffed animal company by the name of North American Bear came out with a bear family called Muffy and Friends. Muffy came in multiple sizes and had a full line of clothes and accessories that even included Halloween, Christmas and Easter costumes. Soon North American Bear's sales eclipsed the older and better-known Gund. Not only was it a missed opportunity for Gund, but North American's sales captured more of the buyers' open to buy dollars, leaving less dollars available for Gund products.

In December 1975 Gund had one foot in the grave. No retailer of consequence wanted its animals. But I was hungry. I went after business wherever I could find it. In the department stores, if one department wouldn't buy from me, I went across the hall and introduced myself to the buyer of another department. I was told, by an internal source, that at one time I accounted for 50% of Gund's overall business. Me, a single rep!

When have you been too generous or super stingy? Why?

As the line grew stronger and Gund's popularity in the marketplace grew, the reps' efforts in finding greater opportunities for Gund product continued. To bring Gund to a greater number and variety of retail stores, we each grew our firms by hiring additional salespeople to make sure we adequately covered the market. By the mid 1980's, in California and Hawaii, I had 15 people in my sales organization, a 2,000 square foot showroom in downtown

Los Angles, and a main office and small warehouse in Northern California.

The typical owner of a manufacturers' rep firm splits commissions with associates 60/40. That is 60% for the associate and 40% for the company. At Michael Luckman and Associates, I made the mistake of being more generous to our associates, making our split about 66/33. That 7% pays for a lot of overhead as well as contributing to company profits, but I gave it away to my associates. What I didn't figure was how expensive it was to run a large organization. I paid for the showroom, office, insurance and all of the various trade shows, plus the salaried employees. Our 33.3% of the commissions just about covered these expenses. My personal income came from my own accounts that I serviced, primarily all of the department stores in California.

Is your business or financial portfolio balanced?

To make sure that my salespeople had the opportunity to earn a lot of money, more and more of my energies were expended finding additional quality companies to represent. We added both toys and children's products manufacturers. In addition, we participated in numerous toy, gift and children's products trade shows in our territory. At the beginning Gund represented about 90% of my income. As my organization grew we were able to reduce that number down to about 50%, but still way too high and dangerous to have so many eggs in one basket.

In 1978 Bruce Raiffe, Herb and Rita's son, entered the business. Bruce was a graduate of the Wharton School of the University of Pennsylvania and the third generation in the family business; neither accomplishment won any great respect from me. I liked to say that a quality business education does not mean that you're smart. Only that you know how to pronounce John Maynard Keynes name correctly. How do you think Bruce and I got along?

Do certain things trigger your instant dislike? What are they?

Bruce's first initiative as the newly minted Director of Marketing, was to create a direct marketing program to Gund's customer base.

Gund would mail out a catalog and price list to every customer across the country. When an order would be received, Bruce planned for Gund to keep all the profits, and not pay a commission to its reps. I mocked him in my mind: "Sounds simple enough. Wasn't that what they taught you in business school, Mr. MBA?"

Have you done anything that came back to haunt you?

In fact, Gund's contracts with its representatives prohibited that. I pointed out that Bruce's initiative was not only illegal but in my opinion: immoral. When I first made my case to Bruce, he scoffed at me. My position was this. Gund had us sign contracts. Although the bulk of our representative agreements favored Gund, we did have a few legal rights. And one of those rights was that any order written in our territory for shipment anywhere in the U.S. was commissionable to us, whether we actually wrote the order or not. And second, my belief is that you don't hire people to represent you and then try to find ways to avoid paying them their just commissions. Once you as a manufacturer gain this reputation, you will never attract the best reps, nor get any reps to work their hardest for you. Especially, if they have to constantly look over their shoulders to see what hard earned commissions they might be losing.

Have you ever lost a boss that you liked and respected?

Bruce relented and his initiative was canceled. But, can you only imagine how he felt about me? It came back to haunt me, for sure.

THE BEGINNING OF THE END

Gund essentially had two product lines. Regular stuffed animals that typically sold in toy stores, toy departments and children's departments, and baby items sold in the infants' department and baby products retailers. As reps, we sold both lines. Around 1987, Gund separated the two lines and placed the infants' products under its own banner, Baby Gund.

It was about this time that Bruce found a heavy hitter to take over the newly created position of Executive Vice President of Sales. Now it wasn't that we weren't being managed up until then. A number of years earlier Gund had hired an industry veteran by the name of George Spangler. George was like a father figure to many of us. We loved the guy. In fact, of all the sales managers that I've worked under through the years, George was by far the best when it came to really liking and helping his sales force. When you needed something you could always count on George to get it for you, exactly when you needed it.

When do you find yourself rooting against someone's success?

George's one drawback – and it was a big one, was that he was a lousy salesman. You could introduce George to the prospect, but that was as far as you'd want it to go.

Bruce replaced him with a heavy hitter from New York, Steve Shapiro. Steve dressed well, spoke fast with a strong New York accent, and was constantly in your face. As you can imagine, I liked and respected Steve even less than I liked Bruce or his father Herb. Steve was about 5'6" tall, and that gave me license to express my point of view: beware of short men with Napoleonic complexes.

Steve came to Gund from Eden Toys where he held a similar position. At the time, I took comfort in the rumor that when the owner of Eden sold his business, Steve was expecting a little something for himself for all the years he devoted to the company, but got nothing. So a bitter Steve Shapiro moved over to Gund where his dictatorial management style was welcomed with open arms. You are probably getting the idea of how my relationship would go with him and the company.

With Steve at its helm, Eden Toys dominated the shelf space in the infants' departments of practically all the department store chains across the country. At Gund, we had made major inroads with our baby line, but we sold product while

How do you respond to change?

Eden sold programs. By that I mean Steve and Eden knew how to sell at the top, to set up strategic relationships with decision makers like vice-presidents who would give Eden real estate in the departments to merchandise their products. I was selling to buyers who were on a strict budget. We refer to this as a buyer's "open to buy," the money available once orders to suppliers like Eden had been placed.

Mr. Shapiro was going to change all that. With California being such a large market, Steve was quickly on a plane to San Francisco. His first stop was Mervyns', a 240-store chain considered to be a mid-level department store. Steve had a strong relationship with the infants' buyer from his days at Eden. It wasn't long before Steve made Mervyns' a house account, meaning he would personally take care of it and take it away from me. Before I opened Mervyns as an account, Gund had never sold them even a single stuffed animal. When Steve made them a house account, I was doing close to $300,000 a year in sales.

How do you respond when you feel you're being treated unfairly?

Unbelievable but true, I thought that Bruce and his family might object to what Steve just did. Coming in and taking my account and making it a house account. In my eyes, Steve was now Sammy "The Bull" Gravano to Bruce's John Gotti. But, in their eyes, they would sell more and profit more. My argument about contractual rights didn't seem to matter this time.

When have you felt desperate? What did you do?

Mervyns' was only the beginning. Steve's next move was to pull Baby Gund from all of the reps selling it to department stores. We could still sell Baby Gund to our other clients, just not to department stores. Steve put on separate infant reps to deal with these stores. Reps he knew from his years with Eden toys. People who owed their allegiance to him and with whom he had trusted relationships and a shared knowledge of how to make money. I just didn't see it that way. I thought of it as a personal attack.

I know that all the current reps took a hit when this happened, but it was particularly tough for Michael Luckman and Associates. Over the years most department stores eliminated their toy departments. All that was left was the infants and children's departments to sell to. When I could no longer sell to infants, my personal income was severely impacted.

By 1991 I was desperate for income. A lot of money came into my firm but very little was going into my personal bank account. Something had to be done. At this time I had three reps working for me in Northern California. Pat Linn, who lived in the East Bay, was my highest earning rep. She thought of herself as the top salesperson in our company, but she wasn't. When Michael Luckman and Associates grew, and I needed to devote more of my time to managing the company, I turned over a number of my accounts to Pat. Within those accounts were several that grew from one or two stores to over a hundred stores under her tenure. Pat's income grew exponentially because of those customers.

When have you done something you knew was unfair?

I had made a mistake in managing my company and my income as well as my relationship with my largest manufacturer, Gund.

I had to do something rash in order to keep the company afloat. Even though I thought highly of Pat Linn, my decision was to let Pat go and take over her accounts. It's ironic that I thought this was perfectly fair for me to do to her, at the same time I felt wronged when it was done to me. I justified it because I had opened a lot of the accounts that Pat grew. I had always accused my employers and manufacturers of disparaging salespeople for not working hard for the huge commissions we earned, and now I was making the same case about Pat to myself.

So from my perspective, somehow it certainly was nothing personal, it was strictly a business decision. I set a meeting for Pat to come into our offices and I explained why I was doing what I felt I must do. I told her I was cutting her out in order to save the company, and save the jobs of all of her colleagues. As you would guess, Pat didn't take this news very well. We weren't a nation and she wasn't a soldier. Why would I think Pat would feel fine about sacrificing herself for us? Within an hour I received a call from Steve Shapiro.

You could probably guess that he wasn't pleased. From the moment Steve joined the company it was obvious that he wanted to replace Gund's longstanding reps with his own. I would be the first. Steve told me that he didn't want me to fire Pat and if I did there would be dire consequences. At this moment, you would think I would have listened to him. My company, my family, my house and everything else I had are hanging in the balance. Did I listen or ask questions? You can guess what I did. I argued.

When have you reacted rashly?

My argument was that I was an independent businessman and I needed to run my business as I saw fit. By the time I put down the phone I was a basket case. I have known fear in my life but what I came away with from that conversation was unbelievable. It was like my world was coming to an end. Everything that I sacrificed for over the last 16 years was now about to end. What would I do if I lost Gund? How would my business survive? How would I replace the income I was going to lose? I would be a failure. I would lose my reputation. Every end-of-the-world thought filled my head. I couldn't sleep. I couldn't eat. And when I wasn't feeling fear I was feeling rage.

The very next day I was at Stanford Hospital. Melissa was scheduled for another bowel resection to remove an ulcerated portion of her small intestine. Melissa was 22 years old at this time, and I had been there with her for every one of her surgeries. I cannot begin to describe the fear a parent feels each time you accompany your child to the operating room door, desperately trying not to let your face show what your mind is thinking. Will the surgery go well? Will there be complications? Is this the last time I'll see my precious daughter alive?

Have you had a time in your life when it feels like the world is caving in on you?

Thank God, the surgery went well and my exwife Phyllis and I got to see Melissa in recovery. For anyone who has visited a loved one in the recovery room after a major surgery it is a scary thing. There lay Melissa, asleep and helpless, with a countless number of tubes entering and exiting her body. Plus, the IVs and the various machines she was hooked up to. Once reassured by her surgeon that everything went well, it was now time to try and save my business.

Unfortunately, it was way too late to create the relationships and goodwill with the people who might have helped me. In my self-righteousness I had argued my point of view with every important person in the Gund organization. And, now I needed their help.

From a pay phone in the surgery waiting room I called Bruce. He took my call and let me know that his confidence was in Steve Shapiro's judgment and he backed him 100%. I next called Herb and Rita. They didn't take my call then or ever. For 16 years I did my best to bring Gund products to as many retailers as possible. Year after year I would pack my van with three huge rolling sample cases and would go on two-week road trips traveling my territory so I could hit every toy store, infant/children's store and department store in my territory. Often missing out on important events in my daughters' lives. But none of my hard work would make up for the way I dealt with the people in authority.

I made the worst call I could make, making a decision to "stand up" to Steve Shapiro and lose everything – in fact, daring him to deliver the dire consequences he promised.

With the fear I felt evident in my voice, I told him that I made my decision; Pat would leave my company and I would take over her customers. His response was swift. He pulled the Gund line from me and gave it to my three Northern California reps. These were people whom I paid more than other firms would have – and yet would have no loyalty from. Not only did I lose my number one line, I now was without anyone to sell for me. With my daughter in the next room and worried about her recovery, I was now pleading for my livelihood. Steve then offered me a bone. He said I could keep the line in Southern California but all of my department store customers would become house accounts.

After losing the bulk of my business I decided after 16 years to close the doors of Michael Luckman and Associates. With sadness in my heart I liquidated my showroom, sold off all the samples and fixtures, and wondered what I'd do next.

It is not the critic who counts, not the man who points out how the strong man stumbled, or where the doer of deeds could have done better. The credit belongs to the man who is actually in the arena, whose face is marred by dust and sweat and blood, who strives valiantly, who errs and comes up short again and again, who knows the great enthusiasms, the great devotions, and spends himself in a worthy cause, who at best knows achievement and who at the worst if he fails at least fails while daring greatly so that his place shall never be with those cold and timid souls who know neither victory nor defeat.

– Theodore Roosevelt

CHAPTER 11

I SHOULD HAVE FOLLOWED MY GUT

We are so fortunate, for the universe has given us the most incredible tool to help guide us along our paths in life. All living creatures possess this gift and rely on it daily. The swallows return every year to San Juan Capistrano. The California gray whales travel thousands of miles south every winter to give birth to their young and then return to the exact same part of the ocean they left behind. This built in guidance system is called intuition. But only man, with his well-developed logical brain, argues with and often ignores this wonderful gift. I certainly did.

Have you ever seen a bus or train that was totally wrapped in advertising, including the windows? Have you ever wondered how that was done? How you could print an image on one side of a film

LUCKMAN'S LAWS
- When your gut is telling you one thing and your mind another, nine times out of ten your gut is right.
- When opportunity knocks it helps to open the door.
- Never own a company with three people on the board. One has only to sway one other person to shift the balance of power against you.

- When someone is with you and tells you things about another, who do you think they talk about when they are with that other person?
- Fear of missing out on something is the number one reason most people go against their gut instincts.
- Don't let anybody bully you, including your own ego.

and see through it from the other side? Well, let me tell you a story.

In the late 1980's I was introduced to a very unique product called ContraVision. ContraVision was invented by an engineer by the name of Roland Hill, located in Manchester, England. Roland's international patents allowed an image to be transferred on to a polyester or vinyl substrate through either screen printing or through a patented transfer system developed by the 3M Company called Scotch Printing. The process was unique in that the finished product allowed the substrate to adhere to glass either on the inside or outside. From one side you saw a full color image. From the other side, rather than seeing nothing through the window, you actually were able to see through the substrate as if you were looking through a window screen.

How long after a major stressful event should you wait before making a significant desision?

I thought the opportunities for this product were enormous, especially the way I wanted to use it. The first product I imagined would be something for sports fanatics to promote their favorite teams, or for alumni to let the world know where they went to college and who they'd be rooting for come Saturday afternoon. Instead of a 4 inch by 12 inch bumper sticker why not something that would cover the entire rear window of your automobile and yet still allow you to see through your back window?

When has your personal enthusiasm clouded your ability to plan with caution?

Once the first product was off the ground and profitable I planned on creating a second company with even greater revenue potential that would sell point-of-purchase advertising space on the inside of freezer and refrigerator doors in supermarkets, drug stores and convenience stores. As the customer walked down the refrigerator or freezer aisle they could still see into the case, but once they opened the door they'd see a full color advertisement for the product within the case, or a competitor's product. As an example, you might be looking for ice cream. When you decided which brand of ice cream you wanted and opened up the door, you might see an advertisement for Cool Whip or Hershey toppings.

Through research (much more difficult then since there was no Internet) I discovered that Avery Films, a division of the Avery Company, held the exclusive manufacturing and distribution rights in the United States for this amazing product. I placed a call to Avery Films and discovered that the marketing manager for the ContraVision product was a woman by the name of Linda Icard. I put in a call to Linda and after a lengthy conversation decided that the best thing to do was get on a plane and visit her in Cleveland, Ohio, home to Avery Films.

Linda and I hit it off right away. She was smart, intelligent, attractive and dedicated to expanding ContraVision products throughout the United States. While in Cleveland she explained how ContraVision worked. The first step in creating a see through product was to take the substrate (film) and add a dark colored background to the back by either printing or by bonding a second dark film to the first. The next step was to add tiny black dots to the front surface of the film that would later be printed. The product was now ready to be printed on by either Scotch Printing or screen printing. Once the substrate was dry the films were shipped to a company by the name of Clear Choice Marketing in Charlotte, North Carolina where they were put through a bath where the ink was washed off all the areas except where it had adhered to the tiny dots. And finally, a self-adhesive glue was added to either the front or the back depending upon whether the film would be attached to the inside or outside of the window.

Linda explained that by using this process the product was quite expensive, but in high volume we might be able to get pricing down to a point where we would could establish a viable consumer product. She shared with me two other important points: One, she and her husband Ben owned Clear Choice Marketing in Charlotte that washed the ContraVision product, and two, Roland Hill the inventor, was very difficult to work with. If you have ever worked with inventors you know that their inventions are like their children. They want to control every aspect of how their product is used in the marketplace. And they have not learned that it is better to receive a royalty of 10¢ per unit and sell a million units, than receive $1.00 per unit and sell only 10,000 pieces. I would soon find out how difficult Roland Hill would be to work with. But before that, Linda invited me to Charlotte to tour her facility and to discuss how we could start working together.

Within several weeks I was in Charlotte meeting with Linda and Ben. They gave me a tour of their factory and walked me through the ContraVision manufacturing process. We then took several samples and went to a local supermarket to test their product. After getting permission from the store manager we were able to begin a test to see if ContraVision product could be used in freezers and refrigerators. It wasn't difficult to adhere the product to the inside of the glass door. Once on the door the test began; could we see through the film? If no the test was over. If yes, how easy was it to identify the individual food items in the freezer/refrigerator case? If we couldn't identify the different food products behind the doors, the stores would get too many customer complaints and refuse to use this form of advertising.

The good news, the ContraVision product worked on both the freezer and refrigerator doors. The bad news it was too expensive in the size we needed to completely cover the door. Using a smaller size would affect how it was viewed from the outside. Part of the door, at least at eye level, would look darker than the rest of the door. Yet where there's a will there's a way. The next thing on my agenda was to get Roland Hill interested in my licensing opportunity. Without an exclusive license I would not be able to raise venture capital funding.

Of course, I thought Roland would jump at the chance to see his products in every retail supermarket, drug store and convenience store in America. Several months after my trip to Charlotte I had the chance to meet with Roland in San Francisco. To strengthen my position I brought along a good friend of mine by the name of Larry Udell. I had known Larry for quite a few years. At this time he was an assistant professor at California State University Hayward teaching entrepreneurship. In addition to his teaching duties Larry had started an organization called Center for New Venture Alliance under the auspices of the school of business at Cal State. The center worked

When have you assumed you would get cooperation and didn't?

with inventors to help them bring their inventions to market. Several times a year the center would sponsor conferences and bring in guest speakers to hold workshops for these would-be entrepreneurs. Years earlier Larry had gotten me involved in the Center and whenever there was a conference I was there to teach a workshop on consumer product marketing.

Larry also was involved in the Silicon Valley Chapter of the Licensing Executives Society, a professional organization whose members are involved in intellectual property licensing. Together we felt we could convince Roland that providing us with an exclusive license agreement for the two categories we were looking at would make financial sense to him. We could not, perhaps because we weren't thinking – we weren't even interested – in his vision for his invention. What I see now is that I failed to prioritize relationship building, ahead of business dealings. I should have learned as much about him as I had learned about his invention. If I had his trust and regard, perhaps he would have let me take his "baby" into the market. Typical of me at the time, I did not see him as a collaborator but just another obstacle in my business development plan.

Roland Hill was very much like an artist. He created his product but had very little consumer marketing experience. At the time, I scorned the way he wanted to micro manage it and the way he viewed the marketplace. Typically, when inventors license their patents to a master licensor like Avery the licensor is then responsible for granting licenses to various individuals and companies to monetize the patent. They charge a license fee called a royalty to the licensee and then split the royalties with the inventor. Now here is the most important part, in order for a licensee to start a company, raise capital and bring a product to market, they must have an exclusive license. Meaning, no one else is licensed by the inventor to do the same thing, nor enter the same market. Roland refused to grant anybody an exclusive license to market ContraVision and to this day his product has languished because of it. If I had approached Roland with a different attitude, would he have changed his mind? I'll never know, because I was a man with a plan, trying to go from point A to point B, without time for the people part of the equation.

Have you ever discounted someone's approach to business?

Without an exclusive license my dreams of starting a company using this unique technology had to be put on hold. In the meantime I fought to keep Michael Luckman and Associates viable. But of course, as I mentioned earlier, I wasn't able to do that. After closing my firm I wasn't sure what I wanted to do. The toy industry was consolidating with fewer manufacturers and fewer retailers to sell to. The next best thing was to become a consultant. Consultants are typically out of work individuals who print up business cards and work out of their homes. So I was now a consultant. Unfortunately, your income goes up when you're on a gig, and down when nothing is happening.

What is holding your dreams hostage?

During this time I was still volunteering as a marketing guru for the Center for New Venture Alliance. At one of our conferences I met a very likable local inventor by the name of Rodney Shields. What made Rod different from other inventors was, 1) he was a prolific inventor coming up with one idea after another, and 2) he didn't fall in love with his ideas. Since we lived only about 5 miles apart we arranged to get together so that I could look at what he had invented and see if there was anything I could help him bring to market. After reviewing his ideas I told him about ContraVision, my challenges in gaining an exclusive license from Roland Hill, and showed him some sample films.

My question to Rod was; is there any way we can create a see-through product that would do the same things ContraVision could do, but not infringe on Roland's patent, and be made cheaper by mass production? His response was, maybe. I gave him a sample to take back to his home workshop and looked forward to hearing back from him. At least a maybe was better than a "no." You know how I feel about "no."

How could volunteer work help you network?

Within a few days Rod got back to me and said he felt there might be a way to create a see through product using punched holes in the film rather than the black dots ContraVision used. We got together once again to discuss this process and it was then that Rod mentioned an exclusive agreement he had with another inventor he was working with to develop products together. That person's name was Greg Ross and Rod felt that with Greg's background in licensing inventions, Rod's talents in inventing, and my talents in marketing we may have the synergy to create a company. At this point I was certainly open to it.

How do you meet people with the credentials and experience to help you?

Greg lived in Santa Rosa and also worked out of his home. Santa Rosa is about 90 minutes north of where we lived in the East Bay. We decided that the three of us would meet at Greg's home and see if there might be an opportunity for us to work together.

Greg lived in a very nice home in an upscale section of Santa Rosa with his wife Debbie and their children. He was originally from Australia and met his American wife at a Club Med resort. We were met at the door by Debbie and ushered in to meet Greg. Greg was very cordial and began by introducing us to two associates who helped him in his efforts to market his inventions. He then showed us some

How do you measure the character of people you meet?

of the things he was working on. He was especially proud of a product that would prevent people from overdosing their medications and to remind them if they hadn't already taken their medicine. It was a thin membrane that could be attached to a medicine bottle that had the days of the week on it or times in a day. When you took your medication you would push down on the day or time and the button would stick down as confirmation. It looked promising but not much better than keeping your medications in a dated AM-PM medicine case.

Rod had already met with Greg and passed on the ContraVision sample that I had given him. We sat down to discuss how we might be able to work together. Each of us had a specific talent that we brought to the table. Rod the inventor. Me the marketing person, and Greg as he explained, had years and years of licensing intellectual property both here and in Australia. It seemed like a match made in heaven.

There was only one problem. I didn't like Greg Ross. There was nothing I could put my finger on. There was nothing that he said or did that caused me to be distrustful of him. But yet, something was gnawing at my gut that said watch out. I went home that day totally conflicted. I liked Rod. I believed that we could develop a see through

Do you typically go with your "gut" or against it?

product that would be unique and different from Roland's product and would be patentable. But still I had these uncomfortable feelings about Greg.

On the way home Rod and I discussed Greg and my wariness about starting a business with him. That was the first mistake I made in this deal. Talking against someone's friend or partner only causes them to defend the person. Of course Rod did not share these feelings and explained that he had been working with Greg for a number of months now and that he was on the up-and-up. But still I wasn't sure.

I was in the midst of a divorce from my second wife Susan who had moved out of the house with her daughter Tracey. So when I returned home there was no one to talk to about my feelings. I did discuss them with a number of friends who said I should go ahead with the partnership. That was the second mistake I made. I was polling people who didn't know the players, didn't have expertise or experience that would help them give me expert counsel, and didn't have a stake in this deal going well. Someone said, "You've got nothing to lose and all to gain." And what was the worst thing that could happen, I thought. We'd decide we didn't have a viable product/company, split up and go our separate ways. But still the feelings persisted.

Who do you ask for input? Are you asking the right people?

So it was decided, we'd form a partnership. Rod would be the President, Greg, Vice President of Licensing and I, Vice President of Marketing. We wanted Rod to be the President so Greg and I, when negotiating with prospective customers, could always say, "We need to discuss this with our President," before giving the prospect an answer. Greg had a relationship with a law firm in Palo Alto that specialized in patents. He and Rod worked with the lawyers while I put together a marketing and business plan. We needed to raise money and these plans were needed as quickly as possible. I named the company ImagoImage. Imago from the Latin meaning vision and of course the word image. We soon incorporated with each partner owning an equal number of shares. A close friend of mine, Ernie Lavagetto, was downsizing his business and had space in his Walnut Creek, CA offices for our fledgling enterprise. Soon we had the makings of a real company. But even though things were moving steadily forward somewhere down deep I had my reservations. And even though my new partners granted me the exclusive license for a separate company to market supermarket advertising I could not shake my uncomfortable feelings.

How do you make sure you're getting good advice and making good choices?

Within several months we had decided upon the process for making ImagoImage see through films and the patents were filed. We developed a strategic partnership with the 3M Company out of St. Paul, MN to manufacture our vinyl and polyester films. Within six months we had found manufacturers to convert our raw product into finished product and we now began selling exclusive and non-exclusive licenses to use our see through films. Our first license went to Linda and Ben Icard and their company in Charlotte, NC to print and resell ImagoImage. Linda was a great help to us in developing ImagoImage, both the company and the product. She had a solid background in screen printing and guided us as we perfected our product.

For each license we sold we asked for an up-front license fee of anywhere from $25,000 to $100,000 depending upon the size of the marketplace, and if the license were to be exclusive or non-exclusive. These funds paid the rent and provided each of the three partners with a modest salary. What we needed to do next was raise $500,000 in outside funding. So with business plan in hand we started contacting angel investors to find the one or two that would see our vision and invest in our young company.

We were fortunate. My future son-in-law Mike LaBarbera and his father Sal were interested in investing the full $500,000 and made us an offer as to what they wanted in return for this half a million dollars. Like all good investors it was a percentage **When is it right for you to get family involved? What are your special obligations?** of the company, so many seats on the board and a phased in approach of how they would dole out the money. Shortly after we had their offer we received a second offer. This one came from Greg's wife Debbie's uncle, Bernie Plack. It too offered us $500,000 except with different terms and percentages. Both offers were good, but I believed the LaBarbera offer was the better choice.

While I was Vice President of Marketing for ImagoImage I also started a second company to market the supermarket point-of-purchase advertising. This one I named See-Thru Advertising, Inc. I needed a strong partner to grow this company with me. I chose my good friend Ernie Lavagetto. Ernie was an excellent financial person. Just what we needed since this company would need a large infusion of cash to get off the ground. And venture capital people are much more comfortable when there is a solid Chief Financial Officer on board.

ImagoImage was now about a year old and moving forward rather nicely, except for one thing. Beginning about our ninth month Greg would come to me and tell me stories about Rod. He believed Rod had plans to take over the company and push us both out. Almost every time we were alone together or when Greg stayed over at my house because the drive to Santa Rosa was too long, the conversation would return to Rod and his ambitions. He even told me to watch out for certain things that Rod would do. And sure enough, Rod would do those very things.

How do you perceive someone who casts aspersions?

Although I was getting more and more leery of Rod, he and I worked together to take the ImagoImage process and use it with a thin sheet of plastic that could be vacuum formed. Our desire was to create a Halloween mask that the adult or child could see through no matter which way they were looking. If you're familiar with the plastic masks that come with inexpensive Halloween costumes you'll note that the mask has but two eyeholes and often the mask will slip on the face and cause the wearer to be temporarily blinded. This could be a very dangerous situation, especially for small children. The ImagoImage mask would solve all that.

When I owned Michael Luckman and Associates I represented what at the time was considered to be the premier Halloween costume manufacturer in the world, Disguise. Their Vice President of Sales, Toby Sheldon, was a terrific guy. I thought of him as much as a friend as a business associate. It was a pleasure to represent this company. They had a line of products that beat every competitor hands down and they always treated us fairly when it came to paying commissions.

With our new Imago Mask I looked to Disguise as the company I wanted to grant an exclusive manufacturing license. Although the principals were based in New York, the company was headquartered in San Diego. I met with Toby and his boss Jerry Berko several times in late 1993 and early 1994, in their San Diego facility. They loved the mask and the fact that it could be painted to look like anything you wanted; a witch, the devil, Mickey Mouse, and the different accouterments that could be added to it. For example: Mickey's ears, a clown nose, or facial hair, or hair sprouting out of the top.

How do you choose partners and vendors?

Disguise wanted the license, and both my partners wanted to grant them the exclusive. The only thing left to do was come to some form of financial agreement. In those days there was a Halloween Show that was held in Chicago every March. This was for retailers who had not seen the line at February's New York Toy Fair. It was agreed that I would meet with the principals of Disguise at the Halloween Show and we would finalize the license. The meeting was planned for the morning of Wednesday, March 23, 1994. We discussed all the pertinent details of the exclusive license: length of time, up-front fees, royalties, minimums, etc. I had already discussed with my partners what we wanted in this agreement. It was just a matter of would they agree.

As I recall the meeting 16 years later, Disguise agreed to almost everything we wanted. They had several points that needed clarification, and once cleared up, we were set to go. We shook hands agreeing we had a deal. Disguise would be our exclusive licensee for both children's and adult's Halloween costumes and masks, for the patent pending Imago Mask. I came away from the meeting feeling on top of the world.

How do you feel about "handshake" agreements?

I caught a plane that night back to San Jose. I had started the trip the week prior, first visiting with members of our strategic partner, the 3M Company in St. Paul, MN and then with manufacturers in the Chicago area that were doing the conversion of the raw 3M product into ImagoImage product. I communicated with my partners Greg and Rod several times each day. I continually apprised them of what was happening in my meetings and strategizing the license negotiations with Disguise.

My last conversation was with Greg that evening as I waited for my plane at O'Hare. We were going to hold a Special Meeting of the Board of Directors the following morning, Thursday March 24, 1994 to formalize the decision to go with the LaBarbera offer to invest in ImagoImage. Greg said he was worried that Rod may not go for the deal because it was with my future son-in-law and his father. His suggestion was that we should surreptitiously record the meeting just in case Rod balked at it and we would later be involved in legal proceedings. I told Greg that I felt it wrong to tape record the meeting and on top on that, thought it was illegal if not everyone in attendance agreed to it. He agreed and said he wouldn't record the meeting, and we left it at that.

When have you thought everything was set, but it wasn't?

The next morning the board meeting started with Greg, Rod and I in attendance. I was looking forward to a very successful meeting and the privilege of telling Sal and Mike LaBarbera that we'd be working together and Toby and Jerry at Disguise that the license was a go. Rod started the meeting and the first thing on the agenda turned out to be the acceptance of the Bernie Plack offer to invest in ImagoImage. I was in shock. Greg, Rod and I had fully reviewed both offers and the LaBarbera one was definitely the better of the two. In return for two $250,000 infusions of cash we would give up a percentage of the company. Simple and straightforward. The Plack offer was part equity and part a line of credit. But the line of credit was only for one year. What would happen at the end of the 12 months? Would we need to go outside to get a loan to pay off the Plack debt? And it wasn't even a straight loan. For with each $100,000 draw down, and there were two, we also gave up equity, an additional 4% and 5% respectively. Plus having the Plack debt on our books could preclude us from getting other business loans if we needed them. And finally

Has anyone ever asked you to do something illegal or immoral? What did you do about it?

the LaBarbera offer asked for 33% of the company and would value the company at $1,363,636 while the Plack offer asked for 40% of the company and would value the company at $714,286.

It was ludicrous, except for one thing that I failed to value: their relationship. I had entered a partnership with two people who had a bond that was greater than I was able to create with either of them. Rod Shields trusted Greg Ross, not me. Of course it probably helped that while Greg was complaining to me about Rod, he was probably complaining to Rod about me.

The second thing we discussed was the Disguise license. Greg was now not sure that was the way to go. He and Rod now thought that we should not grant an exclusive license but the rights to manufacture the Halloween mask should be offered to all manufacturers of Halloween products. This was a complete 180° reversal of what we had discussed just the night before. I was totally confused and in shock. What was happening here? Yesterday we were celebrating a major licensing agreement and today it was shelved. Obviously, I was in the dark.

When have you underrated a prior friendship or relationship?

The last major item of business was to renew See-Thru Advertising's option for the exclusive rights to supermarket point-of-purchase advertising. The very reason I started ImagoImage. Instead, this is what was placed in the minutes of the Board of Directors meeting. "Resolved by a majority that the Agreement from See-Thru Advertising not be signed as the contents of this letter give See-Thru a perpetual Option which was considered detrimental to the interests of ImagoImage Inc. Mr. Luckman was in favor of signing the agreement, Mr. Ross and Mr. Shields were against." Now it became very clear to me…I was being screwed.

What single action do you regret more than anything else you've done at work?

I will admit that what I did next was totally uncalled for and detrimental to my future negotiations with Rod and Greg. I went into a rage. It was totally surreal. One day great things were happening for me, my dreams were becoming reality and the next day I was totally devastated and humiliated. I had to face my future son-in-law and his dad and tell them that they would not be investors in ImagoImage, as they were led to believe. And, I had to tell my friends at Disguise that an exclusive license was not in the cards. To this day my good friend Toby Sheldon has not spoken to me. I yelled and I screamed at Greg and Rod and then I said a really stupid thing. I told them I had a gun at home. My father had died the month before and he wanted me to have his .357 Magnum. I had never shot it or even had it out of its case, but I

Have you ever said anything to try to elicit sympathy?

blurted out right then that I had it at home. I wasn't thinking about shooting Greg or Rod. I don't think I could ever take another human being's life. I feel bad when my car hits a squirrel or rabbit. I was thinking about killing myself. For at that moment my world was collapsing around me, and I felt so very, very lost.

In fact, I had no real intention to kill myself. Once again in my career, I made a pity play to people whom I'd given no reason to care about me. It was clear these men didn't like me or respect me and probably even feared me. Yet, somehow I believed they would feel bad that my life was about to be destroyed. But, I was wrong.

I could probably tell you that I didn't say I had a gun at home. But that would conflict with what Greg recorded. You see, after I told him in our phone call the previous evening that I would not agree to surreptitiously recording the meeting, he went to Rod and got him to agree, since he knew I would be upset with what they had planned. And he was certainly right.

Within several weeks I was forced out of the company and we were embroiled in lawsuits. Within a year Rod Shields was forced out of the company. From the moment we formed our company Greg was hatching a plan to drive both Rod and me out of it. I have no idea what he said to Rod about me, but he was constantly telling me we needed to get Rod out of the company as soon as the patents were all filed. And, I always responded to Greg the same way. I told him that once the company was making money everything would work out well for the three of us.

What I know now is this. If someone maligns a mutual acquaintance to you, then they are probably saying similar things about you to other people. Never let your ego tell you that you are too smart or too good for this to happen.

Now I know what you're thinking, "If he felt so uncomfortable when he first met Greg Ross, why did he go into business with him?" Great question! I'm glad you asked. I went into business with Greg because I was scared. I was scared that I would lose my dream of starting a company to sell point-of-purchase advertising in supermarkets, especially after my disappointing negotiations with Roland Hill at ContraVision. I threw my lot in with Greg and Rod because they were the ones who said yes, we could develop and patent the product and build a company that could dominate our markets. I was scared that if I didn't jump on this opportunity it may be lost to me forever. That this could be my one and only shot. I feared that my intuition about Greg might be wrong; maybe he was an upstanding person and I was not being "fair" with my doubts. And so, I ignored my uncomfortable feelings, and made an awful mistake.

What lessons have you learned in life?

Has this ever happened to you? And it doesn't have to be just business partners. Has your gut told you one thing but your logical mind overruled it? The truth is, it's your job to choose the people you want in your life and my job to choose the people I want in mine. But all too often we get into bad relationships because the clock is ticking, or we believe that we don't deserve better (this is a biggy). We feel frightened that we may wind up alone. So we choose the best of the bunch we see, as if we're picking a banana.

Do you make mistakes when you don't listen to how you feel?

Your gut instinct speaks to you every day of your life. Listen to it. If it's telling you to run, then get the hell out of there. Trust it. If your ancestors didn't trust their instincts you wouldn't be here reading this book.

You can follow your intuition in everything you do. If you're going for a job and after all the interviews you get the offer but still feel uncertain, then walk away. The Universe is telling you that this is not the job for you. Ask the Universe for the perfect job and have faith that it will come to you. When it does your instincts will tell you that this is the perfect job because in your heart you will feel the joy.

Do you have evidence that your intuition is right there working for you?

You know this feeling. When looking for a house or an apartment most of us trust our feelings. We say things like, "It just feels right. I feel very comfortable here." Under these circumstances, we become these very kinesthetic people. However, in day-to-day decision-making only one quarter of the population is naturally kinesthetic. This is how they learn, how they interpret the world around them. They check their feelings before answering a question or making a decision. They check first with their internal partner that communicates with them whether something is right or wrong. But for the other 75% of the population (visual 55% and auditory 20%) we don't have a very sophisticated gut. So what are we to do?

Have bullies played a role in your life? Are some of these bullies among your friends or family?

The answer is not as complicated as you might think. We can develop this natural ability. It's millions of years old and it's just waiting there for us to reawaken it. And how do we do that? Simply by asking. When faced with any type of decision, even answering a question, ask yourself or ask the Universe, "How do I feel about this?" And then wait. The answer will come. And it will be the most perfect answer to your question. The more you do this, the quicker the answers will come. Until the answer will literally come with the question.

Now what can prevent you from using this amazing talent? Bullies. The benevolent bullies in your life. They are often well meaning people who constantly try to bully you into their way of seeing things. They

Who is trying to guilt you?

sincerely believe they know what's best for you. It could be your parents, a spouse, siblings and even good friends. They are full of "you shoulds" and "why don't yous." They tell you what choices you should make in your life. The choices that make them happy. My mother is 91 years old and I am a grandfather, yet she still tells me what I should do, or not do. Like so many mothers, she does it through guilt. The conversation goes something like this:

Mom: I know I shouldn't say this, but……

Michael: Then don't say it.

Mom: Well I wasn't going to say it, but now I think I should.

Michael: Don't Mom.

Mom: I worry about my children.

Michael: Mom, you don't have to worry about us. We are all doing fine.

Mom: I wish that were true. Let me tell you what I'm worried about.

Michael: OK. Let's hear it.

What my mother is really trying to do is to use guilt to manipulate me to do something that she wants me to do. To change my behavior to what she wants it to be. Not necessarily what I want for myself or what's in my best interests.

This seems about the right time to tell you a joke about mothers. And it could be anybody's mother, be they Jewish, Italian, Irish, Polish or any ethnicity:

Mother: Son, I bought you a couple of shirts, why don't you go try them on.

Son: (Tries on one of the shirts and comes out of his bedroom to show his mother) Well, Mom what do you think?

Mother: (Looking at her son) What's wrong; you didn't like the other one?

Of all the animals, man is the only one that is cruel.
He is the only one that inflicts pain for the
pleasure of doing it.

– Mark Twain

CHAPTER 12

It is not that you ask God for too much,
but that you ask Him for too little.

– A Course in Miracles

LITTLENESS VERSUS MAGNITUDE: YOUR CHOICE

I know my parents loved me, but throughout my childhood I was taught that I didn't deserve to have what others had. I worked pretty hard to make that a sad truth, long after my childhood was over. Maybe it was how my parents were raised, but nonetheless, my belief as a small child on up and through most of my adulthood was that I was not deserving of having what I really wanted. So often as a child, whenever I really wanted something, I would hear from my mother, "Gonsig k'nacker (Yiddish for big shot). You want! Why do you think you're so special? Do you really deserve it? You can't have

LUCKMAN'S LAWS
- By your very existence you DESERVE to have the BEST of EVERYTHING.
- You were created for Greatness and nothing less.
- God created an abundant Universe so that you His child would have everything.

- Do not ever feel guilty for asking for what you want. As a child of God you deserve to have, be and do everything you desire. Ask and have faith that your choices will be delivered to you.
- Life is not a zero sum game where if you win someone else must lose. The Universe sees that everyone is a winner.
- Nothing happens until you ask for what you want when you want it.

everything you want." If my mother finally capitulated and got me what I wanted, it typically was not what I REALLY wanted. It was usually a knock-off or it had some features missing; in some way it was a compromise.

Somewhere in her upbringing, she learned we were not entitled to have the best. Why we couldn't have the best, I'll never know. And who could have the best, if not us? Were there people out there who were more deserving? Who were these other people and why were they so much better than us? These are questions I never got answers to. They are questions that have filled me with insecurity and rage.

What do you believe you deserve? Who told you?

The last time I raged was in 1996. I remember it well because at the time I was on a no-rage diet. I was sincerely working on breaking myself of this destructive behavior and had not raged in over a year. I was on the phone with my mother and I could sense that it was turning into one of those conversations that began with, "I know I shouldn't say this, but." And I knew what was coming. Soon my mother would be trying to manipulate me into some form of behavior she considered best for me. Have you ever been in a situation where your conscious logical mind was telling you to get the hell out of there, but something deep inside overruled it?

At that point I should have said goodbye and hung up, but I couldn't. And then they came. The words that flew me into a rage. "Michael, you always want the best!" I was literally shocked by the smack of those words, as if they had come across my face with the back of her hand. What parent doesn't want the best for their children? What parent tells their children that they can't have the best? What parent would deny their flesh and blood the best? What parent tells their child that the best is reserved for others, not them? Why not me? What's wrong with me that I don't deserve to have the best?

After decades on earth, many more of them as an independent adult than a dependent child, these thoughts continued to undermine me. They made me appear aloof but feel inferior, and often got in the way of my having positive relationships with people in positions of power. I transferred my sense of "unfair" to nearly every boss, before we've shaken hands for the first time. Only recently have I overcome what has been a dreadful approach to interacting with others.

How have the messages from your childhood created the attitude you have today?

Two separate incidents in my youth where I was made to settle for less have stayed with me all of my life. And when I think about them I still feel the pain and humiliation that I felt then. The first was when I was 11 years old. It was wintertime and in Chicago that meant walking to and from school in weather that was often below 0°. All the cool kids had this new style gray parka that had an attached hood. The coolest part was that the hood was lined with gray fake fur and had a zipper running through the middle. This enabled the wearer to fold over the two halves to make a four inch stand-up collar of fake fur that pressed up against their ears. I wanted one so bad.

I begged my folks for weeks until finally one day my Dad came home from work with this big box from Robert Hall Clothes. I was so excited I could barely contain myself. I ripped open the box and grabbed my new gray parka. I put it on and ran to the full length mirror attached to the inside of the door in my parent's bedroom. With my heart bursting with joy and love that my parents had shown me by buying me this coat, I looked at myself in the mirror. The coat looked great but the hood was lying down along my back. It would look so much cooler when

Was there a prized item of clothing or shoes that made you "cool"?

I unzipped it and folded it over. I took off the coat and reached for the zipper, but it wasn't there. There was no zipper down the middle of the hood. When I mentioned this to Mom and Dad their response was, "you don't need a zipper. The coat looks nice just as it is." But I need the zipper I protested. And the more I protested the angrier my Dad got. He really didn't enjoy shopping and felt put upon by my mother to have to make the stop at Robert Hall after a long and tiring day at work. Finally he erupted in a rage. Yelled at me that I was ungrateful and that he was not going to return the coat and I should just make the best of it. The only thing left for me to do was to cower in the face of terror and cry. And cry I did.

How did your parents express anger? Did it upset you?

The next day I didn't want to wear the coat to school, but my mother insisted that I not only wear it but I should wear it with the hood up because it was snowing. As I approached the playground I could see all the cool kids and a number of not-so-cool kids wearing their parkas with the hoods folded over and I knew what was coming.

All the kids started laughing at me and my nerdy coat with the hood and there was nothing I could do about it. With tears welling up in my eyes I pushed past them knowing that I was going to go through this same ritual at morning recess, lunch, afternoon recess and at 3:15 when we left school for home. Eventually the teasing stopped, but here I am 54 years later and I still feel the pain. The tears once again well up in my eyes, not so much for me, but for that little boy who only wanted to fit in.

The second incident came in 1964 when I was 18 years old. I was in college as a commuter student, still living at home. I was also working at Kassner's California Men's Shop making enough money to pay my own monthly car payments. The previous fall Chevrolet had introduced the Malibu a beautiful mid-sized car, and I had my heart set on a Super Sport Convertible, yellow with a black top and black interior and

Were there bullies at your school? Were you one of them? Were you a victim?

four-on-the-floor (4-speed manual transmission). Every night until I actually got the car I dreamed of what it was going to be like driving that car through my neighborhood. How cool it would be and how the girls would swoon. There was only one problem standing in my way, the down payment would have to come out of my college fund, and that meant my parents had a say in the decision process. Not only a say, they had veto power.

Did your parents get in the way of your dreams?

I wanted a V8 engine and even though it was a convertible I wanted air conditioning. My parents answer to both was no. "You don't need them," my mother said. And that was it. Actually my Dad didn't care one way or another but he didn't want to get Mom angry at him, so he stayed out of it. It was just Mom who stood in my way. "Why do you want air conditioning when you're getting a convertible, she argued? The air will blow in your face and keep you cool. You don't need a V8. It will only cost you more in gas. And, you'll go faster and get speeding tickets," she added. As much as I argued I couldn't convince my mother that I not only wanted this car with the equipment I desired, but since I was paying for it, I deserved it. "You deserve it, she questioned? You think you're so special? When you're not living in our house then you can buy whatever you like. But as long as you're under our roof you get what we say." And as the saying goes, that's all she wrote.

Have you compromised and received a just fraction of what you really desired?

I bought my dream car with the equipment my mother wanted, and every day I drove it I hated it more. No matter how much I revved the engine and popped the clutch my gorgeous car with its 6 cylinder engine went nowhere. And you can imagine what it was like in the summer of 1964, with temperatures in the 90's and the humidity close to 100%, the top down and the black interior. It was like driving a sauna. I could not wait to get rid of that car.

When it is ingrained in you that you don't deserve to have, be or do what you really want, it can stay with you a lifetime. And it hurts that long, too. For some like me, it can be a major influence in work and personal relationships. People who believe that they aren't deserving of love, happiness, joy, abundance, wealth and success, will often acquiesce their desires to others, believing others are more important than themselves. We often will be people pleasers hoping to get the love that we desperately seek. Afraid to say no when others ask us for things. Always wanting to be liked. And yet, we are unable to build deep relationships because we believe other people will treat us poorly. So, we spend our lives with the proverbial chip on our shoulders and a snide putdown ready to land its blow. We make people feel uncomfortable, angry and resentful.

What do you believe about what you deserve today?

In my consulting practice, I evaluate salespeople by gauging their need for approval. Salespeople with a high need for approval will not plant their feet and go toe-to-toe with a prospect because their need to be liked is stronger than their need to get the order. They won't ask the tough questions nor challenge the prospect when they know they're being lied to. How do I know this? Because I am describing myself.

Do you need to be loved more than you need to succeed on your own terms?

Let me share a story with you. After separating from Phyllis and after waiting 18 months for our Morgan Hill house to sell, I was finally moving to a two-bedroom apartment of my own. I was excited. This would be my bachelor pad so to speak. I would furnish and decorate it completely to my taste.

At the time videocassette recorders were just becoming popular. Video rental stores were opening in my neighborhood where I could rent movies and the thought of inviting friends and dates over for pizza and a movie was very enticing. The only problem was VCRs were selling for about a thousand dollars. Now I could easily afford the thousand dollars but spending that much money on myself was very, very difficult. You see, I didn't believe I deserved to spend $1,000 on myself. If I were still married it would be a given that we as a family would spend this amount of money for the joy of watching movies, but not just for me. It almost became depressing wrestling with this decision. $1,000 is a lot of money. Should I spend this much money on myself? Did I really need a VCR? Maybe I could wait until the prices came down?

I could hear my mother's words, "You want to spend a thousand dollars just to watch movies? You don't need it. Wait, the price will come down. Michael, money always burns a hole in your pocket." I struggled and struggled with this purchase, until I finally decided to go ahead and buy it. $999.00 plus tax. When I brought it home and hooked it up to my TV and then rented my first movie, what thoughts do you think were running through my head? Do you think they were thoughts of joy because I bought what I really wanted? Unfortunately not. They were the complete opposite. Did I really need it? Did I make the right decision? Should I have waited? Did I really deserve to spend this much money on myself? Were they my words? No, they were not. They were my mother's words spoken to me in my voice.

Are your parents voices still in your head? Are they kind or harsh?

The title of this chapter Littleness versus Magnitude comes from a chapter in A Course in Miracles. You may not be familiar with this wonderful book. I have been reading portions of it almost daily for the last 20 years. At practically 1,100 pages it is not an easy book to read, but it reflects my spirituality and my belief in God. A Course in Miracles teaches us that God dwells within us and we in Him. We are His children and together we create our lives and together we create miracles.

For the sake of clarity I am going to change the word Magnitude for one that I believe is easier to understand, and that is Greatness. So our choices are Littleness or Greatness. Now let's see what A Course in Miracles says about these choices.

"Littleness is the offering you give yourself. Everything in this world is little because it is a world made out of Littleness, in the strange belief that Littleness can content you. Chose Littleness and you will not have peace, for you will have judged yourself unworthy of it. For you will be content only in Greatness, which is your home. Every decision you make stems from what you think you are, and represents the value that you put upon yourself. Believe that little can content you, and by limiting yourself you will not be satisfied. For your function is not little, and it is only by finding your function and fulfilling it that you can escape from Littleness. God is not willing that his children be content with less than everything."

You were born into this life to achieve Greatness. It matters not if you were born into riches or poverty. It matters not if you are male or female. It matters not what color your skin or who you pray to. And it matters not if your body is perfect or in some fashion less than perfect. You are God's child and God wants you to have everything.

Why do you think you were born? Why are you here?

When you grow up believing you don't deserve to have what you truly want, then you are going against God's will for you. As a kid I remember my parent's refrain whenever I asked for something, and I asked for a lot. (They would affectionately call me a "chazzer," which is Yiddish for the word pig). So here I was this little boy who just wanted a toy or a plastic model plane or a bicycle and I was compared to a pig, affectionately or not. So whenever I prayed to God my belief was that I should only ask Him for the big stuff, and certainly not toys or things, because if I asked for everything I wanted, he might laugh and call me a chazzer.

Think about it. If God dwells within us and we in Him does God deny himself anything? And the logical answer is no, he does not. But I always felt guilty asking God for too much. As if life was a zero-sum game. If God answered my prayers is there some little boy down the street or on the other side of the world whose prayers are not answered? But what if I asked for a train set and he asked for his mother to get well or his father to come home from war, and I got my train

Are you afraid to ask for everything that you want?

set? Did I ask for too much? Did his mother and father die because I got my prayers answered instead of him?

The answer I was seeking I also found in *A Course in Miracles* – "It is not that you ask God for too much, but that you ask Him for too little."

The quote I shared with you from A Course in Miracles speaks to finding and fulfilling your function in this life. Your function is why you are here. Why you were born to your parents. Why you experienced all the good and all the bad in your life. I know my function. You are holding it in your hands. My 65 years of living and experiencing the sweetness and the bitterness of life was so that I would eventually write this book. And through this book and the seminars I teach, I provide you a pathway to achieving your highest function and your Greatness.

Your function may be as simple as having a child and raising that child where they believed they could have, do and be everything. And maybe that child wins a Nobel Prize in medicine. Or perhaps it is for you to start a business and through the products and services you sell help countless people to live a better and more joyful life. Maybe your function is to be a doctor and volunteer your services in Africa, and some child's life you saved grows up to lead her people to a better life. Maybe it is to be fulfilled as a sales representative, secretary, manager, or parent and be a role model for living a good life.

All plans are grand. What are yours?

Just remember this: God wants you to have everything. God created you for Greatness. Ask God for whatever you want and have faith that what you asked for will indeed be given to you and will manifest itself in your life. And why? Because, you deserve it.

CHAPTER 13

THOSE WELL MEANING PEOPLE WHO RAIN ON OUR PARADES

Has this ever happened to you? You have a wonderful idea; it could be for a new product, a new job, a new business, a move to a new locale or a new direction for your life. You have thought it through and you believe you can achieve this new goal. You feel so good about it, in fact, that it feels as if the Universe has shined its light upon you.

Your mind works feverishly adding thoughts and ideas that solidify your wonderful new idea into a plan of action. You are ready to begin. And then it happens. You share your wonderful new idea with a parent, a spouse, a friend, a sibling, whomever, and in their own "well-meaning way" they begin to convince you why your new idea won't work. Why you won't be able to achieve your success.

LUCKMAN'S LAWS
- Everything you see around you started out as an idea in somebody's mind. The only difference between their idea and your idea is their belief that their idea would come true.
- You have been created by God to create. Don't disappoint Her.
- Well-meaning friends often have a hidden agenda when rationalizing to you why your idea won't work. They're afraid that if you do succeed you will choose not to be their friend anymore.

- One of the key reasons why successful people are successful is because they don't allow negative people into their lives.
- True friends build you up and encourage you to reach for the stars. False friends tear you down by reminding you of all you're not good enoughs.

They in their "loving way" remind you of your past failures. They remind you of all of your not enoughs; you're not smart enough to achieve your dream. You're not talented enough to achieve your goal. You're not rich enough. You're not strong enough. You're not capable enough to make it happen. You are destined to fail. And they'll end it with this ominous declaration: You are just not being realistic. These people are bullies. No, they are not the classic bullies who steal your lunch money. They are the loving and friendly bullies, a more insidious and dangerous species.

Who has told you that you can't succeed?

And how do you respond to their negativity? Of course, you argue point-by-point, against all of their negative comments with why you believe your idea will work. But the damage has already begun. They have planted a seed of doubt in your mind that maybe, just maybe, they may be right. Maybe you aren't smart enough to handle all the challenges you are going to encounter along your chosen path. Maybe you aren't as talented as others who have preceded you. Maybe your past failures are a clear indication that you'll fail once more.

You have planted beautiful flowers in your garden and your "well meaning" friends or relatives have planted weeds. And all too often, just like in your lawn where the weeds choke off the grass, your doubts will choke off your dreams.

Who has planted seeds of doubt in your mind?

You know that their weeds have taken hold when you begin to feel frightened. Nowhere near as sure of yourself and your ideas as you once were. Fear grips you as your mind fills with preposterous thoughts of failure, humiliation, poverty, rejection and catastrophe. The end of the world has come even before you've taken the first step. Your dream is DOA - <u>dead on arrival</u>.

An incident happened to me just recently that brought this crisply into focus. I have a home in Las Vegas where I can get away now and then. My brother David and his wife Sharon live there and Phyllis, the mother of my children, and her husband Jeff have retired there. When the holidays roll around, the family all gets together in Las Vegas. Sharon, knowing how much I miss my mother's cooking, invited me over on a Sunday evening for a traditional Jewish meal of chicken soup with noodles and matzo balls and beef brisket. And it was absolutely delicious. How lucky my brother is. She also invited one of her best friends to join us. I'll call her Cindy. I've met Cindy on perhaps a dozen occasions over the years.

After a bit of small talk she asked me what was going on in my life and I mentioned I was writing this book. "Really," she responded. "What makes you think you can write a book?" With that I lifted up a binder with 145 pages already written as proof that I can write a book. She then asked what it was about. I told her it was about my life and what I've experienced over the years. "Why would you think that anyone would be interested in your life?" she chided. Well, it's more than just my life. It's how I experienced fear for most of my life, and how when I gave in to my fears I settled for less than God wanted me to have. And then, I share how I discovered ways to overpower my fears and live the life I was destined for.

Has "small talk" chipped away at your big plans?

"What makes you such an expert on fear that other people would want to read about it?" she asked. I told her I wrote it because I have always believed that I am every man. That if I'm experiencing fear around some issue, then many, many others probably feel the same thing. And if I could overpower my fears, then maybe others out there might want to know how I did it. As if I was creating a path for them to follow, including the obstacles that I faced so they didn't have to go over the same difficult ground.

Finally dinner was being served and I looked forward to a wonderful meal. I certainly didn't think I would have to defend my writing a book to someone who was almost a stranger to me. But unfortunately that was not to be the case. Her next question was prefaced with, "Let me ask you an honest question." To that I responded with, "So all your questions up to now were dishonest?" "No, no," she said. "But I really want to know this. Did you write this book with the intention to make money or to help people?" By this time I was getting a bit miffed. First of all, that's a very personal question coming from a person I hardly knew. Second, it impugns my integrity. Like I'm looking for just another way to make money. That I would bare my soul just to make a buck. "No," I answered. "I did not write this book just to make money. I have been thinking of writing this book for at least 10 years, but I couldn't do it until I was no longer under the influence of my fears. How could I guide others to live the life that they've only dreamed about if I have not found the tools for overpowering my own fears?" By this time my patience was wearing thin.

Has a stranger or strange question threatened to ruin a special occasion for you?

Cindy's final words forced me to put down my knife and fork. Looking over I said, "Cindy, you are the most negative person that I have ever met in my entire life." Remember, the title of this chapter, *Those Well Meaning People Who Rain On Our Parades*. Cindy's question was like a torrential downpour. Her question to me was, "How do you plan on promoting your book?" My answer was meant to be funny but with a tinge of hope, "I'm hoping that my book will be good enough that Oprah Winfrey might read it and consider recommending it to her audience."

Cindy guffawed. "Oprah? She's in her last season on TV. Your book won't come out in time. Plus, she's not promoting anybody anymore," she lambasted me. Wow! I didn't know that Cindy knew Oprah, or that Oprah had confided in her what her plans were for the future.

After I pronounced her as being the most negative person I knew, she used that old, "Michael, you're just not being realistic!" crap on me. Not being realistic is a crutch that negative people rely on. Reality for these people is to see everything as bleak. The cup is half-empty and maybe not even that much. They don't take risks because they might fail. And they don't want their family and friends to succeed because, one, they would be envious and jealous of our success and two, they might lose us to a better life.

Who has used this weapon on you: the old realistic ploy?

Yes, if you hear that "be realistic," line, remember this. They're afraid that with your success you might move to a better neighborhood. Start shopping in upscale stores. Take wonderful vacations. Send your children to private schools. Donate to charities. In essence, live the life that you create through your thoughts and your belief that you can have everything you want, and more. Your best interests scare the hell out of them. And so, they will tell you that you're a dreamer. Not living in the real world. Not being realistic.

How many people do you know like this? I'll bet plenty. It could be the very reason you remain friends with them, because misery loves company. But what happens when you throw off the shackles of poor me and truly believe you can accomplish great things? When fear does not stand in your way? When the future is made up of countless opportunities? And opportunities will come to you because you will attract them into your life with your newfound optimism? These people will become a weight on you that you will no longer choose to bear. Consider off-loading these people sooner.

Consider the people who surround you. How much misery is there?

Every successful person. Every great inventor. Every person who has ever risen from poverty to riches had to face the people in their lives who would drag them down. We've said to ourselves, I can no longer be close with this person. I can no longer allow this person to hold me down. Successful people do not allow negative people into their lives. <u>Even family</u>.

So how do you bar the door to "well meaning" negative people who plant weeds in your garden. First, consider the source and take an inventory of this person who is demanding that *you be realistic.*

- Are they successful?

- Have they achieved greatness in their lives?

- Are they known for taking calculated risks?

- Have they failed at something in their life, and more importantly, have they picked themselves up, learned from their failure and tried again until they succeeded?

- Is their outlook in life one of possibilities or one of lack and limitation?

- Are they people you admire for their intelligence and common sense?

- Do their words uplift you and increase your confidence in yourself or do they cause you to feel fear and self-doubt?

If you answered No to any of the above questions about someone in your life, then that's a sure sign you must disengage yourself from that person. These people may profess to be your friends, but they are not your friends. Friends build you up and support you. Friends offer encouragement. Friends provide a shoulder to cry on when things get tough, accompanied by words of encouragement that it's always darkest before the dawn and not, "See, I told you so!"

When Cindy asked me all these questions, they didn't affect me one bit. In fact they made me laugh. You see, I asked myself the questions about Cindy that I outlined above and each and every one of them came back a resounding NO!

Was this always the case with negative people in my life? I wish. No, it wasn't always the case. For way too many years I listened to these "well meaning" people. And even if I pushed ahead with my plans, their words left me with some fear, uncertainty and doubt which I call the FUD Brothers. This fear, uncertainty and self-doubt go completely against The Law of Attraction, which is as simple as it is true. Ask the Universe for what you want. Believe that it will indeed manifest in your life. And let go and let the Universe do its work.

So plant your seeds, nourish them with love and desire, bar weeds from taking hold, and expect your garden to flourish. The Universe will shower you with more gifts than you can imagine.

Something to ponder: Our lives would be spent in the dark if Thomas Edison, who persevered through approximately 1,000 failed experiments in creating the light bulb, had listened to his mother who might have said, "Tom honey, why don't you come in from your workshop? That's the 999th time you experimented with that bulb. It's time to be realistic. You're never going to invent the light bulb."

> *All our dreams can come true, if we have the*
> *courage to pursue them.*
> – Walt Disney

CHAPTER 14

Every artist was first an amateur.

– Ralph Waldo Emerson

ANYTHING WORTH DOING IS WORTH DOING POORLY

That doesn't make much sense now does it? The actual adage is; Anything worth doing is worth doing well. So why would I possibly want to do something poorly?

Several years back I attended a real estate investment seminar in Banff, Alberta, Canada where the guest speaker was Keith Cunningham, a famous business coach and author of the bestselling *Keys to the Vault: Lessons from the Pros on Raising Money and Igniting Your*

LUCKMAN'S LAWS
- Life has a way of knocking us down. It happens to everyone. Failure is when we don't get back up.
- How can you know success if you've never known failure?
- If you're an entrepreneur in Silicon Valley and you have not failed at least once, venture capital people will look at you funny.

- A horse won't respect you if after it's thrown you, you fail to get back in the saddle.
- We are what we think, so choose your thoughts wisely.

Business. Keith was also one of the rich dads in Robert Kiyasaki's bestselling series of *Rich Dad, Poor Dad* books. It was from Keith that I learned why I needed to change the old saying from well to poorly.

As toddlers the world is an amazing place. So much to see. So much to do. So much to learn. So much to try. Every day is filled with new adventures. No one has told us we can't do something. So we take the risk and try it. Do we always succeed the first time? Of course not. So we try again and again and again until we do succeed. This is how we as human beings learn. At this point in our lives no one has told us that we can't do something, and so we go ahead and do it. We are in the stage of constant learning.

When did you start trying new things? When did you stop?

As we grow from toddler to preschooler to grade-schooler and beyond something changes in our learning process. We begin to develop an ego, and as I mentioned before, our ego is not our friend. Never has been. Never will be. Our ego tells us it is there to protect us, but that's a lie. Now when we attempt to learn and try something new our ego tells us; beware you may not succeed. It reminds us that if we don't succeed people will laugh at us. They'll ridicule us. They'll call us names and we'll be embarrassed. Our face will flush and turn bright red and we'll feel the shame of failure, and we may even carry that shame with us for all the remaining years of our lives. Just waiting there for our ego to remind us of it.

When was the last time you dared yourself to take a risk?

When we were adolescents we were so very fortunate. We had friends who forced us to try new things and take risks. Whenever there was some challenge we needed to overcome our friends dared us to do it. Now a single dare may not have been enough for us to take the risk, but a double dare might. And if that was not enough there was always the triple dare. Some of your friends may have embellished a multiple dare with "I double-dog-dare you! Or, I triple-dog-dare you." Either way it was meant for us to take a risk and probably do something stupid. But it was not the stupid thing we did that was so wonderful, it was the fact that we pushed through our fears, took a risk and did something. Sometimes it took that dreaded word added to a dare that finally pushed us forward. And that word was "chicken."

But as we got older, daring us to do something or calling us chicken stopped working. In fact, it was almost a blessing to reach adulthood because now we could choose what risks we'd accept and which risks we'd avoid. Unfortunately, what happened to many of us is we began to avoid taking risks and learning new things. The fear that we might fail and feel the sting of embarrassment was just too great.

Keith reminded us of what it was like to learn to drive. Whoever taught us how to drive did not take us out on the freeway the first time we were behind the wheel. Instead they probably took us to a deserted parking lot where we wouldn't run into anything. We were willing to learn something new and take the risk of failure because of two important things. One, the desire for the freedom that having a driver's license would bring us, and two, all of our friends were going through the same anxiety we were. We risked doing something poorly until we learned how to do it well. Isn't that what learning really is, doing something poorly until we've mastered it? If you want to learn something new don't worry about mastering it, you will in time. Allow yourself the freedom to do it poorly at first. Learning is never linear. We learn, then forget, then learn again and over time we aren't doing it so poorly anymore. We are beginning to master the subject, be it a new job, golf, fishing, tennis, computers, dance, you name it.

But unfortunately mastering life skills is not as simple as that. For most adults, once we're out of the educational system, learning becomes much more difficult. It was okay to participate in class because everyone is there to learn the subject. There's a tacit agreement that making mistakes is part of the job of being a student. But when you or I must learn new things on our own in the real world: the real fear takes hold. Your ego reminds you of every past failure and the humiliation that came with them. Your ego will even talk to you, in your own voice, and remind you that you're just not good at (fill in the blank). So when the fear takes hold, instead of working through it, you give in to it. You now begin justifying why it was not such a good idea to begin with. Why it really wouldn't have helped you much. That once you learned this new subject, you probably wouldn't use it. These and a thousand other excuses.

Do you feel free to make mistakes?

Dr. Wayne Dyer said it best in both his excellent book and PBS special, *Change Your Thoughts –Change Your Life: Living the Wisdom of the Tao,* we must learn to think differently. Your thoughts become the things in your life. In fact, you create only through thought. All the good and all the bad in your life and mine, we have created. Of course, most of us would argue that this isn't the case. We'd say, "I would never create these bad things in my life!" And it is true. We would never create bad or evil things in our lives, consciously. And the key word is consciously. Each and every moment of every day our minds are working. They never stop. They go from one thought to another in a steady stream. And scientists will tell you that the majority of those thoughts would be classified as negative. And how do you know that you're thinking a negative thought? You feel it. Negative thoughts create the fears, uncertainties and doubts you feel.

30 DAY THOUGHT DIET

So if we agree that thoughts become things and most of our thoughts are negative, then it would stand to reason that if you changed your negative thoughts to positive ones you would then

Can you stay on a thought diet?

create in your life only those things that you truly wanted and desired. So how do you do that? Where do you start? The first thing is to recognize when you have a negative thought. A negative thought is always accompanied by a negative emotion. Typically one of the FUD brothers. Most likely all of three of them; Fear, Uncertainly and Doubt. So here is what I would like you to do. Buy yourself a spiral notebook. Something you can carry around with you. Perhaps one that would easily fit in a pocket or purse. Then for the next 30 days, you're going to go on a thought diet. Instead of counting calories and tracking your intake you are going to write down each and every negative thought you have. If you can spare the time, you may also want to write down what you were doing at the time of this negative thought. In that way you can see what activities activated your FUD brothers.

At the end of this 30 day thought diet I want you to sit down and read through your negative thoughts that generated your fears, and make this notation next to each negative thought. Did it come true? Yes or No. There are two things you are going to discover when doing this. First, you are going to be very, very surprised at how many negative thoughts you've had in the past 30 days. Second, the majority of what you worried about never came true.

Let's go back for a moment to the concept that you create all the good and all the bad in your life. The Law of Attraction never stops working, and it typically works subconsciously. If you give your subconscious mind a positive suggestion and then believe that it will manifest into your life, it will. You can do this consciously and train your subconscious mind to constantly reinforce it. But since no one has taught you how to recognize your negative thoughts, your fears, your worries, and the things you dread, they too will be handed off to your subconscious mind for manifestation. Something to always remember, the subconscious mind does not know the difference between a posi-

How would you like your brain to bring you what you want?

tive thought and negative thought. It doesn't know the difference between what is true and what isn't true, nor does it care. It is there only to create the things in your life, the good and the bad.

Throughout this 30 day period you are going to learn how to recognize every negative thought you have. Remember: you feel your negative thoughts. So keep in mind how you feel. Once recognized, it is easy to change that negative thought to a positive one. Just say to yourself the opposite of what the negative thought was. As an example, you can change a negative thought like, "I'll never make it through all this work and go home on time." Your positive thought take off is: "This work is a breeze. I'll finish it in plenty of time to make it home on time." Remember don't argue with your positive

Can you commit to 30 days of recording your negative thoughts?

thought. It doesn't have to be true. Your subconscious mind doesn't know if it's true or not. It just accepts it as fact. Simply say it and believe it.

The man who thinks he can, and the man who thinks he can't are both right.
– Henry Ford

What the mind of man can conceive, the mind of man can achieve.
– Napoleon Hill Author of Think and Grow Rich

CHAPTER 15

He has not learned the lesson of life who does not every day surmount a fear.

– Ralph Waldo Emerson

HAVE YOU EXPERIENCED ANY OF THESE FEARS?

You may believe you are unique, so much so that you think that you are the only individual in the entire universe who experiences a particular fear. You're wrong. Absolutely wrong. I mentioned earlier that I was so very fortunate to be in a men's group. For the seven years we were together we shared stories of our childhoods, our parents, our relationships and the fears we lived with. What I learned was that no

LUCKMAN'S LAWS

- A math problem for men: In the past week there were 3 Susie's you wanted to meet. You were afraid to go up and talk to any of them. How many Susie's will you be going out with this weekend?

- A math problem for women: There's a cute new guy at your office building you'd like to talk to but you're afraid you'll stumble over your words. Will you be giving yourself a manicure or a pedicure, or both, this coming Saturday night?

> • Mom and Dad advised you never to talk to strangers. But that was when you were a little kid. Now that you're all grown-up it's okay to talk to strangers.

matter where in the country we grew up, no matter our religion or the culture we grew up in in, we were all pretty much the same. Even the guys who said they were in the most popular groups in school still felt the same fears we all did.

I would like to share with you some common fears that all of us have felt at one time or another.

ADOLESCENT ANGST

Remember those mixers in junior high where all the boys were on one side of the gym and all the girls on the other side. Every boy there wanted to meet a girl and dance the evening away with her. But how many boys actually trekked across the dance floor chasm and actually asked a girl to dance? Not very many. Now, why was that? Fear. Pure unadulterated fear that paralyzed us from even attempting to take that first faltering step. And so we spent the entire evening standing with the other chickens on our side of the gym. Wishing we had the guts to make a move.

Do high school dance memories haunt you?

Did this happen only once in our lives? Not even close! For many men, me included, it is a lifelong affliction. Starting at age 12-13 and continuing for as many years as the man is single.

Let's examine why this is such a common occurrence. Pretend that this junior high dance is a sporting event and two sportscasters are describing 13 year old Michael Luckman attempting his first mating ritual.

Hey Bill, there's 13 year old Michael Luckman looking like he's in the bull pen warming up for an approach. You think he'll do it? I don't know Tom. As I'm reading his mind I see he's got his eye on little Susie

How would sportscasters call the game of your life?

on the other side of the gymnasium. She's definitely interested in him. She's giving him some very interesting buying signals. She's got her head titled to the side and she's slowly curling her hair around her fingers, very positive signs. I wonder if Luckman is picking up on them. What do you think Tom? Well Bill as I too read Luckman's mind I get the feeling that he's really unsure of himself. His mind is filled with all kinds of crazy thoughts. He's really scared. I don't think Susie's signals are registering. From experience I think he's feeling the big panic. You know the what ifs. Yeah Tom, I know the what ifs. What if I walk over to the other side, with every eye in the place watching me? What if I trip over my big feet and fall down right in the middle of the dance floor? What if I go to ask her to dance and my voice squeaks or I don't know what to say and nothing comes out? Or, the big one Tom, what if I walk over without falling, and I do blurt out, "Would you like to dance?" and then she says no? I've got to walk back across the dance floor alone with everyone staring and laughing at me and thinking, what a loser!

Yeah Bill I know the fear. Oh, something's happening here. Luckman's friends are egging him on. They're pushing him to make a move. No, no. False start. He's pushing back. No not today. Luckman's chickened out. I hope for his sake this doesn't become a lifelong slump. It would certainly be a shame. Poor Susie. She was really hoping. Maybe another dance Susie.

SOUND ADVICE FOR SUSIE AND ALL WOMEN

Have you ever heard of the *Learning Annex?* You'll find them in most urban areas. They offer different classes for adults, from creative writing to belly dancing. Usually these classes are several hours in length, generally held in the evenings or on weekends, and usually reasonable in price.

After my divorce from Susan I took one of their short courses on dating. Here I was, a man of the world in his late 40's, learning dating secrets you would think I would have learned in my teens. Remember what I said earlier about a lifelong affliction. It's true. Men seldom overcome their fear of approaching women. And here's the kicker; the more attractive the woman the greater the fear. Go figure. Men

How can you communicate to find a new love or ignite the one you have?

are scared to death and women have no idea why a man who seems interested never actually approaches them. What I learned in that simple Learning Annex class are things women can do to help men overcome their fear. I'm going to share those tips with you now:

✔ Practically all guys are scared. If you want to meet someone take some initiative. Smile at them. If he's interested he'll give you a knowing smile back. If he's still too frightened to make a move, then just walk up to him and say hello. Most guys will be flattered. If he's not interested you'll know pretty early in the ensuing conversation. If you're just as scared as he is then you've both got problems. Someone has to make the first move.

✔ If you're in a bar or club try not to go there with every one of your girlfriends. If it's difficult for a guy to approach one woman, the fear level goes up exponentially by the number of women present. Walking up to one or two women is scary enough. Walking up to three or more he'd rather be storming the beach at Normandy.

✔ You are better off sitting at the bar rather than at a table. A table is often another barrier for the man to cross. He's scared enough to walk across the room feeling every other man's eyes upon him. Will he succeed? Will he fail? A table puts him at arm's length where he has to shout to be heard. If at the bar sitting next to a friend and the guy is coming over to talk to you, your friend should be more interested in her drink then being part of the conversation. After things get moving she can easily join in the conversation. But not before.

✔ If the guy is not a great conversationalist then you carry the ball. Ask him what he does for a living. With follow-up questions of how long he's been doing that kind of work, followed by how he got into that line of work. Remember, everyone likes to talk about their favorite subject, themselves. If he never gets around to finding out about you by asking you questions about yourself, drop him right then and there. Wine and beef get better with age. Not a guy who thinks only of himself.

COCKTAIL PARTIES, MIXERS AND NETWORKING EVENTS

Nothing scares the hell out of more people than going to a cocktail party, mixer or networking event. The very first thing we learn as a toddler when we begin going outside to play with our friends is, "never talk to strangers!" Okay, I could handle that as Little Mike. But Big Mike still feels the fear. It's not easy starting a conversation with a complete stranger. In fact, it's downright unnatural. If God wanted us to talk to strangers he would have given us the very things to say when approaching a stranger. Instead, what actually happens is, our hearts begin to beat faster, our hands get clammy, our mouths go dry and our minds begin to race and then that little voice screams: don't screw it up!

Do you get nervous, clammy, and struck dumb at networking events?

Today people might look at me and say, "Luckman's a great networker. He's a natural schmoozer." But that wasn't always the case. In fact, that isn't even the case today. I am anything but a natural. I never really liked going to networking events. Even today, given the choice of going to a cocktail party or business networking mixer, or staying home and popping some corn and watching a movie, the movie wins hands down.

I really got into going to these various events when I started my Sandler® sales training business 10 years ago. I needed to meet people to grow my business. If it's a choice of going to networking events or cold calling, networking events win every time, they have food, booze and fear. Cold calling just has fear.

I don't really hate these kinds of events. In fact today I really do enjoy them. Mostly because of the things I've learned and have taught my students over the years. So let me share them with you now:

✔ Everyone that's there is there for the same reason you are. To meet new people. At some events you might be looking to meet new friends to socialize with, while at business functions you're looking for people with whom you can eventually do business. So always keep this in the back of your mind; EVERYONE IS THERE FOR THE VERY SAME REASON YOU ARE!!!

✔ I know that a couple glasses of wine on your empty stomach will loosen you up a bit, but beware. The last thing you want to do is slur your words or worse yet, throw-up on someone. Drink moderately. You do want to get invited back. Don't you? Eat and drink separately and eat first. If you've got a drink in one hand and a plate in the other it's difficult to shake someone's hand.

✔ Don't stand in the corner waiting for someone to come up to you and engage you in a conversation. The reason most business networking events are called mixers is because you're supposed to mix with other guests.

✔ Your name tag should always be on the right and not the left. This makes it easier for someone shaking your hand to read your name.

✔ You don't need some magical opening line. Or as my New Jersey friends say, "Fuged aboud it!" Just go up to the person, read their name tag and say, "Hi (insert their name), my name is (insert your name)."

✔ Typically the company they work for is listed under their name. If you are unfamiliar with their company then your next question should be, "What does Nuclear Waste Products do?" This isn't magic. What's happening is that the person you're talking to is becoming actively engaged with you. To keep the conversation going the next questions could be, "What do you do there at "Nuclear Waste Products?" I once was at a cocktail party where we didn't have name tags. I went up to this distinguished looking gentleman and introduced myself. I asked him who he worked for and he replied, IMAX. Well if you've ever watched a movie in an IMAX theater it's quite an experience and I told him so. I then followed with, "What do you do for IMAX?" His reply, "I'm the founder and Chairman of the Board." Wow! I was impressed to be in such good company!

✔ If you're familiar with the company they work for, then just ask what they do there. A good follow-up question might be, "How did you get into that line of work?" This isn't rocket science; it's just the ability to carry on a conversation. Arm yourself with questions that you'd like to ask as if you were just curious about someone. Remember: get them talking about their favorite subject, themselves.

✔ When you introduce yourself also offer them one of your business cards. Hand it to them face up. Usually they will reciprocate with one of their own. Quickly scan the card and then engage with your questions while continuing to hold their business card. If you would like to take notes on the card ask them if they mind if you write on their card. In some cultures it's a sign of disrespect to deface their card.

✔ If it's a business function you can wind up the conversation with the following question, "Who are your ideal prospects?" As they tell you write them down. Then tell them what a pleasure it was to meet them and that you'll keep their card on file and if you run into anyone in need of their products or services you'd be happy to refer them. Then excuse yourself and find someone else to talk to.

✔ One of the best ways to meet new people and overcome your fears is to join an organization. For business people these could include the Chamber of Commerce, the Rotary Club, Toastmasters or a professional organization related to your type of work. For non-business organizations there are the Kiwanis, Lions Club, Optimists, Junior League and many, many others. Here's some sound advice; whichever organization you join, get involved. Join a committee or run for an office or the board of directors. The reason to do this is threefold: One, you'll meet many more people quicker than you would by just attending meetings. Two, the people you will now be associating with are often the movers and the shakers in the community. And three, whenever they have a social event you'll know before you even arrive that there will be quite a few people you know in attendance. This typically will remove a major part of the fear. Plus, as a bonus, you'll probably get a name tag different than the average attendee, stating that you're an officer, or board member or ambassador. I always like to call them my red badge of courage (or white, green, blue, whatever). Wearing the badge allows you to approach any attendee like you were the host. Believe me it works.

✔ One last thing; put your business cards in your right hand pocket and the cards you receive in your left hand pocket. In this way you'll never accidently hand out someone else's card as your own. Or like the banker who handed someone a business card and the recipient said, "I thought you were a banker. This card reads, For a good time call *Trixie and Bubbles*."

✔ And last, don't go to a business networking event expecting to meet your ideal prospect. You will probably be disappointed and never go again. You go to these events to meet people who can introduce you to your ideal prospect. It could be their boss, their spouse, a friend or even a neighbor.

COLD CALLING FOR FUN (LOL) AND PROFIT

Since this book started out as a guide to help salespeople overcome their fears we can't ignore talking about the greatest fear generator ever created by man; the telephone. For with the telephone salespeople can now dial out and call a suspect. For those not familiar with the term suspect, a suspect is a potential prospect and a prospect is a potential customer. The buyer only moves from suspect to prospect when you have qualified them by determining a reason to do business. As you learn from Sandler® training, that reason is some form of pain your suspect endures that you can remedy for them with your product or service.

Years ago I came across a study that said the average company will lose 50% of their customer base over a five year period. Customers will go out of business, merge with another company you don't do business with, or God forbid, buy from your competitors. That means a company's salespeople **Do you know the difference between suspects and prospects?** must constantly be searching for new customers. They must be proactive. Not waiting for marketing to drop some leads in their laps. So if new business is so important to a company's survival why do so many companies allow their salespeople to sit on their butts waiting for something to happen? If a salesperson is not actually meeting with a suspect, prospect or customer, or engaged with them on the telephone, then they should be on the phone making cold calls. No excuses!!!

I cannot begin to tell you how many salespeople I hired and fired over the years who in the interview process said to me, "Michael I'm great when I'm in front of a prospect, but not very good over the phone! Bring me the leads and I'll bring you the **How can you let the phone scare you away from reaching the right people?** business." When I heard that it was like a light bulb would go on in the back of my mind, and I'd think, "That makes sense. I'm not very good over the phone myself." And I'd hire them. Then I'd wait for their business to come in. But it was typically a lot less than what I expected. Whenever I called them I'd find them at home waiting for the phone to ring. In good times the phone did ring. But in bad economic times it did not.

Are you familiar with the acronym Y.C.D.B.S.O.Y.A.? It stands for *You Can't Do Business Sitting on Your Ass!* In the world we live in today all salespeople need to be hunters. A hunter can become a farmer or gatherer when the need arises, but a farmer or gatherer can never be a hunter. They just don't have the abilities or prospecting awareness.

All salespeople need to know how to go after new business. And that means how to use the phone.

I am not going to profess to you that I love cold calling. I don't. I never have loved cold calling and I'm sure I never will. Do I do it? Yes, I do. Am I good at it? Yes, I am. Do I have to push myself to make cold calls? You better believe it. But I do make them.

So what are you afraid of when calling a complete stranger and engaging them in a conversation:

- You're afraid that you are bothering them. That you're interrupting their day.

- You're afraid you'll forget what to say.

- You're afraid that you'll flub your words and then get all tongue-tied.

- You're afraid they'll get mad at you and hang up.

- You're afraid they won't like you, and your ego (which is never your friend) will get bruised.

How do you feel about cold calling or using linkedIn to connect?

Let's take a closer look at those five GIGANTIC FEARS and see if we can knock them down to a manageable size.

1. **You're afraid that you are bothering them.** That you're interrupting their day. Do you believe in your products and services? What do I mean by that? Do you believe that your products and services do what their supposed to do? Do they solve a problem(s) that the buyer is living with? Do you believe that your company offers a quality product or service at a fair price? Do you believe that the buyer's life will improve once they become a customer?

   Now you might say, "Hey, I sell toner and ink cartridges. How is their life going to be better once they buy from me? Okay. Let's pretend they are currently buying their ink and toner from a competitor and your competitor is often out of stock on key products. The buyer is getting a lot

   What are your fears about rejection?

of flak from everyone in the office because they can't make copies or print proposals. The buyer is afraid that if the boss gets wind of it he can kiss his raise goodbye. So if you can guarantee that you'll never be out of stock on the key items your buyer needs, his work environment is going to improve dramatically.

So, does it not stand to reason that if by making that suspect a customer, their life will be better? No more colleagues giving them a hard time. No more fear of not getting a raise. No more kicking the dog and yelling at the kids when they get home. If you believe what you've just read, and you believe that your prospect's life is going to be better because they know you, then you have every right to interrupt their day and talk to them about the pain (problems) they're living with. And then to set a future meeting where you have the opportunity to sit down with them and uncover more of their pains that you can solve.

Do you see how you, your products or services make people successful?

2. **You're afraid you'll forget what to say.** Forgetting what to say is definitely a big fear. But easily solvable. Never, never, never make a cold call without a script. Now, I know what you're thinking, "I don't want to sound scripted." And if you don't practice your script that's exactly what you'll sound like. But let me ask you a question? Have you ever seen a movie or TV show? Of course you have. How do you think those actors knew what to say? They weren't just adlibbing the words they spoke. They started with a script. Memorized it. Then practiced the right tonality with the perfect inflection in their voice. You must do the same.

Which has been your style: adlib or rehearsed?

The greatest no-pressure call script that I have ever used is the one I teach my students. It is the script that I was taught when I began training salespeople in my Sandler® training business. The script itself is worth the price of a one-year President's Club sales training program offered by Sandler® trainers around the world. Learn it. Use it. And you'll schedule more appointments than you ever dreamed possible.

3. **You're afraid you'll flub your words and then get all tongue-tied.** Hey, it could happen so what? We're not in kindergarten anymore. All of us flub words now and then. It's really no big deal. I use to believe that if I screwed up on the phone the person I called would remember it forever. That I was definitely going to be the topic of conversation around that person's dinner table that night. And if I were to call her several days later she'd remember me as the idiot salesperson who **What's the dumbest thing you've said? Are you still alive?** flubbed his words. Not so. Not even close. Most people don't even remember what they had for lunch the day before, let alone some cold calling salesperson they spoke with for less than a minute earlier that day.

    If you're worried about getting tongue tied and not knowing what to say then look to the answer in number 2 above. Use a script. Even though I know my script backwards and forwards I always have it open in front of me when making cold calls, just in case.

4. **You're afraid they'll get mad at you and hang up.** Sticks and stones will break my bones but words will never hurt me. Not true. Words do hurt. And having someone, anyone reject us can knock us off our game. Who are they rejecting? You? Absolutely not. They're rejecting that slick salesperson they think you are. They're rejecting the interruption. That's why, before we even tell them why we called, they tell **When you hear "no" do you hear "not ever?"** us, "Not interested. Don't bother me. We're happy with our current supplier." And a whole host of things just to get rid of us.

The Sandler® script I use and trained my students to use eliminates most of the above issues. I am contractually not at liberty to share it with you in this book. But, I can offer you some suggestions that can help you to overcome some of these issues:

Do you have a great opening?

- Never ask the person you are speaking with, "How are you?" You don't really care how they are. They know you don't care how they are. And you know that they know you don't care how they really are. So don't ask it. It's a sure sign to the person you called that it's a cold call. I once had a telemarketer call me and the first thing she asked me was, "Mr. Lukeman how are you today?" The first thing I did was correct her pronunciation of my name and then I said, "I am so glad you asked. I woke up this morning with this pain in my lower back and it's killing me." It turns out that she's a telemarketer for half the day and a massage therapist the remainder. She gave me some good advice to help my back, but I still didn't buy anything.

Can you get around simple obstacles?

- Always use first names. Asking for Mr. Timothy B. Rogers tells gatekeepers that you don't know Tim. So the next question they'll ask you is, "what is this in regards to?" Now you're trapped. Instead just ask for Tim. If they ask you which Tim then respond Tim Rogers. Make it sound like you and he are good buddies. If you aren't sure if he goes by Tim or Timothy call the company when they're closed and using their internal phone tree get to Tim's voicemail. If his outgoing message says, "This is Tim Rogers. I'm away from my desk…." then you know he goes by Tim. Here's what I say when I get hold of him, "Hi Tim this is Michael Luckman." He'll be thinking: why this guy's name sounds familiar. Then he'll ask himself, where do I know this guy from? Is he a customer or a resource? That's exactly what I want him to think.

- You are on the phone for only one reason; to set a future meeting. If you are an inside salesperson you still want to set a future meeting. Too many salespeople, when faced with a willing suspect, go into sell mode. Then the interested suspect looks at their watch and says, "Whoa, I've got to cut this short, I have a meeting to go to. Thanks for all the information. If I ever need anything I'll give you a call." Boom. It's over.

- If you don't want to be hung-up on don't sound like every other salesperson. If you think telling the suspect all about your company and your products or services are going to convince him to invite you in for a meeting, think again. Why should he? You sound like every other salesperson out there, and when you talk about all your features and benefits you sound just like the company he's currently buying from. If he's satisfied with them why even waste his time with you? And this is where he says, "We're happy with our current supplier. Goodbye!"

Why are so few customers happy with their suppliers?

- Instead of telling the suspect all about your products and services it would behoove you to find out what's not working with his current supplier. Do they ship on-time? What's their percentage of in-stock items that ship complete on the first shipment? Are there quality problems with his current resource? Are there billing problems? Are products coming in damaged? Get suspects talking about these issues and I guarantee you they won't be hanging up on you. Here is a great way for them to start talking about their issues with their current vendor. Ask them, when they say they're happy with their current vendor, "If you could wave a magic wand over your current supplier, what's the one thing you'd like them to do for you, or do differently that they're not doing right now?" Whatever they answer say, "You know I hear that more and more, can you tell me more about that, perhaps give me a recent example?' You now have the prospect talking and

How good a detective are you?

that's exactly what you want. You noticed I said prospect, not suspect. The minute you hear the prospect complaining about their current resource and you can solve their problems, they went from a suspect to a prospect.

5. **You're afraid they won't like you, and your ego will get bruised.** As you read over the previous statement ask yourself if it sounds a bit ridiculous. It sure does to me. Remember what I said in a previous chapter about your ego? Your ego is always comparing you to other people. And when it does you're either going to feel superior to them or inferior, there's no middle ground. If you have a high need for approval, always wanting to be liked, and you're in sales, watch out. It's a deal killer and a career killer. Because your need to be liked and accepted is stronger than your need to make the sale. You won't ask the tough questions and when you know the buyer is blowing smoke, you won't challenge them on it. The sales arena is not the place to get your needs met. Get rid of your ego and your high need for approval will disappear with it.

Are you too interested in pleasing people?

CHAPTER 16

A pessimist sees the difficulty in every opportunity;
an optimist sees the opportunity in every difficulty.
– Winston Churchill

REINVENTING MICHAEL LUCKMAN

In June of 1967 I went to work as a junior salesman for Milton Bradley Company, the world's oldest and largest manufacturer of board games, puzzles and school supplies. I'm sure you're familiar with some of the products I sold: Game of Life, Chutes and Ladders, Battleship, Twister and many other number one selling toys. This was my first real job after college and my entry into the toy industry, where I would remain for 25 years.

Have you been looking for security?

LUCKMAN'S LAWS

- Fear and ego are a lousy combination. Fear tells you what you can't do. And then if you do it anyway and fail, your ego reminds you that YOU are a failure. When in fact it is what you did that failed. NOT YOU.

My parents came of age during the Great Depression where jobs were in short supply and unemployment topped out at 25%. Their advice to me was: find a good job with an established company, work hard, advance and someday retire with a nice pension. Not much different than what my fellow baby boomers were hearing from their parents. It didn't matter if you were a white-collar employee or a union card carrying blue-collar worker. Security was the name of the game.

How many good traits do you bring to work?

And that was my plan in 1967 when I went back to Springfield, Massachusetts in early summer for my initial sales training. My goal was to work through the ranks, climb the ladder and eventually become president of Milton Bradley. And that was my goal until May of 1968 when I was fired.

By now you know that I was a bit arrogant and cocky in my early days. Okay, more than just my early days and more than just a bit. However, I was also hardworking, imaginative, dedicated and the best ambassador I could be for every organization that employed me or that I represented.

At Milton Bradley I was a budding salesman with a solid future. So what, that I didn't always follow directions! Often the dictates from above seemed not to make much sense to my twenty-two year old brain. Although I lacked his worldly experience, wealth or power, I took to heart the words of Frank Sinatra's number one song, "I Did it My Way."

How many bad traits are causing you to undermine your success?

Let me explain what "my way" meant. As a junior salesman my job was to call on Woolworth stores in three mid-western states. I was to merchandise the store's board games display and then sit down with the store manager and present him with our upcoming TV advertising campaigns for his geographic market. Then, I was supposed to suggest he order additional product. And with that I was supposed to be off to the next town and its Woolworth store. For me this plan didn't make much sense. Having worked in retail I knew that once a salesperson left the store without writing an order, the likelihood was next to none that the manager would later write one on his own. My own common sense told me to write the order while I was there. And so I did.

But, you see, that was not in my job description. My job was to visit as many Woolworth stores in a day as I could. And while writing an order made the company money, it took time. Consequently the number of stores I visited in a day was less than my fellow junior salespeople. My immediate boss was frustrated with my performance on the metrics he set out for all of us. But the senior salesperson responsible for the Woolworth account wished he could replicate me throughout the country. I was moving product and helping him reach his bonus. No wonder he liked me, I was doing his job! Unfortunately, I was not doing the job I was hired to do.

What delusional thoughts cause you fear, disrespect or angst?

At that tender age, my ego created some delusional thinking that would hobble me throughout much of my career. I didn't try to understand what my role was. I persisted in believing that my approach was superior to how my manager wanted me to conduct business. Even worse, I globalized that belief beyond this one situation. I decided that management in corporate America suffered from a lack of common sense. From then on, I was skeptical of people above me and that made my life difficult. Skepticism and cynicism made me fear their decisions, including how they judged me. I spent much of my working life embattled, almost always afraid and at the same time pugnacious.

If you're just another corporate asset, how can you increase your unique value?

It took me years to learn that not just anyone is privy to the reasons behind all the decisions, plans and policies made by managers in a company. I learned I didn't need to fear management. In fact, when I showed respect for those above me and chose to learn from people at the top, including how to work with them, my life changed. It was almost magically easy and I was routinely successful.

But the most important lesson I learned is that nothing is forever. Working for one company all your life and then retiring with a comfortable pension is now a myth. That sense of security in a career is rarely warranted. Even hardworking, productive employees are expendable. Sometimes it seems that people are just another company asset to stock up on when times are good and then let go of, when times go bad. I had my own company, so I know what it's like to have to cut back on the people who helped grow your business. And, of course, I've been the person let go.

The baby boomer generation put computers on every desk and a mobile phone in every pocket, and developed hundreds of other inventions that transformed our economy. Yet, we are required to reinvent ourselves along with everyone else in the workforce if we are going to survive. I have been luckier than most. For much of my career I felt all I needed to do was to evolve, not start from scratch. I went from being a manufacturer's salesman to a wholesaler's salesman. From wholesaler's salesman to retail buyer. From retail buyer to marketing executive. From marketing executive to manufacturer's representative. Actually it would have helped me if I had approached each role as a brand new one and given myself the opportunity to learn as a neophyte. But I felt I was simply evolving in my career. That was until ImagoImage.

How comfortable are you with learning and researching?

Clearly, ImagoImage was a revolutionary product. My partners and I were learning new things every day. As the marketing guru, I needed to learn about the industries we intended to sell our product into: transit advertising, retail advertising, point-of-sale advertising, trade show promotion and miscellaneous other retail products. On top of these industries I had to learn about the printing industry and the various ways our products could be manufactured: Scotch printing, screen printing, offset printing, large scale inkjet printing and a host of other technologies. In essence, I had to work in multiple industries and markets, learning as I went along.

These were the days when there was no Internet. Researching an industry required a visit to the main library and hours and hours spent reading trade journals and discovering whom the major players were. But, research was the easy part. My next challenge was to call the key players in each industry; engage them in a conversation and set up meetings to determine how our unique products could benefit not only their individual firms, but their industry as a whole. This was more than just cold calling. This was cold calling blind. I didn't really know their industry, their markets or even if our product would be valuable to them.

If you didn't have the internet, could you survive?

So here I am, everyday confronting my fear of picking up the phone and calling complete strangers and engaging them in conversations about things I was still learning about myself. Nothing could prevent me from feeling the fear - but fear would not stop me. My company's success depended on my making these calls, so I had to devise a way to accomplish my objective. And that way was simplicity itself. I called to ask these industry leaders for advice. I told them I needed their help. Here's a key learning: the majority of people when asked for help will typically stop what they're doing and not only offer help to those whom they know, but to a complete stranger as well.

Are you too shy to ask strangers for help?

I called them as a neophyte. Sharing with them upfront that I didn't know their industry or their marketplace, but had this product that might work better than alternatives now used. I wasn't shy to say that if they could help me, we might be able to determine if I had something for them. I was free of the fear of asking dumb and irrelevant questions because neophytes can ask those types of questions. And through those questions we both could then determine if what my company offered would work in their world. No pressure. No tricks. I came to them with honest curiosity.

What I did is not rocket science. It had more to do with normal human behavior and that includes the innate goodness in people. When asked with humility for help, most people are ready and willing to find the time. Even a cold call can be used for asking for help. If you're a salesperson calling a suspect, rather than blurting out all the facts about your product or service, an approach they probably heard one thousand times before, tell them you're not sure if what you have would even benefit them. And if they can give you just a minute or two, and with their help, maybe the two of you can determine if you have a fit. Try it. It works!

If you went "back to basics" what would that mean?

REINVENTING MYSELF

After leaving ImagoImage, or more correctly my partners and ImagoImage leaving me, I was faced with the challenge of what I wanted to do next. Some things were certain: I didn't want to start another company and I certainly didn't want partners. What I really wanted to do was just go back to basics. And basics for me was to find a company that was looking for an executive sales pro and do what I loved best, selling.

I went to work first for one and then a second international management consulting firm. My challenge: could I sell intangible services? After all, for over 25 years I had always sold tangible products. Something I could put on a prospect's desk, a sample, a swatch. Something that could be picked up, touched and even smelled. Something I could demonstrate. Was I up to selling a dream? For that's exactly what you sell when you sell an intangible. You want to create a picture in the buyer's mind that by purchasing your services you are going to take the buyer, and their company, from where they are now (not a good place) to where they want to be (their dream).

Does fear get in the way of your learning?

My first employer IMPAC Integrated Systems sent me to their Florida headquarters for three weeks of training where I learned their internal system for moving a suspect to a prospect and a prospect to a client. After the second full week of training I was still fearful that I might not be able to do this, in essence to reinvent myself. It's not always easy learning new tricks as an old dog. But by the time I returned home to San Jose, I was convinced I could do it.

There was still one more obstacle to overcome. Every sales call I made was to a "C" level officer. I was used to calling on buyers. CEOs, CFOs and COOs scared the hell out of me. I felt uncomfortable dealing with people I felt inferior to, a leftover from the admonitions and beliefs of my childhood.

Upon returning home from training, my very first meeting with a suspect was with the Chief Financial Officer of APL in Oakland, CA. For those not familiar with the acronym, APL stands for American President's Line, at the time the largest container transportation line in the United States. Was I scared? You bet. Was I worried I'd screw up?

How do you feel about calling and meeting top management?

Absolutely. Did I do well? Yes, I did. I didn't sell them a project but I did learn some very important lessons from that meeting and subsequent meetings with other companies and their top executives.

First, top executives for the most part are very nice people. They've climbed the corporate ladder and typically don't have to prove to anyone why they sit in the captain's chair. They are big picture people who don't want to get bogged down in details. If they like what they see and it makes sense to them, they can pull the trigger or introduce you to the people who can make the decision. For the most part they are ordinary people with exceptional business talents. But keep in mind, their time is limited so use it wisely.

Bottom line: I would much rather call on a company's "C" level officers than any other employees within the organization. If you are not calling at the top because of fear, you need to work your way through it. A major benefit of calling at the top is that you'll close more business in less time with fewer headaches, and you'll beat your competition who will be working their way up to the level you started at.

How do you need to change your self image so others see a more confident you?

Selling intangibles to the executive suite did require me to reinvent myself. It wasn't always easy and I will admit I did meet with some very intimidating people. But overpowering my fears altered more than how I sold or to whom I sold. Overpowering my fears changed the way I viewed myself.

At the beginning I felt inferior to these senior executives. I thought their success was due to their being smarter, better educated, and more talented than me. That made me nervous. But the more I got to work with these people the more I realized I didn't have to be measured by how I compared to them, whether that was favorable or not. I was there to do my job. They were there to do theirs. In fact, when I stopped my ego from running my mind and simply turned my attention to their needs, I turned out to be just as smart and just as talented as I needed to be. And I found out I belonged in their paneled offices sitting across from them. That I had every right to be there and had every right to their time and attention.

Do you have a list of A-list companies to prospect?

I enjoyed selling management consulting projects. I was good at it. Amongst the companies I worked with were U.S. Steel, Mazda, Crown Paper, plus a number of lesser known firms. I was content to live out my days just doing what I loved best: selling, and selling at the top. That was until I was introduced to Sandler® training.

I had never heard of Sandler® before I was introduced to their unique selling and training methodologies, although they have been around since the late 1960s. A business acquaintance shared with me that he was taking this great sales course and I should look into taking it myself. So, curious as to why he was so excited about this sales training, I checked them out. The more I looked the more I liked, including the fact that there was a business opportunity here. I could be a franchisee and become a Sandler® trainer. So in late 2000 and for the next 10 years, my firm Achievex Corporation trained hundreds and hundreds of salespeople to dramatically increase their success rate. It was not unusual to have students within a year double their incomes. Some tripled, and one even quadrupled his sales.

It was as a trainer, coach and mentor that I realized as good as the training was (and I consider Sandler® to be the best available) there was still something missing. Why did some students see incredible results (100% and more) while others achieved only average results (25% to 50% increases)? The more I debated this with friends, business associates and colleagues, the more I came to realize it isn't the training that makes the salesperson succeed. It is the student putting the training to use on a daily basis that is the determining factor.

Looking back on all your training and education, is there something missing?

Those who experienced outstanding results used every bit of what I taught them and used me as their coach and mentor to reinforce the lessons learned. Others learned the very same things but used only selective portions of what I taught them. Now why was that?

Much of what I taught these sales pros moved them to the very limits of their comfort zones. I was forcing them to take action and say things to the prospect that struck terror in their hearts. Their biggest fear was that they would say or do something that would cause the prospect to get mad at them, thus rejecting them. They were afraid of losing something they never had, an order. And where could you find this fear? Always between their ears. It was a classic case of delusional thoughts preventing smart and talented people from reaching greatness.

What about selling or business strikes fear in your heart?

Let me give you an example. I would work with every student early in his or her training, writing a custom no-pressure cold call script. This script was the best that I've ever used. **It gets meetings.** I've taught this script to every student, from semiconductor equipment manufacturers to remodeling contractors. It works in every industry. But, every once in a while a student would come and tell me the script didn't work for them. The prospect would hang-up; tell them they were happy with their current supplier or any number of other excuses suspects use to get salespeople off the phone. When I'd hear this, I would always suggest they cold call me in role, so we could determine why the script wasn't working for them. Since I knew this script like the back of my hand I knew exactly what they should say and the order in which it should be said. Typically, within the first 15 seconds I would stop them with a time-out and say, "what happened to 'blank, blank, and blank?'" And the answer would always be, "Oh, I can't say that." Then, I would ask why. "Because the buyer will get mad at me." Why do you think that? "Because I would get mad at a salesperson if they said that to me." Or, they'd say, "I shortened the script because I thought it was too long and the suspect would get antsy." They hadn't actually heard this from anyone. They just *imagined* that someone would have that reaction – despite the benefits of using a proven sales system customized just for their needs.

How often do you role play?

Can you see how your own delusional thoughts create fear, and how that fear reaches into your pocket and steals your money? And worse yet, gives it to your competition.

The year 2010 was my last as a Sandler® trainer and you probably are interested in why I gave up my license. Every five years Sandler® requires us to renew our franchise agreement for another five year term. In May of 2010 I began to write this book with the express purpose of helping people to overpower their fears - all fears. I am giving online seminars, coaching and traveling the world putting on live workshops to directly help people through the exercises and programs that I have designed. So as my last term ended with Sandler® Training, I let go of the past to enter this new phase of my life, developing the material that I've had a lifetime to learn myself: overpowering fear.

What are you doing now that will lead to your life purpose?

REINVENTING YOURSELF

When did you last think about who you were, and what you wanted to do with the rest of your life? Was it in college? Were you about 20 years old? Typically, that's when we must declare our "majors." After that, we hurry towards proficiency in an industry and profession, ostensibly to dedicate all the remaining working days of our lives. What craziness! How at 20 years old can you chose a career path and commit the rest of your life to it? The last generation to commit to this fantasy was the baby boomer generation, and I can bear witness to the rude awakening so many of us have faced. Nothing is forever. And the sooner we embrace that the richer and easier our lives will be.

When did you last think seriously about your ideal occupation?

I know teachers who are now sales representatives, lawyers who became business people, PhDs who have bought retail and business franchises. Life is not linear. What we are today may not be what we are tomorrow. Studies have shown that the average college graduate today will have seven distinct careers in his or her lifetime. And for many the choice to change careers may not be their own, but arises from circumstances beyond their control.

The one thing we can be assured of is that every life changing event comes with fear. How you handle that fear will be entirely up to you. If you accept the fear, manage it and then overpower it, you'll find you will meet the challenges that come with any career or life change. But if you wallow in your fear and let it overwhelm you to the point of paralysis, then expect a difficult road ahead.

How do you handle change?

Remember, life is nothing but a series of choices. Ask God that you may choose wisely.

In life we don't get what we want,
we get in life what we are.
If we want more we have to be able to be more,
in order to be more you have to face rejection.
– Farrah Gray

SECTION THREE

CHAPTER 17

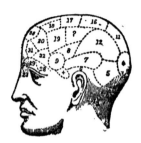

LUCKMAN'S LAW OF ATTRACTION

Everything you create or download on your computer, including emails, documents, photos, images, music files, and videos are typically saved onto a hard drive – which stores them as bytes. This drive is magnetic, and if it doesn't crash or otherwise fail: this information is in place forever. Now, for a moment, think of the universe, which is everywhere – an inch in front of you or one billion miles into space. Think of the universe as a vast magnetic energy field storing all the knowledge that ever was, and ever will be. It could be considered something like a universal mind, with endless memory and billions of people contributing information, opinions, ideas, music, art, photos, graphics and all kinds of reflections and representations.

Do you believe in a "universal mind?"

Now I want you to think of yourself as computer that never crashes, and a constant source of information and energy connected to our universal mind. Through your daily life, your experiences, your emotions and your thoughts, which all vibrate at different frequencies, you are adding to that vast storehouse of knowledge. Remember, it's not just you alone out there. Every human being who lives or has lived contributes to this incredible universal mind.

Who contributes to your thoughts and beliefs?

The universe is saving every thought mankind has ever thought. Like the Internet, but not requiring any visible or wireless connectivity, the universe is an incredible storehouse of knowledge that any one of us can access at any time. And we actually do it 60,000 times a day. That's the number of thoughts scientists say each of us thinks in a day. Whether you are just walking around or even sleeping: you are thinking. You are making connections from your brain to this universal mind.

Different thoughts have different types of energy, in much the same way each musical note vibrates at its own frequency. It's through vibration that we hear and interpret each note as distinctly different from every other note. To analyze these differences, scientists proved when you transmit a musical note into fine sand, each note forms its own unique symbol. Whether you're watching the sand experiment or simply listening to your favorite song, you know that when a composer put notes together we have music.

Which are more powerful, your thoughts during the day or ones while you sleep?

Our thoughts go out to the universal mind in exactly the same way, each has a unique frequency. Now think of this unique frequency as magnetic, traveling into the far reaches of the universe to attract other like thoughts that are vibrating at the same frequency. Some scientists and many spiritualists refer to this magnetic process as the Law of Attraction. You know about this powerful concept if you read The Secret or saw the video, or experienced the work of Esther and Jerry Hicks, who channel a spiritual guide they call Abraham.

You may not believe this because we as humans don't always believe in the unseen. We believe, often beyond the shadow of any doubt, in what we see, hear, feel, smell and taste. And yet, we acknowledge that dogs hear at frequencies beyond our abilities. We know bats are blind, yet science has proven they know exactly where to fly without running into objects. Birds and whales travel thousands of miles every year

Do you only believe what you can see, smell, hear, taste, and touch?

and come back to the exact spot they started from. If someone were dumb enough to place their arm in a microwave oven they would not see or hear the microwaves, but they certainly would feel the effects of them. So, the facts are in that there's a whole lot going on around us that we cannot directly sense.

The Law of Attraction proclaims we are constantly creating our life. Not just some aspects of it, but everything about it. What comes into our lives, all the good and all the bad, we create. Thoughts are the basis of that creation, and with approximately 60,000 thoughts for each of us every day – a lot can go on: good and bad.

Thank goodness not every single thought manifests into reality. You certainly wouldn't want that since you might cause utter mayhem and destruction with some of your thoughts. For example in traffic you might get cut off by another driver. Out of your fear and anger, you reflexively wish they'd crash into a tree. How would you feel if the next thing you saw was that car actually heading straight towards a tree?

What are your thoughts when you feel angry?

Not every thought – certainly not your fleeting ones – manifests itself. So how do you create all the good and all the bad that does manifest itself into your life? By consistently thinking certain thoughts and igniting emotions that attach to them.

Thought + Emotion creates the things and circumstances of your life.

Let me give you an example. Suppose you'd like to buy a new car. With the current economy you're not sure you can afford it, but you'd really like something more reliable, more exciting or just something with that wonderful new car smell. You've gone beyond a fleeting thought – you've got some desire and some emotional energy tied to that thought.

The universal mind now answers that desire in ways you may find hard to believe. You go visit your dentist and as you seat yourself in the waiting room you see on the table next to you the newest issue of *Car and Driver*. As you read the cover you realize they're reviewing a new model from one of the manufacturers whose cars you've always liked. You pick up the magazine and start reading the review. As you're reading, positive emotions are rising within you. You're thinking about how great it would be to own this car. In your mind's eye you even see yourself driving this car. You can almost feel the exhilaration surging through you, but you still have some doubts about whether you can afford this car. A few days later as you're driving you see YOUR car; the model that you want and in a color that brings your blood to a boil. You've got to have this car....but money still is a concern. When you get home that night you do some research on the Internet to determine what your current vehicle is worth. You discover its trade-in value is higher than what you thought. Now you're really excited. Just maybe you might be able to purchase the car of your dreams. That weekend as you're reading the Sunday paper you see an advertisement for this car you are now dreaming about, and the manufacturer is offering 0% financing. You pull out a calculator and figure out that if you can purchase this car for $30,000 you can afford the monthly payments. With that in mind you pile the family into your old car and drive to your local dealer. You negotiate with them but can't get them to your $30,000 selling price. But you know you're going to own this car and nothing is going to stop you. So undeterred you head to the next dealer, and the next until finally you find a dealer willing to sell you this car for $30,000. That night as you drive home in your new car, feeling the joy that new cars bring, you have just proved how the Law of Attraction works. And it all started with a single thought that you'd like to buy a new car.

You shouldn't be surprised that this law also works when you give thought and emotion to what you don't want. As you now know, research shows the vast majority of our thoughts are negative. You

How often do you focus on what you desire?

Do you spend time really working out the details of geting what you want?

think about and worry about the very things that you don't want in your life. And, lo and behold, you attract into your life the very things you don't want. So what does this mean? It means you must be vigilant and guard against the negative thoughts you allow to take root in your mind.

How do you know when you're thinking a negative thought among the 60,000 you think each day? It's quite easy, as you may recall. Check how you are feeling! Negative thoughts always produce negative feelings. If you're feeling sad, dejected or depressed stop and check your thoughts. It's a sure bet you were thinking of the very things you don't want in your life.

How many negative thoughts are preventing positive outcomes for you?

Now you should be able to see how the Law of Attraction is affecting you. Want it to work for you intentionally? I recommend you take ownership of it like I do. Put your own name in front of the Law of Attraction. It's a great first step.

Now you're going to see how you can turn up your positive thoughts and choke off the negative ones in order to create the life you want, starting with the ten exercises that follow.

Imagination is the beginning of creation. You imagine what you desire, you will what you imagine and at last you create what you will.

– George Bernard Shaw

C H A P T E R   1 8

THE END OF "IF ONLY" AND "SOMEDAY" THE BEGINNING OF THE LIFE YOU CHOOSE TO CREATE

As we looked back on the sometimes painful stages and difficult events in my life, you probably related to them by thinking about your own struggles, frustrations and disappointments. I revealed my story to you, in order to help you be completely candid about your own story. I want you to know you can move quickly to what I know NOW – that I did not know then. To learn my lessons, you do not need to live them yourself. You may borrow my life experience to move swiftly to the joy and peace of mind that I love living now, which is a re-

Are you willing to "borrow" life experience to avoid mistakes?

sult of my overpowering fear. Because it is fear that stood in between me and all that I could have enjoyed during all those years. It is the absence of fear that allows me to create the life I enjoy today.

What replaced fear as the controlling force in my life? It is my knowing there is a source – something greater than myself - that connects me to everything I desire. And, I do mean everything. That might be abundance, adventure, security, peace of mind, generosity, loving relationships, supportive friends and even the best parking

Are you ready to commit to having delight and abundance? spot at the mall during the holidays. I have a relationship to the greatest force of positive energy that I often call "Infinite Spirit." I also control the thoughts that create my reality. I do not leave anything to chance. I am pleasantly assured that what I want now and what I want in the future, continues on its way to me.

I want you to have that same wonderful sense of confidence and delight about your life. There are two fundamental choices I want you to make. One: choose to overpower your fears. Two: choose to have a very deep and personal relationship with Infinite Spirit (although you may choose another name for this unending source of positive life experiences and achievements).

Say goodbye to all of your "If onlys," and "Somedays." And welcome all the other wonderful events and delightful life experiences you have put off because of the fear, shame, or negative thoughts you have suffered until now. In this section, you will take part in exercises that uncover what you have been trying to hide from yourself. These are the thoughts, feelings, beliefs, and unconscious actions keeping you from the life you truly want –and deserve.

How many times have you heard someone use the term "if only" to excuse why they're not more successful, richer, happier or even healthier? "I could be more successful if only I went to a better college." "I could be the branch manager **What is on your list of "if only?"** if only I weren't a woman." "I could own my own business if only the bank didn't have these policies and procedures." "I could have a happy marriage if only my husband did everything the way I want it done." "I could be healthier if only my wife didn't keep buying those chocolate chip cookies that I love."

Do you notice that there is a common thread running through all of these excuses? The common thread is not just "if only." The common thread is "I could be" and its closely related cousin, "I could have been."

Perhaps you have heard people use these expressions. And more importantly, perhaps you use them yourself. What are you really saying when you use the term "if only?" You are saying, "I am powerless. I am nothing. Just a leaf in the wind, blown from one street corner to the next. I have no control over my life. I am always a victim of circumstance."

But are you really powerless? Yes, you are, as long as you believe you are. Henry Ford once said, "The man who thinks he can and the man who thinks he can't are both right!" Life is nothing more than a series of choices. Every day you are faced with a myriad of choices. It's as if you came upon a fork in the road every 15 minutes. The life you are living at this very moment is nothing more than a culmination of all the choices you have ever made in your life up to this point. Tomorrow will bring you exactly what you choose today.

If life is just a series of choices, how do you feel about yours?

Now, you may read the above statement and say, "Obviously, I have made bad choices in my life. "If only" I had made better choices. "Oy vey ismear (Oh woe is me)." Does that make you feel self-pity, or do you suddenly see with great joy, the gift just handed to you? You just got the gift of change, and the almost magical powers that change delivers. Just because you made bad choices in the past does not mean you have to make bad choices in the future. The choice is yours alone, although YOU are not alone.

The Universe is here to do your bidding. But the Universe can't even bring you something as simple as a toothpick, if you don't first ask for it. You've heard that old Bible saying, "Ask and you shall receive."

That's what this last section of the book is largely about. I'm giving you the tools to uncover why you've been stuck in the life you've created up until now, and the tools to create the life you want now and in the future.

It is not enough to just overpower your fears, although you will enjoy the release from such a powerful and negative force. You don't want to remain in limbo – no fears, and then what? The "what" is what really matters in creating the life you desire. The "what" is the force that joins with your desire, and creates the experiences, success, and the fastest, safest route to whatever is your heart's desire. The Universe is available to help you make perfect choices in your life. Ask this force to help you at all times: when the best choices are simple to see and when they seem difficult and hard to decipher. The Universe does not know which request is more important to you. It just provides the answer. In the morning I like to ask for a perfect day, and so I ask, "Infinite Spirit I ask that you bring me a perfect day, a day where everything goes my way and where everything comes my way." Once you have made your request there is nothing more you need do. Just relax and wait for all the perfection you asked for to come to you.

> **When you overpower fear, what will you have left to guide you?**

I use the words Universe and Infinite Spirit. Sometimes I use God, or Holy Spirit or Universal Subconscious Mind. You may also want to use Jesus or the Christ within. The name is your choice. Use the term for your higher power that you're most comfortable with. Your higher power and my higher power are the same, although we may call them by different names. What you are actually doing when asking for what you desire in your life is connecting with your higher power. Your request will manifest itself in your life; there is no need to worry. They say a watched pot never boils. The reason is, as you watch the pot of **not boiling** water your mind is asking the Universe for exactly what it sees, a pot of **not boiling water**, rather than a pot of boiling water.

You are about to find out how to get the water at exactly the temperature you desire, along with virtually everything else you choose, once you are free of fear.

And one last thing: **CHOOSE WISELY**. You are about to claim your real life, the life that is waiting for you to design and enjoy. I'm going to guide you. And, you are going to succeed.

Ready? On to the exercises!

Destiny is no matter of chance.
It is a matter of choice. It is not a thing to be waited for,
it is a thing to be achieved.
– William Jennings Bryan

– Exercise #1 –

What Do You Fear?

When you turn the page, you'll see your first exercise: What do You Fear? Sit down in a quiet space. Write down ALL the things you're fearful of. You may want to duplicate the form on several sheets of paper, because your list of fears may amount to more than the space allotted.

Instructions

1. Just list your fears as they come to mind. Don't prejudge what you are writing down. As an example: If you feel that a fear is stupid for a person of your age you might feel self-conscious about listing it. Remember no one is going to read this but you! Open your mind and check your gut to get at every fear you experience on a regular basis.

2. Prioritize your fears from your biggest fear to your smallest. To do this read over your entire list, then go back and place a number 1 next to your greatest fear. Place the number 2 next to your second greatest fear. Do this until all your fears have a number next to them.

You are going to learn a number of tactics to overpower your fears, but for right now you need to just get them out so you can evaluate them. This is your starting point.

First of all, let me assert my firm belief that the only thing we have to fear is fear itself – nameless, unreasoning, unjustified terror, which paralyzes needed efforts to convert retreat into advance.
– Franklin Delano Roosevelt

Exercise 1: What Do You Fear?

Priority	Fear

— Exercise #2 —

What Have You Lost Out On?

Fear has its costs. When you succumb to fear, you sacrifice the things you really want in life. In sales, fear stops you from earning the income you deserve. You lose out on all the wonderful ways you can spend that income, and you diminish the quality of your life. Fear makes you sacrifice security, comfort, peace of mind, fun, freedom and adventure – or whatever you want to enjoy or provide for yourself and your family.

Here's an example that affects most sales representatives. You fear cold-calling, which is simply reaching out to people who don't yet know you or your company. The cost of letting that fear control you cannot be over-estimated. Everything in the selling process depends on your finding new prospects, so you get meetings to make presentations and demos, write proposals and close new business. All that opportunity to create wealth and success is sacrificed because you fear making a call to someone who might be qualified and interested in your products and services!

What do you do instead of facing your fear?

When confronted by a fear, most people devise ways to get around it. They do all kinds of things to avoid facing the fear directly, and never overpower it. In sales you might concoct "make work," to avoid making cold calls. This is work that may or may not need to be done. But by doing this "make work," which takes time, you just don't seem to ever have enough time to make those dreaded phone calls.

What do you lose?

What do you lose because you're afraid to pick up the phone? You can't afford to move into a nicer neighborhood. Your kids get a poor education, because you can't get them into a better school. No chance of sending them to a top-tier college. No special vacations with your spouse to get some rest and relaxation. What do you get? Money arguments that create a wedge between you and your spouse. You feel depressed, worried, filled with self-doubt, embarrassed and maybe angry – just because of fear.

What is the price you pay?
Everything has its price, so what is the price you are paying by not overpowering a fear in any aspect of your life? Was it a wonderful boyfriend or girlfriend? The perfect job? Higher income? Success? Owning your own business? Higher education? Travel? Remember that not facing your fears often has a domino effect. In the case of the salesperson, not prospecting leads to not earning a large enough income. It's not the income the salesperson loses out on, it's the things that income can buy, and the positive feelings that come with success.

Refer to your list of fears from Exercise #1. Right now you'll be working with your top three.

Instructions
1. List your top three fears on the worksheet that follows these instructions.

2. How often do you feel this fear?
    Check the box next to Occasionally, 2-3 times a week, or daily.

3. How do you avoid facing this fear?
    In about 3-5 sentences write down what things you do to avoid confronting your fear. What do you do differently so as not to face this fear? What compromises do you make with yourself? What excuses do you offer yourself?

4. What family problems or personal problems are you suffering from, that are related to this fear?

5. What have you lost out on by not overpowering this fear?
   In 3-5 sentences describe the things that you have missed out on
   by not overpowering this fear.

*Twenty years from now you will be more
disappointed by the things you didn't do than by the ones
you did do. So throw off the bowlines. Sail away from the safe
harbor. Catch the trade winds in your sails.
Explore. Dream. Discover.*

\- Mark Twain

FEAR #1:

_____

How often do you feel this fear?
❏ Occasionally   ❏ 2-3 times each week   ❏ Daily

How do you avoid facing this fear?

_____
_____
_____
_____
_____
_____
_____
_____

What family or personal problems are you suffering from that are
related to this fear?

_____
_____
_____
_____
_____
_____
_____
_____

What have you lost out on by not overpowering this fear?

_____
_____
_____
_____
_____
_____
_____
_____

FEAR #2:

_____

How often do you feel this fear?
❏ Occasionally   ❏ 2-3 times each week   ❏ Daily

How do you avoid facing this fear?

_____
_____
_____
_____
_____
_____
_____

What family or personal problems are you suffering from that are related to this fear?

_____
_____
_____
_____
_____
_____
_____

What have you lost out on by not overpowering this fear?

_____
_____
_____
_____
_____
_____

FEAR #3:

_____

How often do you feel this fear?
❑ Occasionally ❑ 2-3 times each week ❑ Daily

How do you avoid facing this fear?

_____
_____
_____
_____
_____
_____
_____
_____

What family or personal problems are you suffering from that are related to this fear?

_____
_____
_____
_____
_____
_____
_____
_____

What have you lost out on by not overpowering this fear?

_____
_____
_____
_____
_____
_____
_____

— Exercise #3 —

Cause and Effect

What kind of world do you see yourself living in? Is it a chaotic world where things, both good and bad, just seem to happen to you? Or, do you live in an ordered world where you have complete control over things, both great and small?

If your belief is that things just happen, then your life will be one of unexpected triumphs and surprising defeats. Each day will be a new adventure. You'll never know what to expect. Will it be a good day or a bad day? Will it be accompanied by joy and happiness or sadness and dejection? Are your days best described as; same stuff, different day?

My belief is that you and I live in an ordered universe where we can create the lives we each desire. Where every day can be filled with miracles. Where joy, happiness, abundance and success are there for the asking. Where by knowing the laws of cause and effect you can control your own destiny and create a perfect day, every day for the rest of your life.

Cause or causation defines why some event happened. Effect is the event and explains what happened. Let's use Billy "Always be Closing" Evans as an example. Billy is a salesman. He knows that to meet his income goals he needs to have 10 new meetings a week. He knows from experience that he will make 1 appointment for every 4 prospects he speaks to on the phone, and to speak to 1 prospect he must make 5 dials. Using this example Billy would have to make 200 dials a week or 40 dials each and every day. Suppose that Billy hates making cold calls. Each day he must force himself to sit down and attempt to make his 40 dials. Some days he succeeds but other days he makes less than 40 and there are even days he makes none. At the end of the year Billy gets his W-2 income statement from his boss and sees in black and white how much he fell short of his income goal. Now the choice is his. Does he rail at the heavens that the universe conspired against him and the reason he didn't meet his goal was 1) the bad economy, 2) his products weren't good enough, 3) his buyers didn't want to see him, or 4) the competition was giving it away? Or, does Billy take responsibility for his shortfall, accepting the fact that he didn't do what he knew he must do (make 40 dials a day) to successfully reach his income goal?

In this example the *effect* (what happened) is that Billy did not earn the income he set as his goal. The *cause* (why it happened) is that he did not make the number of phone dials he knew would generate enough conversations to yield the number of new meetings that would guarantee he would reach his income goal.

If we look past the immediate effects of Billy's income shortfall, we can see all of the things Billy and his family missed out on by not generating the income he believed he could have earned. Billy and his wife had to postpone once again the honeymoon they were never able to take. Their son would have to delay for another year the orthodontics he needed to straighten his teeth. Billy's wife would have to settle for a used car rather than the new one she had her heart set on. And the deepest disappointment of all, they had no money to put into savings for a down payment on a house. All because Billy feared making cold calls.

Here's another example of cause and effect. Julie is a bright young woman of 25 years, working as an assistant copywriter for a major advertising agency. It is her dream job and she's very fortunate to have gotten this position. Julie also likes to party and goes out clubbing with friends every weekend and once or twice during the week. Julie's problem is that it's difficult for her to get out of bed the next morning, frequently causing her to be late for work. Her boss had warned her that he was no longer going to tolerate her tardiness. This particular morning, after being out late with friends the night before, her alarm rings. She automatically presses the snooze button for another 10 minutes of sleep. When it goes off again she presses it once more. Finally, she drags herself out of bed and then rushes to get to work, only to be late once again. This time Julie's boss fires her. She is now out of work in a tough economy.

The *effect* is Julie was fired and has no income. The *cause* is her continually coming in late to work. In this example I'd like to go both forwards and backwards in her cause and effect. Let's first go forward with some additional effects. Because Julie has no income she is late paying her rent. Her landlord eventually moves Julie and all her possessions out onto the street. Julie must move back home and live with her parents. She also has been late with her car payments and is shocked when her car is repossessed. Now she must either take public transportation or depend upon friends and family to get around. On top of all of that Julie is finding it difficult to secure a new position. Every advertising agency she applies to is curious as to why she lost her previous position with a top tier agency. Further effects of her tardiness are that her credit score has taken a hit, causing her untold grief.

Now let's go backwards on the cause of Julie's problems, her being late to work because she couldn't get out of bed in the morning. If we go back to the cause of why she couldn't make it to work on time, we'd see she was tired from only having half the amount of sleep she needed. And the cause of not having enough sleep is she stays out late partying and has too much to drink.

Pretty simple. Life is nothing more than a series of cause and effect situations. In fact, everything you do or don't do is a cause that will have its effects. And often the effects have lasting ramifications on other people in your life. Your spouse, your children, your co-workers, your boss, your church, your community and on and on.

Now here is the lesson I want you to take away from this exercise. Every cause was preceded by a choice. Billy had a choice whether to sit himself down for an hour or two each day and make his 40 dials, or he could choose to do something that was less painful and more to his liking. Julie, when asked to go out clubbing on a weekday or Sunday evening had a choice. Stay home and get a good night's sleep or not disappoint her friends and go out to have fun. Both Billy and Julie made choices with bad consequences, in both the short and long term.

Every day you are faced with a myriad of choices. Each choice will lead to a cause and each cause to its effects. If you want to change your life, begin by making better choices. Albert Einstein has been quoted as saying, "The definition of insanity is doing the same thing over and over again and expecting different results!" Now ask yourself why would someone do the same thing over and over again? It's because they had free will and chose to do the same thing over and over again. I want to say that it was a conscious choice but I think I'd be wrong. It was more of a lazy choice. The choices we make without giving them much thought.

Make your choices consciously, with the end effects in mind. You create your life, sort of like the elaborate designs people make with standing dominoes. Push the first one over and all the rest will follow. You must think about the ramifications of your choices while you are making them, by asking yourself how will this choice affect me? How will it affect my family? My work? My friends? My social standing? My country? Once you understand the effects of your choices down the line, only then are you really ready to choose.

In this exercise, you have the opportunity to consider how cause and effect works in your own life.

Instructions
1. Describe a recent experience you had where the outcome was not to your liking.
2. What were the negative effects of this situation?
3. What was the root cause of this experience?
4. What other choice could you have made that would have made this a positive experience?
5. What would have been the positive effects of this new choice?

Shallow men believe in luck. Strong men believe in cause and effect.
- Ralph Waldo Emerson

Exercise 3: Cause and Effect

1. Describe a recent experience you had where the outcome was not to your liking.

_____
_____
_____
_____
_____

2. What were the negative effects of this situation?

_____
_____
_____
_____
_____

3. What was the root cause of this experience?

_____
_____
_____
_____
_____

4. What other choice could you have made that would have made this a positive experience?

_____
_____
_____
_____
_____

5. What would have been the positive effects of this new choice?

_____
_____
_____
_____
_____

— Exercise #4 —

Today is Yesterday's Someday

Have you used the word someday recently? Maybe in a conversation with a friend, co-worker or spouse? Perhaps the two of you were talking about what you would like to do or have in the future, and you casually said, "Someday I'm going to do (blank)" or "Someday I'm going to have (blank)" or "Someday I'm going to go to (blank)." These are rather innocuous statements. Ones that you may not even realize you are saying. But often they hold a much deeper meaning in your life than you give them credit for.

Typically, when you use a "someday statement" what you're actually saying is, "I'd really like to have that in my life," or, "I'd really like to do that" or "I'd really like to go there." These are more than just passing thoughts. Often, they are the things that you truly want and desire in your life. But, instead of saying, "My goal is to have (blank)," you revert to "Someday I'd like to have (blank)." So what's the difference you might ask? A goal or someday mean the same to me."

But they're not the same. Let's take a closer look at what a goal is. Websters defines goal as: the end to which a design tends, or which a person aims to reach or accomplish. Typically goals are well thought out. They have a beginning and a well-conceived ending, and measurable points along the way. Good goals are always in writing. They are specific, measurable, attainable, realistic and time bound. What we typically refer to as SMART goals.

And what is a "someday?" A someday is a wish. A hope for something you consider good to come into your life. "Somedays" make you feel that you are not wasting your life. You want and desire your somedays, but you often don't know how to achieve them or worse yet, secretly believe that you don't deserve them. Somedays bring you both comfort and fear.

Somedays are usually predicated on achieving some nebulous milestone in your life. Someday when I'm older I'll start investing.

Someday when the kids are in grade school I'll go back to work. Someday when my life settles down I'll take up painting. Someday when my business gets off the ground I'll spend more time with the kids. Someday when I've got more time I'll go on a cruise around the world. Someday when I retire I'll go back to my first love, teaching.

My most recent someday was to buy a house in Las Vegas. It's where I desire to retire. My sister Ramona and her then husband moved from Los Angeles to Las Vegas in the mid-1990s. Every time I would visit her we'd go out looking at new homes, and there was always plenty to look at. We'd go from one new subdivision to the next. In the mid-90s homes there were relatively inexpensive compared to California real estate. I fell in love with one particular local builder, American West Homes. I liked their designs and the amenities they included in their homes. Every visit to Las Vegas I would visit their newest offerings.

My dream was to someday own a home, built by American West, in Las Vegas. But of course life frequently got in the way. I got a divorce from my second wife Susan, then lost one business only to start another one and be betrayed by a partner, then my father died, and then and then and then. So when it came to discussing my future with anyone it sounded like, "Someday I plan on owning a home in Las Vegas, as soon as life settles down." But would it ever settle down or was I just fooling myself? Was I too afraid to face reality and make my someday into a goal? And then of course have to stick to my goal until I actually accomplished it? A very scary process.

I mentioned earlier that Somedays are both frightening and comforting. They are comforting when they make you believe you actually have a plan for tomorrow. It's like you carry around a large bag labeled Somedays, and every time you have a wish or desire you put it into this bag. Then wherever you go you carry this Somedays bag with you. Thus, whenever you are in a conversation with someone you can then reach into your bag and pull out as many Somedays as you need to convince that person that you are a well-grounded human being with a solid plan for the future. But is that true or are you only deceiving yourself?

Somedays may also cause you to feel fear. It happens when you look into your bag of Somedays and you realize that you are never going to turn your Somedays into actual things, experiences and events. You then look at these Somedays as false hopes and discarded dreams. Things you would like to have accomplished, if only. If only you were smarter. If only you were rich. If only your health were better. If only you were older. If only you were younger. If only you were more talented. If only you were more attractive. If only you were thinner. If only you were married. If only you weren't so depressed. So you do all you can to not look too deeply into your Somedays bag.

So what do you have to do to turn your Somedays into reality? First, you must go through your bag of Somedays and determine which Somedays you really want to come true in your life, and which ones you need to discard. Someday I would like to play tight end for the San Francisco 49ers. That's never going to happen. First, I'm way too old. And, second, even when I was younger, I didn't have the talent. Once you've cleaned out and discarded the Somedays you know don't make sense, you are left with the Somedays that you really want. And you'll know which ones you really want in your life. They're the ones that bring you joy when you think about them.

Let's go back to my Someday having an American West Las Vegas home. Every time I thought of living in this home my heart would sing. I could picture in my mind's eye furnishing it just the way I wanted. I could even see my wife Arleen and me entertaining friends and family there, and celebrating the holidays with my children and grandchildren. Every day I asked God to bring me my perfect home. On one of my trips to Las Vegas I picked up an American West Homes brochure and chose the home and location I'd like to have. I put this drawing up on my bulletin board next to my computer. A place where I couldn't help but see it 100 times a day.

But to make your Somedays come true you have to do more than just dream about them. You have to turn them into a goal. And creating goals are always frightening. Frightening because they cause you to make a commitment. And, once I made that commitment to buy a house in Las Vegas, I couldn't turn back. Goals need to be time bound. So in late 2005, when I made my decision to buy, I needed to pick a date when I would buy my house. I believed that by mid-2008 I would have the money saved for both the down payment and the things I would need to purchase once I moved in.

My goal needed to be specific. That meant I needed to determine how much I wanted to spend and where in Las Vegas I wanted to live. I knew that I wanted to be close to the airport so when I came into Las Vegas or left to go back to San Jose I wouldn't run into a lot of traffic. I knew that American West had built three separate subdivisions in an area called Coronado Ranch southwest of the Las Vegas strip, and actually only 15 minutes from the car rental facility. So that's where I instructed Wendy Dana my Realtor to look. And with the stipulation that I wanted to spend between $400,000 and $450,000.

My goal needed to be attainable. That meant that I could look in Coronado Ranch but only if I could find a house for what I was willing to pay. When Wendy and I started to look at homes within that price range there were a number that fit the bill. We were looking at the mid-priced subdivision, Promontory. Like Goldilocks, I found that in one subdivision the homes were too big, and in the other they were too small. But in Promontory they were just right. And they were priced within the range I was willing to spend.

Now was my goal realistic? I had saved $100,000 to buy the house and cover all the expenses after I moved in. The less I would have to put down as a down payment the more I'd have to spend on the interior. Once we started looking at used homes we determined that the owner occupied ones wanted too much money for the home, and those that were bank owned in foreclosure, had a lot of things that needed fixing. It was then that Wendy suggested we go to the builder and see if they had any inventory of homes already built, but unsold. As it turned out they had two homes sitting vacant where the deals fell through. We went to look at the first one but it was my least favorite of the five models. We then went to look at the second one, which happened to be my favorite model, but it's interior might look horrendous, if my tastes and the couple who originally bought the house clashed in our idea of decor.

As we drove up I was excited. The house was painted in the very colors that I would have chosen myself, and it was the exterior I really liked with a small balcony off the second floor master bedroom. The front yard had upgraded landscaping and the previous buyers had decided upon a stained glass front door. So far so good. As we entered the house I held my breath, would the interior be as impressive as the exterior? As we stepped inside the large tiled foyer with its curving staircase leading to the second floor, I exhaled with a "wow." The house was everything I wanted it to be and more. It was beautiful. I loved the tile, the carpet, the color of the paint and all the upgrades the previous buyers chose. It was now just a matter of negotiating the best price I could.

The first buyers had signed a purchase contract before the house was actually built, for $572,300, which included $33,350 in upgrades. They then backed out. The builder was now asking $448,500. I offered $425,000. They countered with the fact that the now going base price for this model, without any upgrades, was $448,500, and would not sell this model for less than what a newly built one would sell for. It was now up to me to accept the price of $448,500 or find some way to negotiate a better deal. I told Wendy, my realtor, to counter with the following offer; I would pay their asking price of $448,500 with a 30 day close, but I wanted the following to be included; a built-in KitchenAid refrigerator with matching cabinet inserts, a second oven in the kitchen, a matching washer and dryer, pay all my closing costs and landscape the backyard and include a custom brick patio. They accepted and I got my dream house. We closed June 6, 2008.

I turned my, "Someday, I'm going to purchase a house in Las Vegas where I will eventually retire," into a reality. Was it magic? No. Did I turn water into wine? Only the reds. Can you use the exact same process to create your dreams? Absolutely! And this is how you do it. Just follow the instructions as you complete this exercise.

1. Open your bag of Somedays and take a good look inside. There are going to be a lot of things that made perfect sense when you put them in there, but are not the things you want to create in your life now. Pick two or three Somedays that you have this absolutely burning desire to manifest in your life. You'll know which ones because the thought of attaining them makes your heart sing with joy. God and the Universe do not discriminate by size or complexity. They will create with you anything you ask for. ANYTHING! Write these two or three Somedays on the *Someday I Will Create This In My Life* form.

2. Next I want you to look over these two or three Somedays and decide upon the one you want to create in your life first. Write the one you want under, *This Someday Is Now My Goal.*

3. Take inventory. Write several sentences in the area marked Inventory: *Where I Am Now* to capture your status relative to achieving your goal. If your goal is to purchase a house like mine was, where are you in the process? Have you decided where you want to buy? Have you determined how much you want to invest? Have you started saving for the down payment?

4. As a child of God he promises you everything. Your job is to define everything. The more specific your goal the easier it is to manifest in your life. Instead of asking God for food and he provides you with grits and ham hocks, ask him for a 12 oz. New York strip steak medium rare; a baked potato with butter, sour cream and chives; creamed spinach and French fries; hearts of Romaine salad with creamy Italian dressing and for dessert a big slice of strawberry topped cheese cake. If I missed anything make sure you add it. Under *My Specific Goal* write down exactly what you want in as much detail as you can.

5. In order to create your dream you will first need to determine a time frame for achieving it. Although this is the last letter in the SMART goal acronym it is something you will need to decide upon at the moment you turn your *Someday* into a goal. Write down under *My Goal's Time Frame – The Day I Will Complete*

My Goal exactly when you want this goal to be achieved. If you can achieve your goal in a relatively short period of time, without much effort on your part, you have asked God for too little. Remember whatever you ask for shall be given to you. And remember, the size of your goal does not matter.

6. Your new goal needs to be measurable, and to be measurable you will need to have a means for measuring your progress. If your goal requires money you will need to know how much money you'll have to amass and in what time frame. If like me, you need $100,000 to achieve your goal and you've given yourself 4 years to accomplish it, then you'll need to save or acquire $25,000 each year, which comes out to $2,083 each month or $481 each and every week. In the area marked *How I Measure My Progress* write down how you are going to measure your progress and what numbers you are going to use.

7. Is it realistic? Based upon what's happening in your life at this moment is it realistic to believe that you can achieve this goal in the time allotted and for the money you choose to spend. Write down under *Is My Goal Realistic?* why you believe it is.

8. Is your goal attainable? And, by that I mean, have other people in your particular situation, achieved this same goal in the time frame you've chosen and for the amount of money you plan on investing? If the answer is no then maybe you need to adjust your goal so that it is attainable by you. Write down under *Is My Goal Attainable?* why you think you can attain it.

Hell begins on the day when God grants
us a clear vision of all that we might have achieved, of all
the gifts which we have wasted, of all that we might have
done which we did not do.
- Gian Carlo Menotti

Exercise 4: Someday

"Someday" I Will Create This In My Life

_____

_____

_____

This "Someday" Is Now My Goal

_____

_____

_____

Inventory: Where I Am Now

_____

_____

_____

My Specific Goal

_____

_____

_____

My Goal's Time Frame - The Day I Will Complete My Goal

_____

_____

How I Measure My Progress

_____

_____

Is My Goal Realistic? Why?

_____

_____

_____

Is My Goal Attainable? Why?

_____

_____

_____

– Exercise #5 –

The Ego Has Landed

LUCKMAN'S LAW:
*How you feel in any given moment
is always the result of what you're thinking
at that moment.*

At birth you have no ego. But as you grow up, you begin to develop your ego to help distinguish your being from others. For example, you see yourself as separate from your mother even though she may be the one who takes care of you and provides nourishment, at an age when you cannot do this for yourself.

Eventually, you become aware of what others think about you. Do they like you? Do they want to be your friend? When the answers are yes you feel good about yourself. But if you're rebuffed, it is your ego that gets bruised and you feel sad and alone. As you get older your ego helps you to understand more about yourself, by comparing you to others. Am I taller than Roger? Am I as pretty as Molly? Is Tom smarter than I am?

Your ego is not your friend. It never has been and it never will be. Its job is to constantly compare you to others. If it decides you are better than another, you feel good about yourself, often with a false sense of pride and superiority. If your ego judges you to be less than someone else, you feel an unpleasant shock to your system. You feel fear, and with fear comes a loss of self-esteem and self-confidence. And when that happens you are unable to function at your best.

My belief is that our egos are destructive and cause us untold grief. If we could but eliminate our ego we would be so much happier, and probably even healthier. We each would be delighted to be who we are, and feel great that other people are who they are. What a thought! We would all be free of the jealousy, frustration, shame, anger, depression, worry and fear that there is some universal standard of excellence and someone else has set the bar, which the rest of us can't measure up to.

In this exercise, you'll go about getting out from under your ego.

Instructions

1. Describe a time when you compared yourself to another person and you came up short. What did that feel like to you? How did that affect your self-esteem? Your self-confidence? How long did it take you before you felt good about yourself again?

   Reread what you wrote in the top box. As you read through your description, let the fear rise in you. Your fear may change to anger. Anger directed at the person you compared yourself to, or anger directed at yourself for some long forgotten reason. That's okay. Let it rise.

2. Now take a few moments to consider what thoughts are going through your mind at this moment. Then, write down those thoughts. Your thoughts may provoke rage, self-doubt, misery, anger or fear, or some other feelings.

3. Once you are clear about which thoughts are causing your negative feelings, write a positive affirmation to eliminate those thoughts.

   I like to use any of the positive affirmations below:

   • Infinite Spirit, I cast this burden of fear of _____

   _____ on you. And I go free!

   • Infinite Spirit, I cast this burden of anger towards/about

   _____ on you. And I go

   free!

   • Infinite Spirit, I no longer feel fear about _____

   _____. I now feel totally fearless

   when it comes to _____.

   • Infinite Spirit, I no longer feel anger towards/about _____

_____. I now feel only joy,

happiness and love whenever I think about _____

_____.

You may substitute Infinite Spirit with God, Holy Spirit, Jesus, Universe, Universal Subconscious Mind or whatever you call your higher power. Repeat each positive affirmation from 3 to 5 times. Repeat whenever you're thinking negative thoughts accompanied by their negative emotions.

Exercise 5: The Ego Has Landed Exercise

1. Describe a time when you compared yourself to another and came up short. What did that feel like to you? How did that affect your self-esteem? Your self-confidence? How long did it take you before you felt good about yourself again?

_____

_____

_____

_____

_____

_____

_____

_____

_____

2. Now write down every thought that is racing through your mind at this moment. These thoughts are causing your negative feelings.

_____

_____

_____

_____

_____

_____

3. In the space below, write one or both of the positive affirmations from the previous page.

_____

_____

_____

_____

_____

— Exercise #6 —

Seeing is Believing

All great athletes will tell you that before they take the shot, before they swing the bat, before they position themselves for the lay-up, they have a picture in their mind of exactly what's going to happen.

Several years ago I attended a guerilla business seminar where Bill Bartmann, former billionaire, was a guest speaker. At the height of his wealth in the 1990s Bill was interested in purchasing the NBA Chicago Bulls. He was invited to sit on the Bulls bench and tells the story of a discussion he had with Michael Jordan prior to the game. Jordan boasted that he could sink a free throw with his eyes closed. Bartmann didn't think it were possible. During the game Jordan was fouled and stepped up to the free throw line. Looking over at Bartmann he winked, closed his eyes and made a perfect shot.

What Michael Jordan used is what we call visualization. How many times in his life had he made that shot? 10,000 times, 50,000 times, 100,000 times. Michael Jordan, in his mind, saw the basket. He saw his movements. He saw himself making the basket. He didn't need to see with his eyes. His mind saw perfectly.

All great athletes utilize visualization. They picture in their minds what they want themselves to do physically, and then they do it. Because they have the physical skills, what they accomplish is near perfect. Great generals in wartime use the same visualization skills. They see their armies arrayed in front of them. They see their enemies' armies. They picture in their minds how the battles will play out and they see themselves winning. We too, can create the things we want in our life just by changing the pictures in our minds, and we can use this wonderful tool to eliminate the things we don't want in our lives.

It's been proven that the subconscious mind cannot distinguish between visualization and reality. Your subconscious mind responds to suggestion. Whatever you (your conscious mind) suggest will in time manifest itself into your life.

Now I know you're going to ask, "If that is so, why doesn't it work for me? I picture in my mind all the time what I want but it never seems to get delivered." The reason this happens is you don't hold the picture in your mind long enough. One day you're thinking you want this, and the next day it's something else. In order to use visualization successfully, you need to picture in your mind exactly what you want and never waiver from that image. If it's a beautiful new home you desire, you need to do more than just picture the exterior of the house. You must **<u>experience</u>** your new home. You must walk inside and step into each room. Picture how it will look furnished. Cook a meal in the kitchen. See yourself with your family by your side in the family room watching a movie on a big screen flat panel television. Go outside into the back yard and picture yourself having a barbeque with your friends and family. Get filled with the emotion of having it all. When you can generate emotion by seeing in your mind exactly what you desire, it will indeed manifest in your life.

In this exercise I want you to create a picture in your mind of you overpowering a specific fear that you have. As an example: If it's a fear of public speaking picture yourself standing on stage in front of a lectern and speaking to a large audience. Describe what's going on. Exactly where are you? What are you doing? What are you saying and to whom? How do you feel about what's transpiring? Do you see and feel yourself as powerful, in command, in control, and relaxed? If not, what else do you need in order to bring on those thoughts and feelings? Do this once right now and then over and over again for every fear that you have and for everything you desire to manifest in your life. Remember seeing **<u>is</u>** believing.

Instructions

1. Bring to mind a specific fear that has been troubling you for a long time. It might be a fear that is best phrased as, "I fear Monday mornings because my boss always comes to work angry." Or your fear might be about dealing with your clients. That might sound like "I fear meeting with my current clients because our competitors are

dropping their prices and I don't know how I will compete for their upcoming orders." Or, "I fear the morning sales meeting because someone else is always doing better than I am, and he makes it seem so easy."

2. Imagine overpowering this specific fear. Create a scenario where you are acting without fear, because you are doing exactly what you need to do, comfortably and confidently.

3. Describe what's going on in that scenario. Where are you? What are you doing? What are you saying and to whom? How do you feel about what is transpiring?

4. Do you see yourself as powerful, in command and very relaxed? If not, what else do you need to visualize doing or saying, so you enjoy those thoughts and feelings?

To visualize is to see what is not there,
what is not real — a dream. To visualize is, in fact, to make visual lies. Visual lies, however, have a way of coming true.
- Peter McWilliams

Exercise 6: Seeing is Believing

1. My fear

_____

_____

_____

_____

_____

_____

2. My visualization of overpowering that fear

_____

_____

_____

_____

_____

_____

3. What's going on in that scenario

_____

_____

_____

_____

_____

_____

4. Do I see myself as powerful? What else can I add to enjoy the feelings of being powerful, in command and very relaxed?

_____

_____

_____

_____

_____

_____

– Exercise #7 –

You Shouldn't Talk to Me Like That!

> ### LUCKMAN'S LAW:
> *We are all born perfect –*
> *then our egos get a hold of us.*

Do you talk to yourself? Actually we all do. You, like most people, may hear your own voice saying you aren't very smart, you're unattractive, a klutz, a loser, worthless, not very good at _____, whatever.

What you say to yourself is devastating. You wouldn't be friends with someone who spoke to you in such hurtful ways. What you say to yourself comes from the, often unintentional, programming done by your mom, dad, siblings, schoolmates, teachers, and those who knew you as you were growing up. They judged you and told you what you lacked and what your limitations were. And the worse part of it was…**you believed them**. They programmed you from the day you were born. It was lies. **Yes, lies.** Lies told to you by others to compensate for their own insecurities and lack of self-esteem.

The process works like this: 1. Programming creates beliefs. 2. Beliefs create attitudes. 3. Attitudes create feelings. 4. Feelings determine action. 5. Actions create results. And certainly, a lack of taking action creates results as well. You wind up with the things you don't want in your life. Let me give you an example. Let's say you were lead to believe that you were uncoordinated, a klutz. So, 1) your belief is that you're a klutz. Constantly knocking over things. Tripping over yourself. Terrible when it comes to anything athletic. Then 2) your attitude would be "I'm no good at physical things - sports and that kind of stuff." And 3) your attitude creates feelings of inferiority. Fear would well up whenever you faced a physical challenge. Then 4) your feelings determine your actions. For example, you're going to a picnic and will almost certainly be asked to play volleyball. You'll probably decline with some lame excuse about a sore ankle. And finally, 5) the results are you don't partake in too many picnics for fear of having to play some sports.

My biggest fear was that I wasn't very smart. This dates all the way back to the first grade. I remember it being the first day of class; a hot September day. The teacher asked us to write out numbers from 1 to 100. I never learned to count past 10. I was lost, full of fear and embarrassment. This fear that I wasn't very smart stayed with me all my school days and beyond. Well into my adult life, I always felt others were smarter than me. And then of course, better educated. I always felt inferior to my classmates.

For as long as I could remember my parents would come home from every parent teacher conference and recite the same thing, "Your teacher feels you're not working up to your potential." Well you could have fooled me. I thought I was doing the best I could. It also didn't help that my parents were raised to believe they weren't too smart either, and for me that old adage *the apple doesn't fall far from the tree* was true. Actually, my parents were both very smart. They just didn't believe it. Again back to their childhoods.

Now, it's your turn. Let's get out the negative self-talk, search for its origins, and launch a plan to undo the damage, and replace the negatives with positive affirmations. You may need more room than the space in this book, so get extra paper ready because now is the time to get this negative self-talk out of your brain. Notice that right now you'll be working on steps 1,2 and 3. Then, there's a bit more reading, and you'll return to the same chart and complete it with steps 4 and 5.

Instructions:

Steps 1, 2 and 3

1. Write down a negative statement that was said to you when you were a child. For example: "You had better learn a trade because you're not college material. Or no matter how hard you try you'll never be like your older brother."

2. What were the circumstances? Who first told you this lie was "true" about yourself? How old do you think you were at the time?

3. How do you feel when you repeat this lie to yourself?

Notice that there are two additional categories in the chart, one for writing down all the reasons why what you were told is not true and another for a positive affirmation to neutralize the lie – we'll get to those when you've completed sections 1, 2 and 3.

A lie told often enough becomes the truth.
– Vladimir Lenin

Exercise 7: You Shouldn't Talk to Me Like That

1. Write down a negative statement that was said to you as a child that you now say to yourself.

_____

_____

_____

_____

Who first told you this was "true" about you? _____

How old do you think you were at the time? _____

How do you feel when you hear yourself telling you this lie?

_____

_____

_____

_____

Write down all the reasons why you believe this statement is false.

_____

_____

_____

Write down a positive affirmation that neutralizes the above negative statement. _____

_____

_____

_____

2. Write down a negative statement that was said to you as a child that you now say to yourself.

_____

_____

_____

_____

Who first told you this was "true" about you? _____

How old do you think you were at the time? _____

How do you feel when you hear yourself telling you this lie?

_____

_____

Write down all the reasons why you believe this statement is false.

_____

_____

_____

Write down a positive affirmation that neutralizes the above negative statement. _____

_____

_____

_____

3. Write down a negative statement that was said to you as a child that you now say to yourself.

_____

_____

_____

_____

Who first told you this was "true" about you? _____

How old do you think you were at the time? _____

How do you feel when you hear yourself telling you this lie?

_____

_____

_____

Write down all the reasons why you believe this statement is false.

_____

_____

_____

Write down a positive affirmation that neutralizes the above negative statement. _____

_____

_____

Using Positive Affirmations and Actions To Re-wire Your Brain: Steps 4 and 5

There's a wonderful way to overcome this negative self-talk. You do it with positive affirmations and then catching yourself in action, actualizing the positive messages you are now programming in. You are going to neutralize or erase the lies you have heard. You will replace them with the truth about how you actually are. You'll enjoy your new self-image and abilities. Affirmations are a wonderful way to overcome negative self-talk. There's a great book where I learned to do this. It's **What To Say When You Talk To Yourself** by Shad Helmstetter.

Here are examples of how others have used affirmations and taken action.

Jack is an 18 year old boy and for the most part, he's heard people say he's a great guy, but not overly bright. He's made only average grades in school. Teachers don't see him as college material, always good naturedly suggesting he learn a trade instead. But, deep down, Jack would like to go to college. Of course he's scared it may be too difficult. He's afraid of being embarrassed in class. The idea of flunking out haunts him.

Jack wrote down several reasons why he believes the negative statement is false, including;

> *I am enrolled in a college preparation course where I quickly picked up new study skills and test-taking strategies. Each week, I see evidence of how smart I am.*

Jack's positive affirmation is:

> *I was lead to believe by others that I wasn't smart enough to go to college. That's an absolute lie. I am smart with an above average IQ. I have a quick mind and am always learning new things. There is nothing that I cannot learn and master if I want to. I know I will excel when I get into college.*

Marie is a 42 year old woman, who has always been praised for being a genius, but at the same time not someone with great social skills. Her older sister was the vivacious one, and Marie grew up hearing she is a wallflower. She's decided to leave her corporate job and go into business for herself. She knows that networking is critical to her success, but the thought of meeting strangers terrifies her. She's believes she's not a very interesting person. She's afraid she'll stumble over her words if she has to introduce herself. She's certain she'll feel ashamed that she actually thought she could own her own business.

Marie wrote down several reasons why she believes the negative statement is false, including:

Everyday, I read the news and I regularly check business websites to see what's new. I love going to movies, watching television and visiting popular websites so I'm up-to-date and ready to have conversations with anyone.

Marie's positive affirmation might be:

I no longer believe that I'm socially inept. I now believe that I am smart, talented and up on current events. And, I am a very interesting person with a lot to say. I can now carry on any type of conversation with anyone that I meet. I am a great conversationalist.

Steps 4 and 5

Now, it's your turn. For each negative statement on your chart, write down why you believe the negative statement is a lie. Then write down a positive affirmation. Here's a tip. I like to begin the affirmation by saying either, **I no longer believe** or **I was lead to believe by others**, either one works. It's a strong platform for your new positive talk track.

Do you want a deeper discussion on this? Okay!

How long have you suffered from your fears? For me it was all my life. From early childhood through my teens, as a young adult and even into my mid-fifties. I didn't know there was another way to live. I didn't know what it was like, or that it was even possible, to live a single day without feeling some fear. I bumped up against my fears each and every day. Sometimes winning, sometimes losing.

If you're like me you have spent a major part of your lifetime reinforcing your fears, which are an integral part of your belief system. What you believe true about yourself is often the beliefs of others about you, given to you at an age when you could not even challenge their validity. Since these "truths" came from adults who you loved and respected, they must be true, and you accepted them without question.

Years may have gone by since you first heard the negative appraisal. The person who convinced you of these "truths" may have passed away. But it really doesn't matter. These lies that you accepted as being true are a part of your own belief system. You don't need the originator of the lie to even be in your life anymore. You do a pretty good job of reminding yourself daily who you "really" are.

If as a child you played with Lincoln Logs or Erector Sets and every time you got stymied and struggled to figure something out on your own, Mom or Dad would come to your rescue and say something like, "Don't worry son that's a bit tricky, let Dad help you out with that." You would grow up believing that when it came to building something or reading directions, you just weren't that adept. As an adult when faced with the challenge of assembling something, Christmas toys for the kids or projects around the house, your fear of failing or fear of embarrassment would cause you to make excuses. Something like, "Oh, I've never been good at putting things together. I'm just not good with my hands. Why don't we just pay extra and have it assembled at the store." What just happened was you reinforced the "original" lie about yourself. You accepted it as truth and buttressed it in your mind as a rock solid fact about yourself.

If as a teenage girl learning how to drive, your father convinced you that you were "just like your mother" when it came to figuring out left from right, and north from south, you would grow up with the belief that you just couldn't navigate your way around town. This "lie" would be reinforced every time you headed off to a new location, if you insisted you must have written instructions to your destination, for fear you might get lost. And what would typically happen is... you'd get lost.

In both examples the individuals might be quite capable of doing the very things they believed they could not do, but it really didn't matter. In fact, when they became adults, spouses, co-workers, friends or even a boss said, "Of course, you can do this!" they wouldn't believe it. Because negative beliefs, repeated time after time, year after year, are hardwired into the brain. So, we need to rewire our brains. But how do we do that?

Remember when I said, the universe gives you exactly what you ask for? Do you believe that your self-deprecating statements go unheard? Of course not! Every time you make a statement that repeats one of these lies about yourself, the Universe provides you with proof that the lie is true.

For the man who grows up believing he couldn't even put his toys together, we can see why he is already fearful and embarrassed when he gets a barbeque grill as a housewarming gift. He opens the box, lays out all the parts and then unfolds the directions. Before he starts reading, he silently states to the Universe "I hope I can put this together and not screw it up." What does the Universe hear? "I'll probably screw it up." And what happens? The grill he puts together somehow has a number of parts leftover and of course, it doesn't work.

We can assume that every time the woman gets into her car, loaded down with turn-by-turn directions to her destination, she says to the Universe, "I hope I don't get lost." The Universe hears this as: "I'm going to get lost." And what happens is this woman typically gets lost and arrives either late to her destination, or not at all.

So how do you rewire your brain? How do you eliminate the negative beliefs you now hold about yourself and replace them with new positive beliefs? The answer lies in Step #4 and #5 of this exercise. In an earlier chapter I talked about opposites. That everything in life has a corresponding opposite; small versus large, hot versus cold, day versus night, etc. In Step #5 you are asked to ***write down a positive affirmation that will countermand the negative statement*** you wrote down in Step #1. In essence: you are commanding the opposite of your negative statement. Put another way, your negative belief has been saved, and resaved thousands of times to a place on your hard drive (brain). You must delete the negative belief from the drive and imprint a new positive belief. Then you must say it and "save it" over and over. But it won't be easy. And that's where faith comes in.

Faith is your belief in the unknown. And that's where the difficulty lies. We, as human beings, believe what we can see, hear, feel, taste and smell. It's hard for us to believe in something that our five senses can't recognize. That's why we believe in the old axiom I'll believe it when I see it! But we do have blind faith in several unknowns; that the sun will rise every morning in the East, that the oxygen we breathe will mix with the sugars in our blood to provide food for our cells, that the light turns on when we throw the switch on the wall, that water comes when we turn the tap, that unseen radio and television signals travel through walls. So it's not that we don't have faith in the unknown, but that we find it difficult to find the faith within ourselves that will help us change our lives when our hardwired brains tell us the exact opposite.

So what must we do to rewire our brains? First understand that each of our old beliefs took years and years and thousands of negative thoughts to become a negative belief. Don't expect change to happen miraculously overnight. It will take hard work and diligence on your part. Writing that positive affirmation in Step #5 is the place to begin. Now you have a choice in which to believe; your negative thought in Step #1 or your new positive thought in Step #5. Next you must create or look for evidence of the actions that show you this new positive belief is true.

You also need to monitor what you say to others about your abilities. These negative statements uttered through your lips sound like: "I'm just not good at _____!"
"I always get lost when I drive around town!"

"I believe I have two left feet, always tripping over things!"

"I can't sing!"

"I can't dance!"

"I'm such a klutz! You probably wouldn't want me on your team."

"I'm not good at playing games!"

"Math has always been difficult for me!

"I can't _____!"

Do you see the negativity in each statement? You're telling the Universe what is wrong with you, rather than what is right about you.

Let's take another look at the example where we met Jack, an 18 year old boy who wants to go to college.

I was led to believe by others that I wasn't smart enough to go to college. That's an absolute lie. I am smart with an above average IQ. I have a quick mind and am always learning new things. There is nothing that I can't learn and master if I want to. I know I will excel when I get into college.

The first and second sentences are used to delete the negative belief (from your hard drive brain) that was given to you by others. It's a declaration to the Universe that it is not true. In fact it is an out-and-out lie. Now I know what you're thinking, "It's not a lie. It's what I believe." Of course you believe it. You've heard it all your life. You don't know any better. To get past this you must now lie to yourself. Yes, I'm asking you to lie to yourself. Vladimir Lenin, father of the Soviet Union said, "A lie told often enough becomes the truth." You must lie to yourself until you believe the truth about yourself.

The next four sentences are **your new truths.** These are going to be the new recordings in your mind, recorded over the lies people wanted you to believe. These are the positive truths about you. And when told to yourself, by yourself, and often enough–they become your truths.

The next question, "How often should I repeat these new positive affirmations?" And the answer is, as often as possible. Say it in the morning while taking a shower. Say it over and over again while you're commuting to work or school. Say it during breaks. Say it on your way home at night. And, definitely make it the last thought in your mind as you go to sleep at night. And, one more thing, say it out loud whenever possible. Your subconscious mind needs to hear these positive declarations to create them in your life. Remember the subconscious mind does not know the difference between what is real and what is not. It always responds to suggestion and provides you with **exactly what you want in your life!**

Jesus, the greatest metaphysician in history, knew how to use this Universal Law of Deliberate Manifestation. When he placed his hands upon a sick person and declared: "You are healed!" he did exactly what this exercise does. His "new belief" was that this person was healed of the illness. He didn't say, "I hope this person gets well." He stated with conviction, "You are healed." His absolute belief was that this person was now well. The only difference between what you do in this exercise and what Jesus did was that Jesus was so attuned with God and the Universe he could manifest change immediately. For us it takes longer and with more repetition, but what we are doing is exactly the same.

Here is a little trick I use to keep me on-track with my affirmations. As I'm stating my new beliefs I picture in my mind the words of my affirmation in large letters displayed on a giant stadium TV screen similar to the one in the new Dallas Cowboys stadium. When I see these words flashing at me they are definitely hard to ignore.

– Exercise #8 –

What You Hear Is Not What I'm Saying

*It is the province of
knowledge to speak and it is the
privilege of wisdom to listen.*
- Oliver Wendell Holmes

Most of us suffer from hearing things that aren't actually said. It's sounds nutty but everyone has this experience, some of us more than others. Sometimes you're asked a simple question that makes your heart pound and your head spin. For example, your manager questions an item on your expense account reimbursement request. He says: "I don't understand the cab fare expense. I thought your hotel was right on the airport and it had a shuttle." Fear and embarrassment flood your brain. You believe he's questioning your honesty and integrity. You worry you're being called out as a cheater. All of that gets in the way of your answering with the simple truth, "I thought it was too. But I found out there are two Marriott hotels in the airport area. I mistakenly booked the one that was further out and didn't have a shuttle. I was lucky to get a cab and make the plane."

I recently had an epiphany and knew you would benefit from my sharing it with you. This exercise arises out of a recent and uncomfortable situation that arose with a business consultant I work with.

I rely on Sandy as a coach and consultant to help me in my everyday business affairs. I pay him a monthly fee and meet with him weekly on the phone for approximately 2 hours. Sandy is easy to talk to, and in fact I gain more by just talking to him about a whole range of subjects than any specific business questions I have. He definitely stimulates my mind and I think of him as more than just my coach, but as a friend.

Sandy sends me my monthly invoice by email, with the balance due within fifteen days of the invoice's date. Over the past year I twice had to advise Sandy that his office person failed to send me an invoice. The second time, I mentioned to Sandy that once again, I hadn't received an invoice for the month. He thanked me as before. The next day, I received an email with my invoice attached. It was dated two days earlier, the date I should have received it. Within the week I wrote Sandy's company a check along with three others to various creditors, and mailed them. Sandy's check should have arrived within the 15 day payment window, as my other three checks had. Unfortunately, it didn't. During our next coaching session Sandy asked if I had sent the check. I replied I did and that he should be receiving it the next day. I didn't think much about it after that.

A week later, I received an email from Sandy written the prior evening. He mentioned he still had not received the check and he wanted to postpone our session until the bill was caught up. I was stunned as I read his email, and beginning to get angry. No, I was more than angry, I was livid. Being involved in the sales of consumer products it was not unusual that a retail account would be put on credit hold, with no new product shipped to them, until their past due invoices were paid up. But that usually happened after their outstanding balances became 60 to 90 days past due. Not when you're 4 days past due. To me the "punishment" of suspending our weekly conversations was not consistent with the "crime." Sort of like sending a SWAT team to arrest someone for past due parking violations, or killing ants with a 16 pound sledgehammer. Definitely overkill.

Why was I livid? Why did my brain make analogies to crime and punishment? Why was this tantamount to a police force making an arrest for no reason or insects being bludgeoned to death? Why wasn't it a simple matter of figuring out how to get the bill paid, since the check hadn't arrived?

Now, let me explain why I was feeling so angry and outraged. I was taught at a young age to be responsible when it came to money and credit worthiness. In good times and bad it was always important for me to pay my bills on time and to maintain a good credit history. This is what I was taught and this was what I believe. Today my credit scores are in the 800s and I intend to keep them there. The inference that I "read" or "heard" in Sandy's email was that I was a DEADBEAT. Someone who NEVER PAID HIS BILLS on time and someone you should watch out for. To me it was embarrassing. I also inferred from the email that I was a LIAR when I spoke to Sandy and told him that the check was in the mail. All-in-all it was a very uncomfortable position for me to be in. I didn't like what I was feeling and I didn't like what I was saying when Sandy and I finally spoke later that morning.

I let him know how I felt about "being called" a deadbeat and a liar. Sandy was surprised that I "read" that because he didn't say that in the email he'd sent or in the conversations we'd had. He felt that I was raging at him (he should have seen me in my raging days, only then would he be able to appreciate the difference between anger and rage). Sandy explained that it was his common practice to postpone meetings with people when they were late paying a bill. As a businessperson I could understand that. Unfortunately, my personal beliefs caused an emotional firestorm. I told him he used a NUCLEAR option. He replied he had simply postponed a meeting. I was offended especially since I viewed Sandy as a friend, even though our relationship began as a business arrangement and had a business purpose.

As I made my point somewhat heatedly in an unscheduled phone call to Sandy, he was going into another meeting. He had to break off the conversation. His tone remained calm as he said good-bye.

I sent Sandy an email – actually a very long email detailing my thoughts and feelings. After sending the email and feeling the adrenalin spike of emotion that accompanied the torrent of words I let go, it occurred to me that the situation could be fixed by simply authorizing Sandy's office to charge my credit card for the payment, at the same time each month. When I wrote a second email outlining that solution, it made sense to Sandy, too.

Sandy thought that the scenario might be a teachable moment for this book. At first I didn't see it, but then it came to me. Yes, there is an extremely important lesson to be learned here.

We Interpret the World Through Our Own Set of Filters

One of the first discussions you have with your new spouse upon returning home from your honeymoon is which way toilet paper should be placed on the roller. Should it hang along the wall, or should it come over the top? It sounds pretty stupid but it happens. If each of you were raised in a household that did it differently, each time you are sitting next to the roll, looking at it and knowing it's on the roller backwards, you remove it and turn it around, only to find that your spouse changed it back after discovering what you'd done.

We are the people we are because of our thoughts and experiences. No two people are alike. Even identical twins, although biological clones of each other, are different because they have distinct thoughts and experiences. Our "truths" about the world come from our individual circumstances.

If a person is so politically inclined, watching Fox News is an inspiring and educational experience. Every pundit's comments could be received as nearly biblical gospel. But if you held different political views, then watching Fox News could be dangerous to your health since anger and rage cause countless heart attacks and strokes every year.

Is the person who enjoys Fox News right and the one who rages at the TV screen wrong? No. Of course not. Our thoughts and experiences create our beliefs. And it is through these beliefs that we filter new experiences. We can then determine if these new experiences resonate with our ingrained beliefs, and if not, deal with how these experiences affect us.

Amplifying the magnitude of my disagreement with Sandy about when an unpaid bill should cause or not cause a delay in our meeting schedule is my belief that I am a good citizen who always pays his obligations on-time. I also believe that people who don't pay on time and try to manipulate the system by lying about the check being in the mail, are deadbeats. So when my check didn't arrive and Sandy postponed our coaching session for that reason, what happened? My long held beliefs about myself felt under attack. Anger and fear filled me with rage. Instead of calmly trying to determine what happened to my check and devising another way to pay Sandy, I instead unleashed that fear and anger on him. We often refer to this response as a knee jerk reaction. Quick, and often over the top. Not well thought out and often not useful.

You may now be wondering about how often your perception has impacted your ability to respond to others appropriately. How often have you had an oversized reaction to a simple situation? How have your thoughts and experiences affected your ability to problem-solve? Now it's your turn to consider other filters through which you see the world.

Instructions

Consider the last time you had an oversized reaction to an interaction that involved a disagreement. Then, use this worksheet to gain insight about your capacity to hear accurately, and how you can do a better job of tuning in without turning on your beliefs and emotions.

Exercise 8: What You Hear Is Not What I'm Saying

1. What happened? What did the other person say that kicked off your reaction?

   _____

   _____

2. How did you react?

   _____

   _____

3. What did you feel was being said, beyond the words that were spoken?

   _____

   _____

4. What beliefs about yourself were being violated?

   _____

   _____

5. What else could the person have actually meant – if there were no intention to insult you or hurt your feelings?

   _____

   _____

   _____

6. If you could go back and do it differently, what would you say?

   _____

   _____

7. How would your different response change the result?

   _____

   _____

   _____

8. What is the lesson to be learned here?

   _____

   _____

   _____

   _____

– Exercise #9 –

What Me Worry?

If you can solve your problem, then what is the need of worrying? If you cannot solve it, then what is the use of worrying?
– Shantideva

It's been said that 97% of what we worry about never happens. And yet, for some of us, it's seems almost impossible to put a stop to worrying. What is worry? The psychiatrist Carl Jung characterizes worry as a substitute for legitimate suffering. In other words, it's neurotic, not helpful and a waste of time. Worry is when your thoughts run wild, sometimes to the point of being delusional and out of control. One negative thought attracts another, followed by another and so on until all you can see on your path is disaster. Everything is absolute, and everything is a catastrophe.

How does this happen? Why is worrying likely to cause a tailspin or downward spiral? When you start with one negative thought put out into the universe, the thought is like a magnet, attracting like thoughts. The level of vibration in a negative thought finds similar thoughts because they are vibrating at the very same frequency. Suddenly you have a bundle of worries, creating fear and depression. What you feel in any given moment is always the result of what you're thinking at that moment.

Recently a friend of mine was selected to give a speech at an upcoming charity event. Betty is a highly intelligent and accomplished woman well known in her field, which is why she was asked to speak. Betty wasn't thrilled, in fact she was petrified. Very much as I was when I was in New York to accept the Best Toy Store award for Magic Village. And just like me this woman could think of nothing but catastrophe. What if I forget what to say? What if my voice cracks? What happens if I lose my place? What happens if I mispronounce a word, or worse yet, someone's name?

In the weeks prior to the speech all she did was worry. Now think about this. She allowed herself to be consumed by fear and worry for weeks leading up to the event. Were these happy times for her? Of course not! Her worrying overshadowed everything she did in those weeks; her job, time with her family and friends, the pleasure in her romantic relationship, and her peace of mind. And, for what? Nothing. Worrying was a waste of her time, energy and happiness. Did she do well when she actually gave the speech? Absolutely, she was great. Did any of the things she worried about come to pass? Yes. Her mouth was a bit dry at the beginning and she felt a bit dizzy walking up the stairs to the podium. Then, she took a sip of water, took a deep breath and looked out at her audience. She suddenly realized she was just human, the same as everyone sitting in front of her. If she made a mistake, and she did, she still felt the thrill of getting to talk to so many people about why she supported the charity, and why the organization means so much to her.

Nobody asked for perfect, and you never have to show up perfect. We're human. We will make mistakes. It's all part of life. I've spoken to hundreds of groups over the years and I will tell you this, not a one of those talks was perfect. I made mistakes. As long as I live I will continue to make mistakes. So what? Who cares?

Dale Carnegie is one of the original thought leaders on how to gain self-confidence, and he remains an icon in the art of engaging people. In his bestselling book, *How to Stop Worrying and Start Living*, he offers some excellent exercises to put a stop to worrying. The one I like the best and use the most is asking myself: "What's the worst that can happen?" When you're worrying about some future event, ask yourself this question, "What's the worst that can happen if I don't succeed? I may fail. So what if I fail, it won't be the first time. I'll be embarrassed. And? My ego will be bruised. So what?"

Compared to the final ending of death, every other consequence or event is miniscule. No one dies for mispronouncing a name or for-getting to mention a key point or even the main message. The goal is to attract and accept great opportunities, then spend time beforehand getting prepared and excited about the joy you will experience.

Instructions

Consider 3 upcoming events, appointments, meetings, conversations, phone calls or another opportunity that is currently causing you to worry. For each one, follow these instructions.

1. What upcoming event are you currently worried about?
2. What specifically are you worried about?
3. What's the worst thing that could happen if you don't succeed?
4. Ask yourself, so what if this happens? Write that down. Continue to ask that question each time you have an answer, until your answers run out and you stop worrying.

> *I have been through some*
> *terrible things in my life...some of which*
> *actually happened.*
> – Mark Twain

Exercise 9: What Me Worry?

1. I am worrying about the following upcoming event:

_____

_____

_____

What specifically are you worried about?

_____

_____

_____

_____

What's the worst thing that can happen if you don't succeed?

_____

_____

_____

So what if this happens?

_____

_____

_____

So what?

_____

_____

_____

2. I am worrying about the following upcoming event:

_____

_____

_____

What specifically are you worried about?

_____

_____

_____

What's the worst thing that can happen if you don't succeed?

_____
_____
_____

So what if this happens?

_____
_____
_____

So what?

_____
_____
_____

3. I am worrying about the following upcoming event:

_____
_____
_____

What specifically are you worried about?

_____
_____
_____
_____

What's the worst thing that can happen if you don't succeed?

_____
_____
_____
_____

So what if this happens?

_____
_____
_____

– Exercise #10 –

Tapping Your Way to a Fearless Life

Have you ever had acupuncture or acupressure therapy? These 5,000 year old treatments are the heart of Eastern medicine. While Western medicine focuses primarily on the chemical make-up of the human body and uses drugs to manipulate it, Eastern medicine concentrates on the body's energy system. Our bodies are made up of thousands of tiny wires we call nerves. Every signal the brain sends out through these tiny wires results in a response somewhere within our bodies. Most signals we're not even aware of. For example when you reach out your hand to grasp a fork and then manipulate the fork to spear a piece of food and raise it to your mouth, you hardly give it a second thought. But, it was all done through electrical signals from your brain. Some signals you are more aware of than others. For example, you touch a hot stove and immediately pull your hand away, and feel the pain.

The Chinese discovered the body has a complex system of energy circuits called meridians. Each meridian is responsible for a different part of the body. By manipulating these various electrical circuits through the use of needles, pressure, massage or chiropractic adjustments, practitioners are able to heal the physical body. In 1980 Dr. Roger Callahan, a psychotherapist, was treating a patient for her fear of water. He discovered that by tapping at the end of one of these meridians he was able to get his patient to immediately overcome her fear.

A number of years later Gary Craig took up the study of this fascinating treatment. He named it the Emotional Freedom Techniques® or more widely known as EFT. You can go to his website www.emofree.com and download a 79 page manual, absolutely free.

Gary realized that, "The cause of all negative emotions is a disruption of the body's energy system." What he calls a zzzzzzt. He dedicated his life to bringing this incredible healing process to those who suffer from negative emotions and poor physical health. And one of the best things about EFT is that after you learn to use it, it only takes a few minutes to do.

Instructions

I am going to begin by teaching you the recipe for using EFT. There are four parts to the Basic Recipe: 1) The Setup, 2) The Sequence, 3) The 9 Gamut Procedure, and 4) The Sequence again.

Let's begin with The Setup. Gary believes that through our serial negative thoughts and their accompanying negative emotions, our energy system gets out of whack. Sort of like putting new batteries into a flashlight but reversing the polarity. The energy is there but the flashlight doesn't work. Gary calls this Psychological Reversal and it must be reversed to its proper state in order for EFT to work.

The first thing I'd like you to do is to find a sore spot on your chest, but not just any sore spot. Find the U shaped bone at the bottom of your throat (where your collarbone starts). Now go down 3" and then over 3" to the right or left. If you rub this area you'll find that it's a bit sore. The reason for the soreness is lymphatic congestion occurs there.

Stop rubbing for just a minute, because you're going to say an affirmation while rubbing the sore spot. The affirmation is; Even though I have this fear of (insert your fear), I deeply and completely accept myself. For those who have a fear of cold calls it would sound like; Even though I have this fear of making cold calls, I deeply and completely accept myself.

This will work for any fear you might have; snakes, spiders, rejection, embarrassment. And it also works with anger, depression, nightmares and even physical pain such as headaches, backaches. An affirmation for physical pain might be; Even though I have this pain in my lower back, I deeply and completely accept myself.

OK let's now begin The Set-up. Find that sore spot. It doesn't matter right or left side. Say your affirmation 3 times while you rub the sore spot. That's it. Before we begin, if you find it difficult to rub the sore spot, or you can't find it, there is an alternative. If you were to give someone a Karate Chop you would use the fleshy part of the outside of your hand below the ring finger. Take the first two fingers of the other hand and tap continuously on this spot while repeating your affirmation.

Once The Set-up is done we can begin The Sequence. We are going to use the index and middle finger of the opposite hand to do the tapping. We'll tap approximately 6-10 times on each meridian end point – I'll show you where they are as we go through the sequence for the first time. It's interesting to note that each meridian has two end points, but tapping on one will suffice to balance out any disruptions in it. All end points are close to the surface of the skin, so tapping hard is not necessary. Are you ready to begin? Good, let's go!

We'll start by tapping the eyebrow (EB) at a point closest to the nose. Remember to tap 6-10 times, but not too hard. Next the side of the eye (SE). Now under the eye (UE). Our fourth spot will be under the nose (UN) then the chin (CH) mid-point between the lower lip and the chin. We'll now move down to the chest. Once again find the U notch in the collarbone (CB) at the base of your throat. Go down 1 inch then left or right 1 inch, and tap. Next go under the arm (UA) and tap at a point approximately 4 inches below the armpit at a point even with the nipple for men and in the middle of the bra strap on women. I often find this spot to be sore. Now move to 1 inch below the nipple (BN) for men and on women where the under skin of the breast meets the chest wall. Remember to tap each of these meridian end points 6-10 times.

Next we are going to move to the hand. You are going to tap on your thumb and three fingers, each at a point even with the bottom of the thumbnail. First, tap on the outside of the thumb (TH). Next tap on the index finger (IF) on the side facing the thumb. Now the middle finger (MF) and last the little finger (LF). And finally we are going to tap the Karate Chop (KC) part of the outside of the hand midway between the wrist and the bottom of the baby finger. Now you've learned The Sequence.

Let's move on to part 3 of the four part recipe, The 9 Gamut Procedure. As I describe this procedure, you might think, "This is stupid! The other stuff was bad enough, but this is really stupid." So let's all say in unison before we begin, "This is stupid!" OK?

First we need to find the Gamut Point. This can be found on the back of the hand midway between the ring finger and the little finger above the knuckle. Everybody find it? Good. Now come the 9 actions that make up the procedure that you'll do while tapping on the gamut point:

1. Eyes closed

2. Eyes open.

3. Eyes hard down to the right while holding your head steady.

4. Eyes hard down to the left while holding your head steady.

5. Roll your eyes in a circle going clockwise.

6. Roll your eyes in a circle going counter clockwise.

7. Hum 2 seconds of the Happy Birthday song (or any song).

8. Count rapidly 1 to 5 and then 5 to 1.

9. Hum 2 seconds of the Happy Birthday song (or any song) again.

Got it? Would you like to know why we do the 9 Gamut Procedure? The reason we do the 9 Gamut Procedure is to "fine tune" the brain by eye movement, humming and counting. Through connecting nerves, the brain is stimulated when moving the eyes. The left side of the brain, the logical side, is stimulated when we count. And, the right side, the creative side, is stimulated when we hum a song. It's as simple as that.

Now you're probably thinking, "How does this tie in with my fears?" Good question. While we are doing The Set-up, The Sequence, The 9 Gamut Procedure and The Sequence again we need to remind ourselves of the fear or pain we are attempting to overcome. So remember, as you did in The Set-up you are going to repeat the affirmation, Even though I have this fear of (insert your fear), I deeply and completely accept myself. For those who have a fear of public speaking it would sound like; Even though I have this fear of public speaking, I deeply and completely accept myself. So you will need to remind yourself as you do the EFT procedure, what fear or pain you are eliminating. And you don't need to repeat the whole thing, just the words fear of cold calling, fear of speaking in public, fear of failure, you know the rest.

For most of your fears and physical pains you should be able to eliminate them the first time you use EFT. But, some may require subsequent rounds of the basic recipe to work on the remaining problem. Since we use the affirmation to address the subconscious mind we need subsequent rounds to have slightly different words in the affirmation. The Reminder Affirmation will sound like, Even though I still have some of this (insert fear) I deeply and completely accept myself.

That's it. Make sure you go to Gary's website (www.emofree.com) and download his free 79 page manual and while you're there check out his fantastic array of DVDs for further study of the Emotional Freedom Technique®.

Take This Opportunity To Have it All

Congratulations on finishing Overpowering Fear and completing the exercises. You are now on your way to creating the life that you have always wanted, and that you so justly deserve.

The common belief among trainers and speakers is that once you've read the book or taken the course you believe that your learning is over. You'll put the book, course materials, audio CDs and DVDs up on the bookshelf and over time forget about them. I would hate to see you do this with my book. So I am going to challenge you.

Go to my website www.Michael-Luckman.com. You will receive instructions on how to download three free audio CDs designed to keep you on your new path.

You'll also discover more about a one-day Overpowering Fear intensive coming to a city near you. And, you may join Michael's Inner Circle program where you'll join me for 60-90 minute live discussions via the Internet and phone. These conversations will reveal the twelve key areas, that when mastered, give you the life you have always dreamed of. They are:

Overpowering the Forces of Failure	Taking the Reins of Positivity and Power
• Triumph Over Ego	• Controlling Your Subconscious
• Victory Over Victimhood	• Loving Yourself & Your Career
• Beating Down Blame	• Exchanging Respect & Admiration
• Shutting Off Shame	• Preparing For Greatness Everyday
• Destroying Self-Doubt	• Experiencing Success
• Overpowering Fear Now	• Living Your Dream

I hope this is just the beginning of our relationship. And that you will allow me to be your guide, teacher, mentor and friend as you leave the darkness of fear and walk confidently into the glorious sunshine of your new life.

A Course in Miracles says that God wants you to have everything. Not just sometime, but all the time. And to that end; I wish you constant happiness.

– Michael

Contact Michael Luckman for more about his
speaking, training and media appearances.

Email: Michael@Michael-Luckman.com
URL: http://www.Michael-Luckman.com
Phone: 408.404.6764 Ext.2

CPSIA information can be obtained at www.ICGtesting.com
Printed in the USA
LVOW040059110112

263281LV00003B/7/P